CEAC

AUG 2023

CONCRETE HOUSES

FORM, LINE, AND PLANE

STEVE HUYTON
AND CHERYL WEBER

Other Schiffer Books by Steve Huyton:
Modern Masters, ISBN 978-0-7643-5384-0
Luxury Design for Living, ISBN 978-0-7643-5421-2
Australia Modern, ISBN 978-0-7643-5812-8

Schiffer Books on Related Topics:
Designing for Disaster, Boyce Thompson,
ISBN 0-978-7643-5784-8
Anatomy of a Great Home, Boyce Thompson,
ISBN 0-978-7643-5465-6

Copyright © 2022 by Steve Huyton

Library of Congress Control Number: 2020952755

All rights reserved. No part of this work may be reproduced or used in any form or by any means—graphic, electronic, or mechanical, including photocopying or information storage and retrieval systems—without written permission from the publisher.

The scanning, uploading, and distribution of this book or any part thereof via the Internet or any other means without the permission of the publisher is illegal and punishable by law. Please purchase only authorized editions and do not participate in or encourage the electronic piracy of copyrighted materials.

"Schiffer," "Schiffer Publishing, Ltd.," and the pen and inkwell logo are registered trademarks of Schiffer Publishing, Ltd.

Written by Cheryl Weber
Project research by Steve Huyton

Interior and cover design by Molly Shields

Front cover photo by Sam Noonan.
Back cover photo by FG+SG

Type set in Brandon Grotesque/Cambria

ISBN: 978-0-7643-6277-4

Printed in Serbia

Published by Schiffer Publishing, Ltd.
4880 Lower Valley Road
Atglen, PA 19310
Phone: (610) 593-1777; Fax: (610) 593-2002
Email: Info@schifferbooks.com
Web: www.schifferbooks.com

For our complete selection of fine books on this and related subjects, please visit our website at www.schifferbooks.com. You may also write for a free catalog.

Schiffer Publishing's titles are available at special discounts for bulk purchases for sales promotions or premiums. Special editions, including personalized covers, corporate imprints, and excerpts, can be created in large quantities for special needs. For more information, contact the publisher.

Architecture goes beyond utilitarian needs. You employ stone, wood, and concrete, and with these materials you build houses and palaces. That is construction. Ingenuity is at work. But suddenly you touch my heart, you do me good, I am happy and I say: This is beautiful. That is architecture. Art enters in.
—Le Corbusier

CONTENTS

6 *Foreword by Vibeke Lichten*

 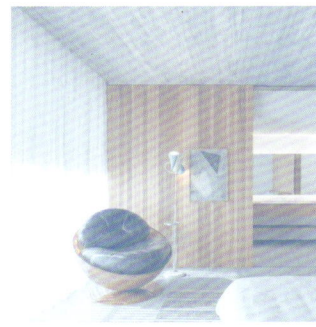  

9 **Patio House**
Karpathos, Greece

25 **Casa Bruma**
Temascaltepec, Mexico

39 **PR House**
Adelaide, Australia

53 **Kloof119A**
Cape Town, South Africa

71 **Casa Madri**
Mérida, Yucatán, Mexico

85 **Casa BT**
Buenos Aires, Argentina

101 **Mexican Contemporary House**
Melbourne, Australia

113 **Concrete Square Tube House**
Kyoto, Japan

123 **Eco House**
Long Island, New York

137 **River House**
Ketchum, Idaho

151 **Casa Plana**
Porto Feliz, Brazil

169 **F Residence**
Hyogo, Japan

183 **Frame House**
Minorca, Spain

197 **E20 House**
Pliezhausen, Germany

215 **La Mira Ra**
South of France

229 **Ark House**
Kraków, Poland

247 **Casa Sierra Fria**
Mexico City, Mexico

263 **Mermaid Beach Residence**
Gold Coast, Australia

279 **R Torso C**
Tokyo, Japan

293 **Shell House**
Australia

FOREWORD

This book is an ode to the world's most widely used humanmade material. Its pages showcase twenty extraordinary homes from around the globe that make art out of concrete. The endless options to form, model, and imprint make concrete a great tool for creativity. Architects can use it to create astonishing design effects, from tinting it in hues from white to black, to exposing the stone and glass aggregate, not to mention the possibilities for using recycled, locally available aggregate materials.

Concrete is as old as civilization. There is evidence of its use by ancient cultures, and some of these structures survive to this day, such as the Mayan concrete ruins in Uxmal, Nabatean settlements in Syria and Jordan, ancient Greek ruins, and Egyptian structures, some dating to 1400–1200 BCE. The Romans were the first to discover concrete's great potential. Their widespread use of concrete mainly involved using masonry cladding on a concrete core, without the use of structural steel. The Pantheon, the largest unreinforced concrete dome in the world, has lasted more than 2,000 years.

In addition to its longevity, concrete has other appealing attributes, including strength, plasticity, and resistance to fire, earthquakes, and tornadoes. The 1960s produced many concrete buildings in the US, some of which are being given a second life. By renovating and adapting them to new uses, we are saving them from demolition—an act of conservation. These twentieth-century structures are a testament to concrete's durability, playfulness, malleability, and beauty—all tenets of sustainability.

Twentieth-century modernist masters such as Le Corbusier, Oscar Niemeyer, Louis Kahn, Eileen Gray, Eero Saarinen, and Frank Lloyd Wright used concrete for their residential projects. Back then, we believed natural resources were limitless. Today, as the need to reduce greenhouse gasses becomes urgent, iconoclasts such as Jeanne Gang, Tadao Ando, Zaha Hadid, Frank Gehry, and Elizabeth Diller, as well as the architects within these pages, have to also address concrete's high carbon footprint.

Choosing the right construction material can be challenging. Architects are often caught between a rock and a hard place, having to balance innovation with the judicious use of resources. While satisfying our need for places in which to live, work, and play, we must take up less of the earth's surface, practice resource conservation, and make mindful use of primary materials in a circular economy.

Concrete is concrete, no matter where you go in the world. It is a composite material made from a very simple formula, within which there are many variations. Every home in these pages is made from the same four ingredients: sand, aggregate, water, and cement. Portland cement, the most common type of cement, is made by heating limestone at high temperatures for a very long time. To reduce carbon emissions, efforts are being made to switch from fossil fuels to other energy sources in the fabrication process. New materials and technologies are being developed that can lighten the environmental impact, including the use of recycled materials. Coarse stone can be replaced with post-consumer glass, plastic, and paper waste. "Green concrete" uses recycled concrete debris, slag from steel plants, silica fumes, or captured fly ash in place of limestone in the production of green cement. Using recycled concrete keeps these waste products out of landfills.

Additionally, allowing concrete's expressive surfaces to remain exposed outside and inside eliminates the need to apply exterior cladding and interior finishes. In cold regions where concrete is exposed, sandwiching insulation between the inner and outer walls helps conserve energy. In both cold and hot climates, thick concrete walls create a thermal mass that modulates interior temperatures by storing energy and releasing it slowly.

I considered concrete's pros and cons when I constructed my own Eco House several years ago. My project in this book is tripartite: the main house, a three-bedroom poured-in-place, all-concrete structure; the garage/pool house with an additional two bedrooms, a three-story hybrid of concrete and conventional construction; and the one-room architect's atelier, built on a smaller, poured-in-place concrete foundation and footing that acts as a counterweight to balance the cantilevered studio.

By acting as the architect, general contractor, owner, and end user, I was able to shepherd the project into construction three months after the design documentation and permits were in hand. The use of poured-in-place concrete for the main house allowed it to be occupied nine months after construction began, right on time for the spring season.

Using the same consulting engineers, concrete fabricator, and construction trades allowed for a smooth transition to a finished house in record time. The main house and the garage/pool house were fully complete in one year thanks to the ease of building with concrete.

The project's aim was to achieve agility, durability, and low maintenance. Leaving the concrete exposed on the exterior and partially on the interior helped mitigate the carbon footprint over the life of the building. Other "pro" considerations were that the concrete house is completely fireproof and can withstand future weather-related disasters due to climate change.

The latest addition to the project is my own detached work studio on the edge of the property. And I do mean on the edge. The smallest of the three buildings, the studio is anchored in place by a solid counterweight—a dense concrete pedestal composed of poured-in-place concrete walls and recycled concrete fill, which allows for the upper portion to cantilever over the sloping terrain. The upper portion, built with conventional wood framing and floor-to-ceiling windows on three sides, reveals expansive views designed to encourage expansive ideas.

For me, this small, hybrid concrete-and-timber building is a representation of the visual balancing act that designers and architects must perform in today's increasingly sustainability-led world. Our ability to influence the use of materials in economically intelligent ways will lead the construction industry into a more robust and responsible green future.

We must have a concentration of purpose in the ways we build. We are at a crucial moment, an urgent moment, where sustainable design can safeguard the resources of the planet; we are required to be honest stewards of the earth for future generations. It is possible to design modern, comfortable living spaces that are good for us and good for the environment. This book captures the best of concrete residential design with warmth and elegance.

Vibeke Lichten
Atelier Vibeke Lichten
New York, New York

Karpathos, Greece | 2018

PATIO HOUSE

OOAK Architects

Photographs: Yiorgos Kordakis and Åke Eson Lindman

Perched on a craggy outcrop on Karpathos, Patio House overlooks the emerald-blue Aegean Sea and Afiarti Beach, one of the best windsurfing spots on the Grecian islands. That's what drew the clients of Stockholm-based AAOK Architects to this spot. Serious windsurfers, they asked for a simple and durable house with access to the beach below, but one that would also let them appreciate the windy site from inside.

This dramatic landscape is difficult to sculpt. "Every man-made alteration is visible," says principal Maria Papafigou. "The site was so special and fragile. The minute you start digging around, it would be destroyed." For that reason, the design team drew a single-story structure made of reinforced, poured-in-place concrete that sits lightly on the land. The concrete forms rest on piers inserted "like acupuncture" between the shrubbery and trees. That structural move also allowed the building to cantilever beyond the ridge, creating a sensation of floating over the extraordinary site. The home's flat gravel roof reinforces the feeling that it is part of the geological surface, protruding from the cliff.

FIRST FLOOR
1 Entry courtyard
2 Bedrooms
3 Kitchen
4 Living room
5 Outdoor dining patio

SECOND FLOOR
1 Guest quarters

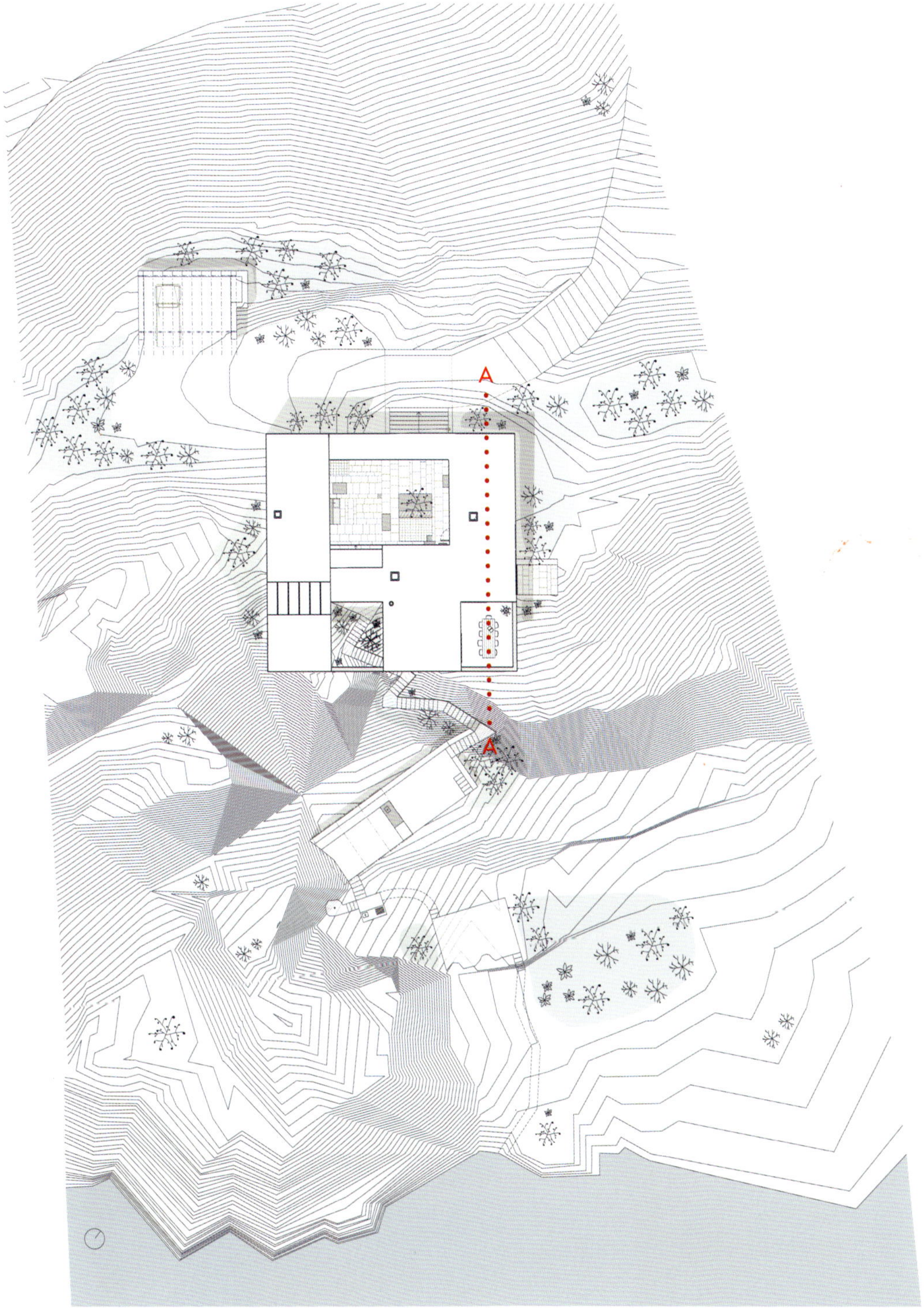

SITE PLAN

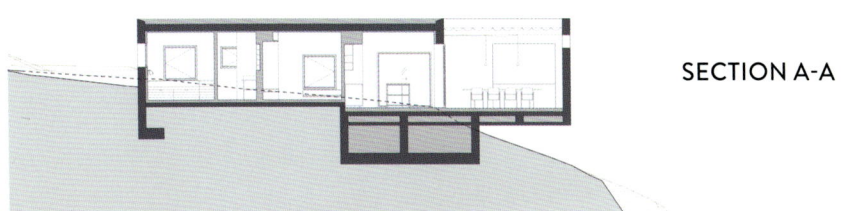

SECTION A-A

Patio House • Floor Plan

Indoor-outdoor lines are so blurred as to be almost imperceptible. The 2,152-square-foot house sits on a plateau, with the main road coming up behind it. From the parking area, a short run of wide stairs lands visitors at a sliding oak door. Inside is an open courtyard sheltered from the wind, with the living spaces rotating around it. To the right, independent guest quarters are elevated on a small hill. Underneath it, down a few steps from the main courtyard, is a basement for surfboard storage. Beyond the entry courtyard is another glassy in-between space. From there one can enter the house or head straight down to the beach via a switchback staircase carved into the rock, with the house floating above it. Midway down the slope is

the only designed outdoor area, a pergola-covered kitchen overlooking the sea.

Interiors are warm and summery. Deep, punched windows are lined with oiled oak, adding a layer of softness to the hard shell. The courtyard's seagrass limestone connects it to the limestone cliffs, and some of the bricks in the courtyard are recycled from old construction. On the interior flooring, the seagrass limestone has a more refined finish. OOAK designed much of the furniture, which was built with local labor and materials. The simple floor plan contains three bedrooms, two baths, and, off the main living space, a partially walled dining patio open to the sky.

Built in the midst of Greece's economic crisis, OOAK Architects was eager to use local workers and construction knowledge. That too made concrete a sensible choice. Whereas in Sweden, where the firm's other office is located, this type of construction would have cost a lot of money and been complicated to explain, Papafigou says, concrete is produced on the island and is familiar to the workers; it also withstands the region's earthquakes.

It was the right material for the right place. "Concrete ticks a lot of boxes for architects in that it's versatile and interesting," Papafigou says. "Although it's difficult for us to support, knowing the damage concrete does to the environment [in its manufacturing], we said to ourselves that there was a social sustainability in supporting the local community; we didn't need to transport wood or other materials from far away to this remote place. And we know it can last several generations. Like shell in a rock, the house and land will eventually become part of each other."

14   Patio House

We knew we couldn't have a perfect surface, because we were using formwork the local workers already had, not casting on plywood. That's why we complemented the building with wood and more-refined details to contrast its roughness.
—Maria Papafigou

18 Patio House

20 *Patio House*

Like shell in a rock, the house and land will eventually become part of each other.

22 Patio House

Temascaltepec, Mexico | 2017

CASA BRUMA

Fernanda Canales and Claudia Rodriguez
Photographs: Rafael Gamo

"It was a strange commission," says architect Fernanda Canales. "Our clients wanted a small weekend house for their family of four, but both of them have a large extended family, and then they realized that they needed to have independent spaces to house the cousins, parents, and in-laws." A hundred miles southwest of Mexico City, Casa Bruma's 6,500 square feet are cleverly meted out among nine board-formed concrete cubes. Canales and codesigner Claudia Rodriguez, who helped create the development's master plan, were also responding to the community's mandate to preserve every tree on the 2.7-acre site, which contains old-growth oaks.

Like a small encampment around a central patio, the ad hoc one- and two-story blocks address the sloping topography, views, and need for privacy. Counterintuitively, the architects reserved the flat middle portion of the lot for a central patio and tucked the buildings into the trees around it. "Development in the community had just started; we knew people would build houses around it but not where and how views would be compromised," Canales says. Plus, "the lot was steep and the vegetation seemed impossible. That's when the idea for an exploded house came up."

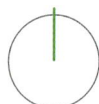

FIRST FLOOR

1 Courtyard
2 Kitchen
3 Dining
4 Living
5 Study
6 Kids' bedroom
7 Guest room
8 Garage
9 Utilities
10 Caretaker's apartment

SECTION 1

SECTION 2

SECOND FLOOR

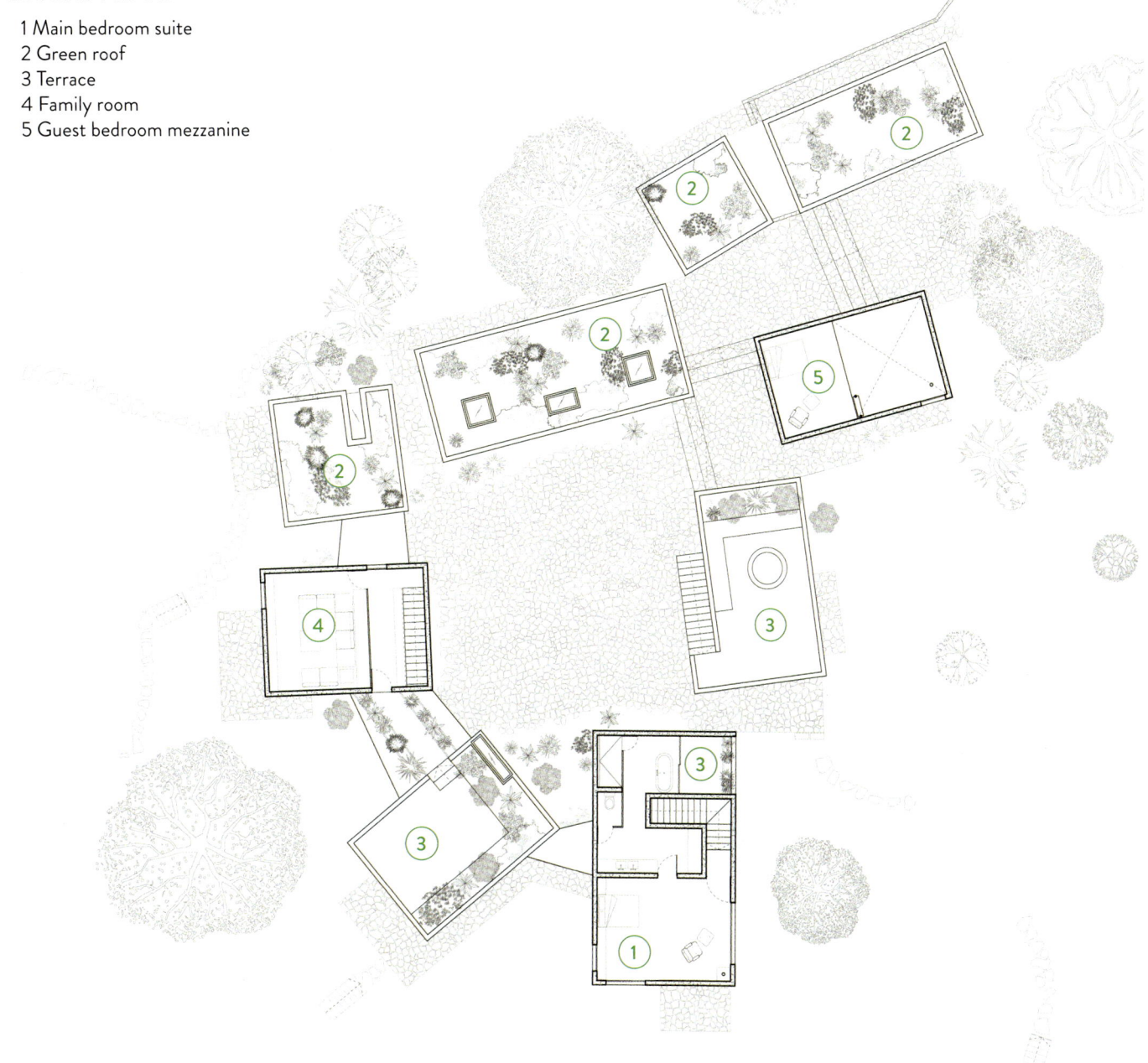

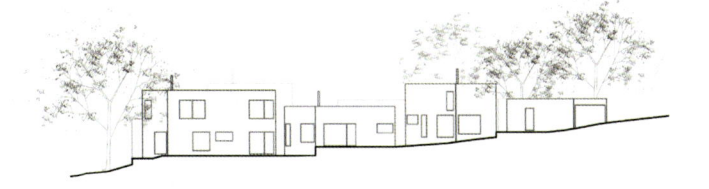

1 Main bedroom suite
2 Green roof
3 Terrace
4 Family room
5 Guest bedroom mezzanine

EAST ELEVATION

Casa Bruma • Floor Plan

28 *Casa Bruma*

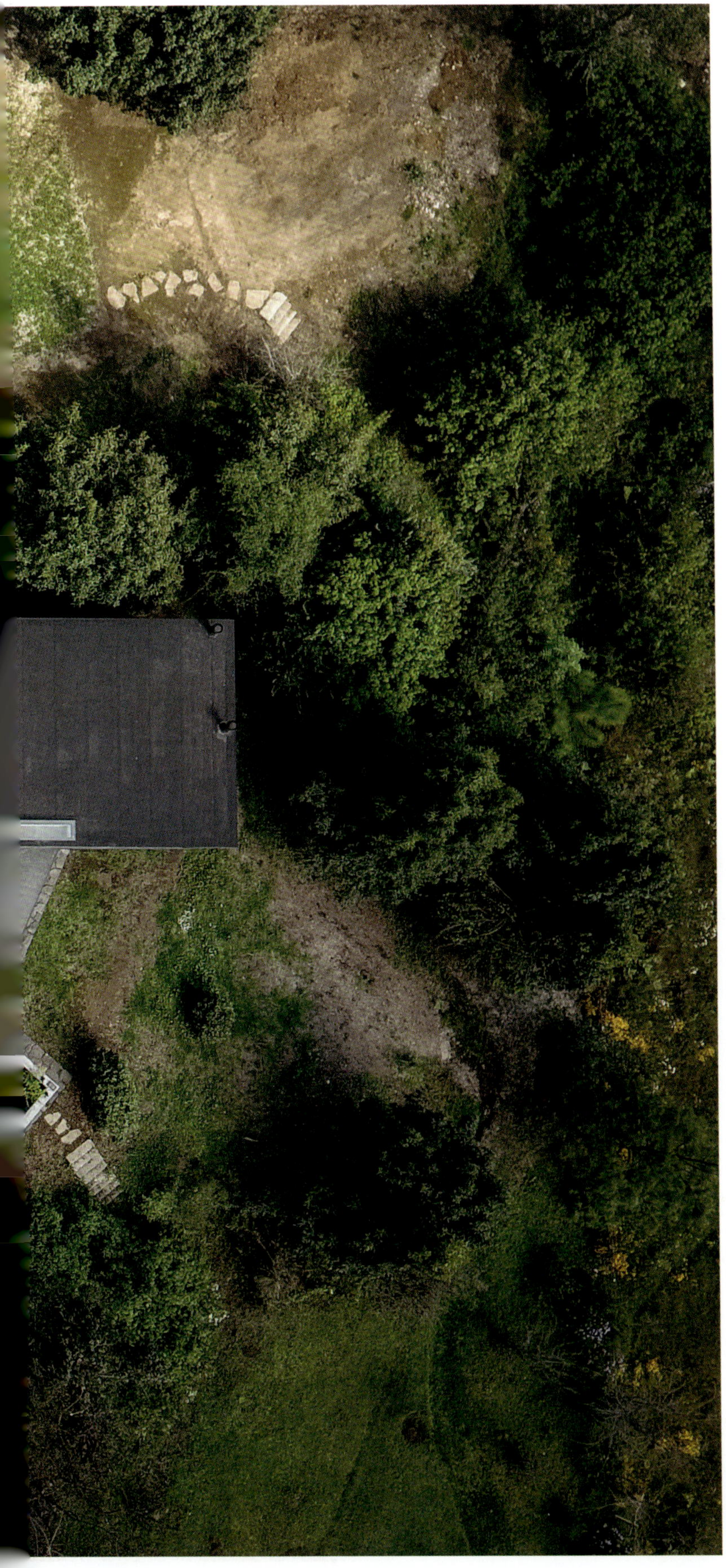

This strategy had another benefit: the buildings recede into the forest, and more so because they are black. At the bottom of the site, the main house is a string of four boxes linked by glass walkways. They contain the kitchen, the dining room with an upstairs studio, the living room and roof terrace, and the bedrooms, consisting of a first-floor kids' bedroom and study, and a second-floor primary suite with a roof terrace above. The other five buildings include a garage, a utility space, two guest rooms, and a two-bedroom apartment for a caretaker who tends the family's vegetable garden and chickens.

An added advantage of multiple small buildings, of course, is that each space can be turned toward the best sunlight and views. Almost every cube has at least two solar exposures through large, operable windows or glass doors that admit cross-breezes. These passive strategies, along with wood-burning stoves and fireplaces, keep the rooms comfortable without mechanical systems, despite temperatures that can swing almost 30 degrees Fahrenheit from morning to evening.

The 8-inch-thick insulated, poured-concrete shell helps mitigate heat and cold too. Concrete was the obvious material choice given the site's remoteness, the lack of skilled labor, and the clients' request for easy upkeep, Canales says, adding that more than

29

70 percent of houses in Mexico are self-built using concrete. Trucks were not needed because small quantities were mixed by hand. The concrete was mixed with black pigments that will weather differently depending on exposure to sun and shade. "We thought of the buildings as rocks, with variations in color and texture," Canales says. Inside, oak ceilings, stairs, and doors made by local artisans add warmth and richness to the dark walls.

Four green roofs and two planted roof terraces reinforce the impression that the architecture is an extension of nature. In fact, it literally is. Abiding by the community regulations, all of the household water comes from rainwater collected from the roofs into a cistern under the central courtyard, and solar panels supply electricity.

What began as a house for a couple with two young children became a house for four or five families, and one that restores and preserves the land's ecology. "It was supposed to be a weekend house, but he spends half the weeks there," Canales says. "He's a lawyer, and views and patios weren't part of his language or ideas, but he says they've changed his life. He's aware of the tress and passing of the sun."

32 *Casa Bruma*

34　Casa Bruma

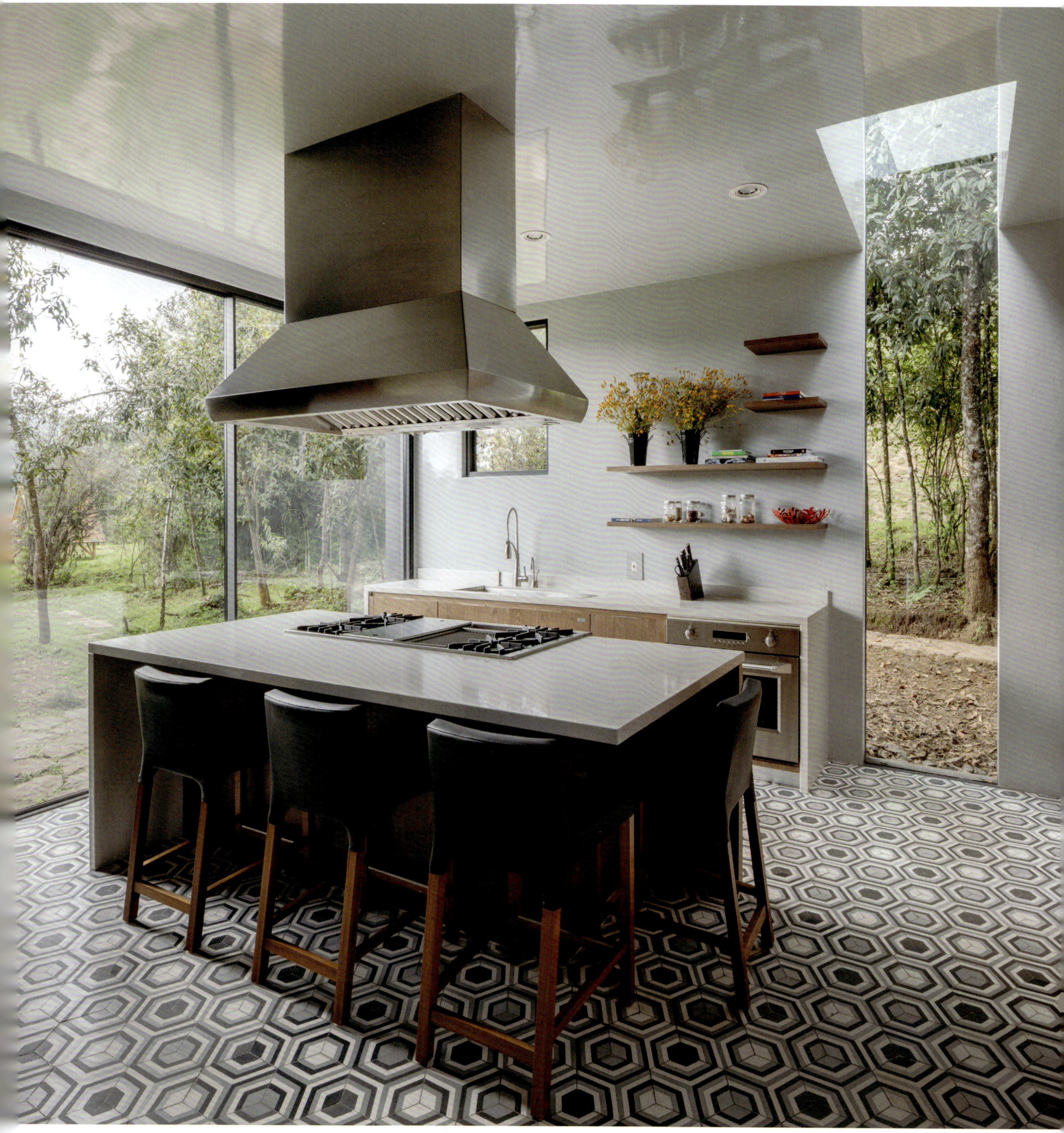

Concrete is a very basic structural element; there is no difference between foundation, structure, and interior. It is the solution to a place where you don't want to have different materials to put together. It was also a way to build something on-site without the complexity of how something arrives and the risk of materials getting damaged in transit.
—Fernanda Canales

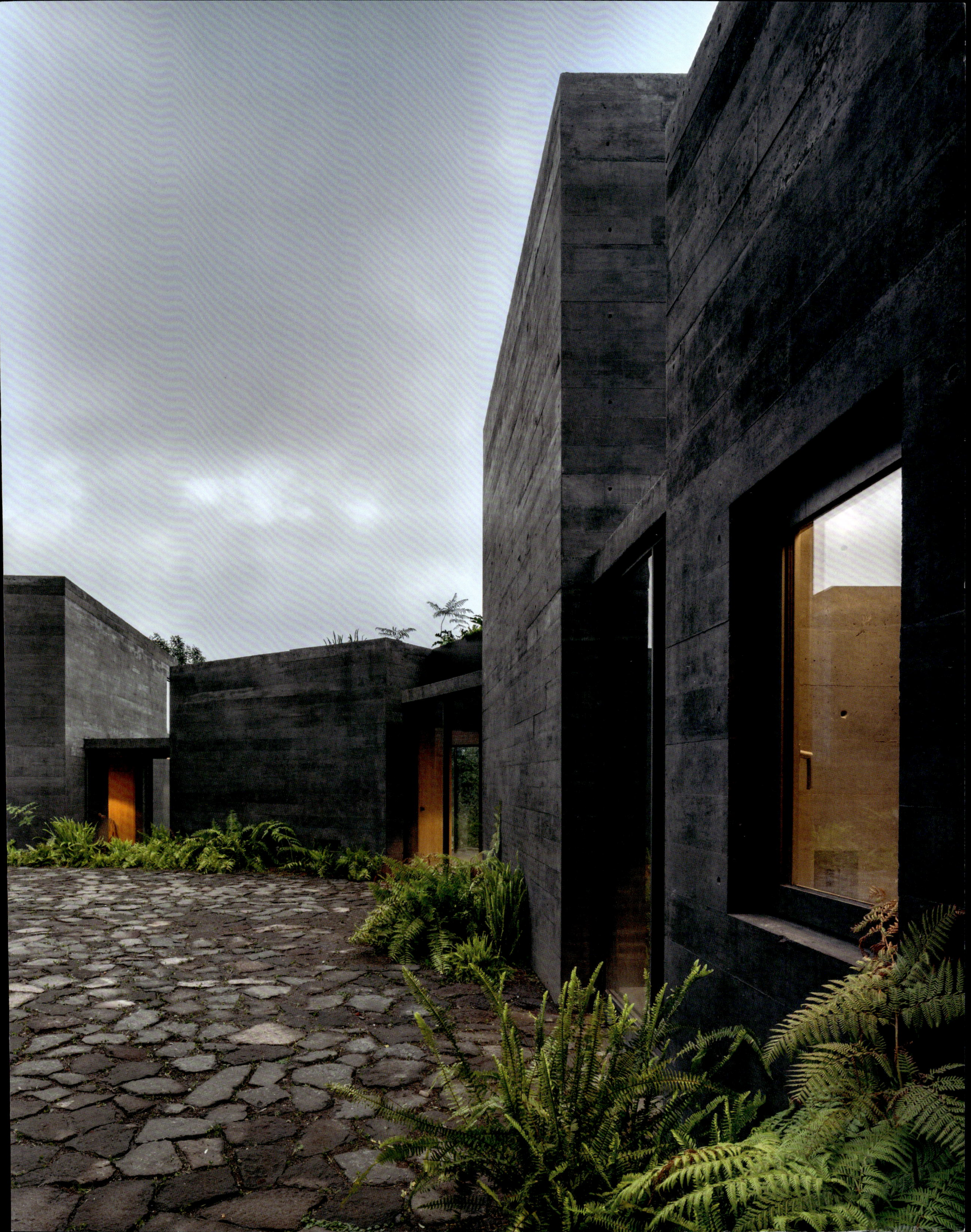

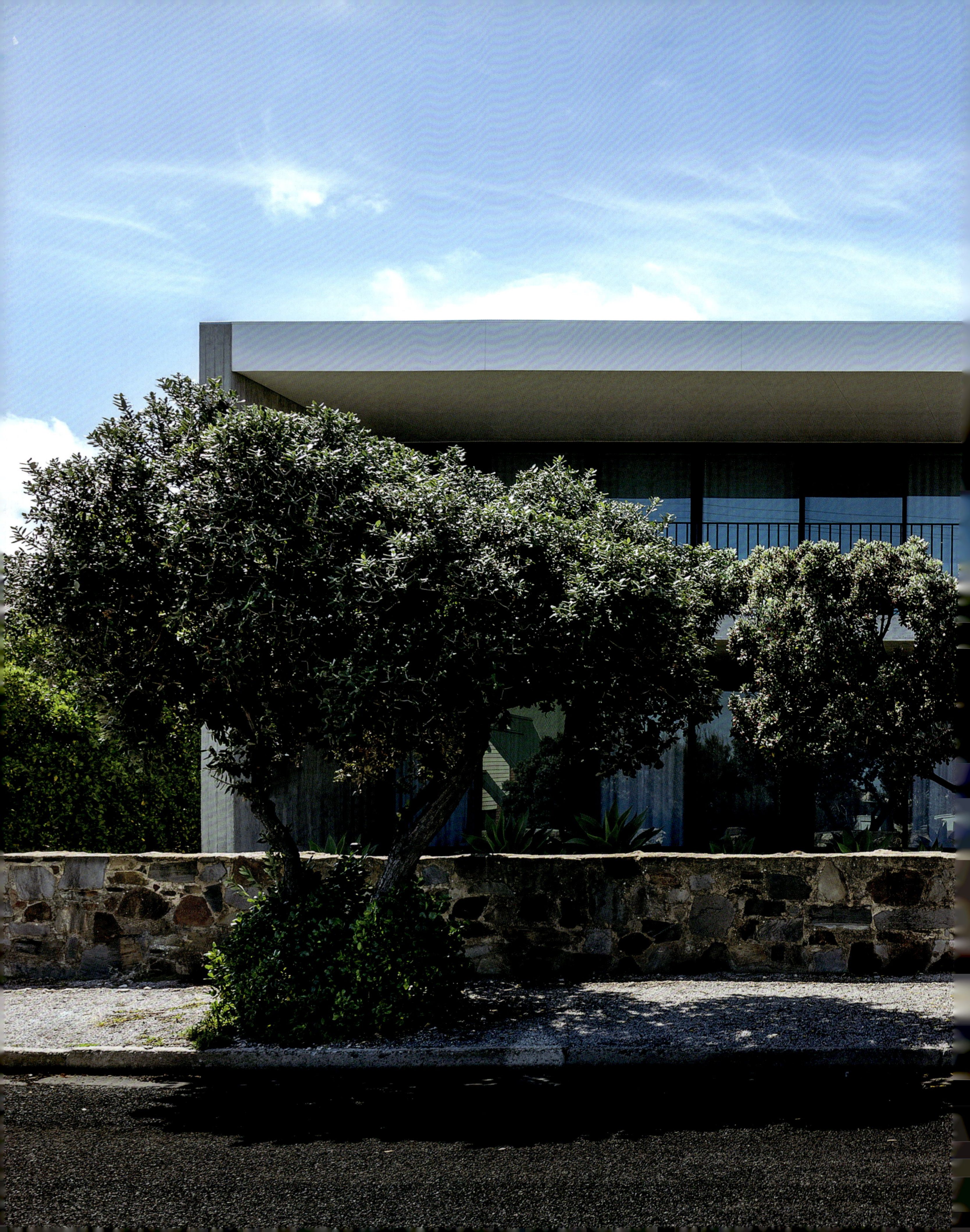

Adelaide, Australia | 2017

PR HOUSE

Architect Ink

Photographs: Sam Noonan

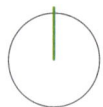

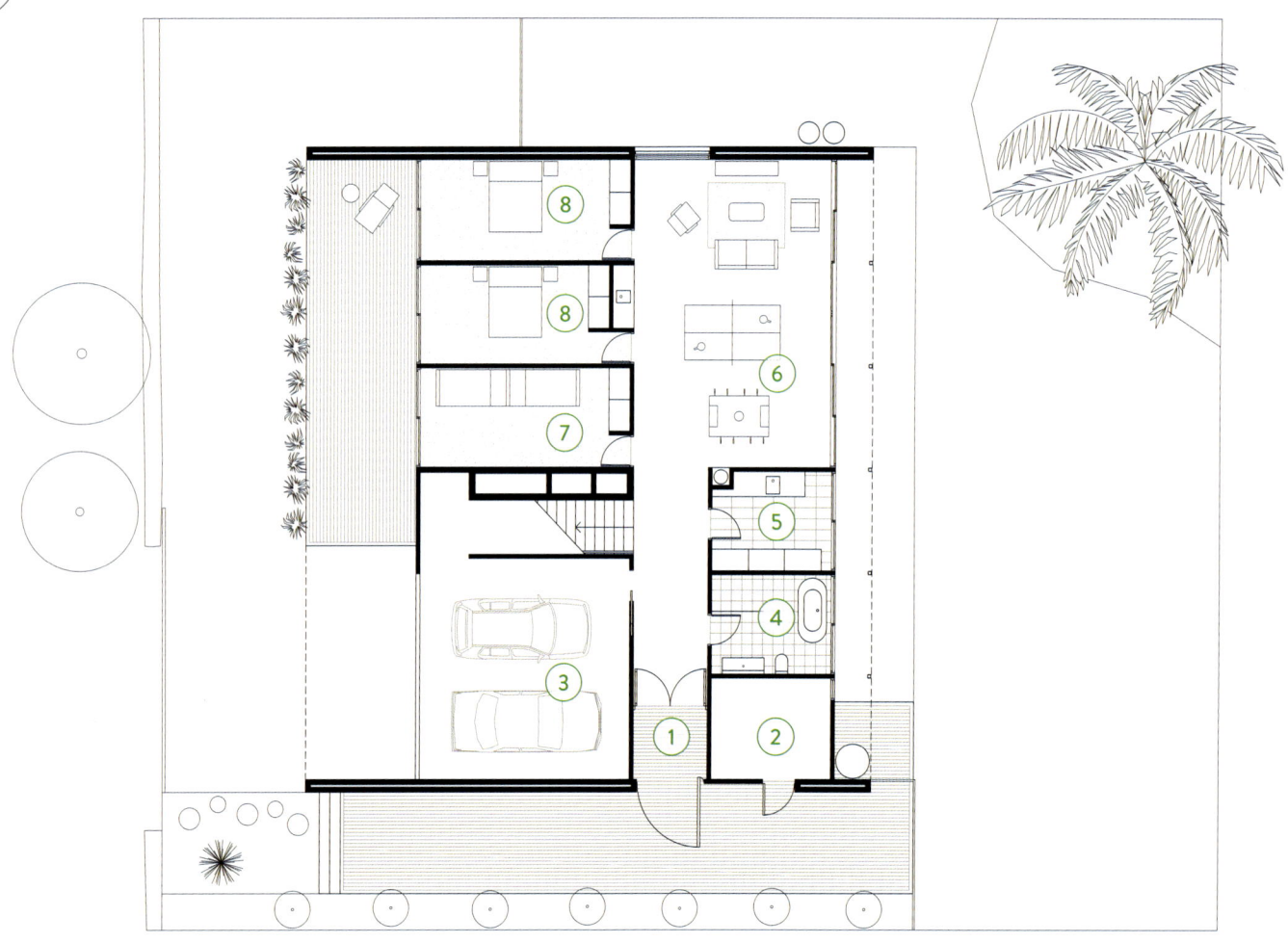

FIRST FLOOR

1 Entry
2 Storage
3 Garage
4 Bath
5 Laundry
6 Lounge
7 Kitchenette
8 Bedroom

SECOND FLOOR

1 Main bedroom
2 Main bath
3 Powder room
4 Stair hall
5 Family room
6 Dining
7 Kitchen
8 Balcony

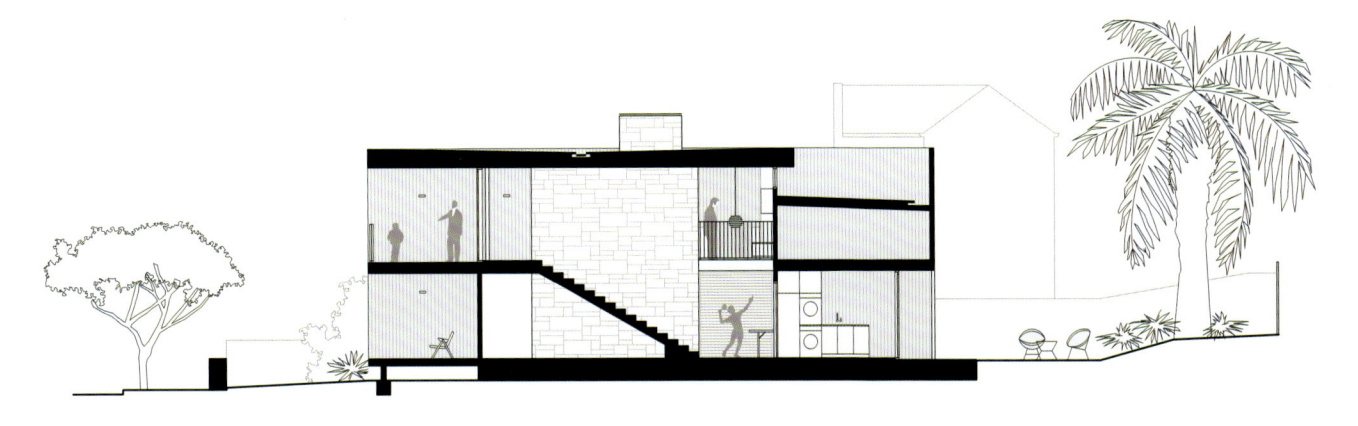

SOUTH ELEVATION

PR House • Floor Plan 41

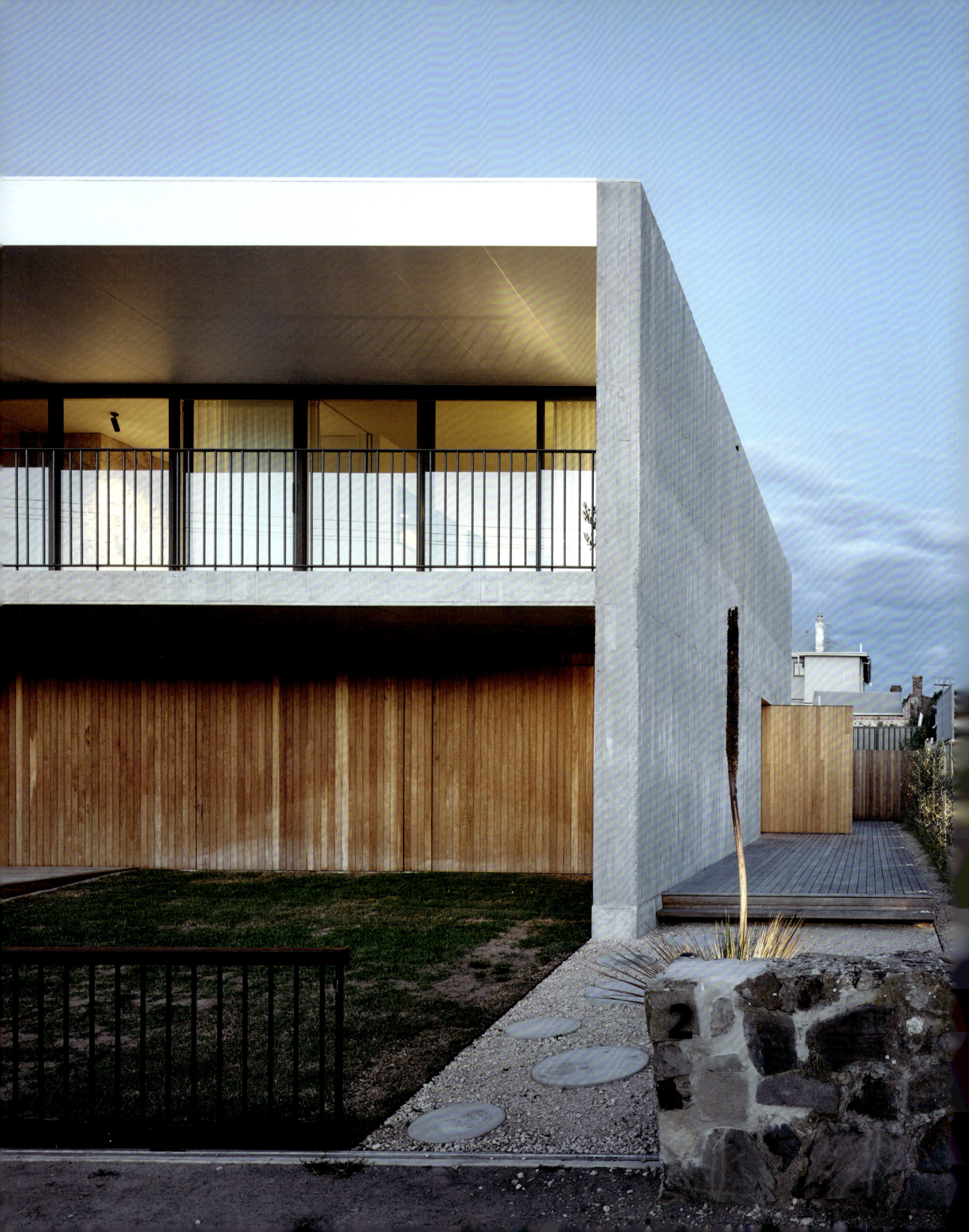
2

For decades starting in the 1920s, fiber-cement siding was a common building material on Aussie beach shacks. Cheap, lightweight, and easy to transport and install, it also was fire resistant and practically impervious to salt air. The asbestos-and-concrete material, or fibro, as it was called, stopped being made after the 1980s, but its use helped define the character and architectural language of countless cottage communities—an aesthetic now seen as nostalgic.

It was this vintage quality that appealed to the owners when they purchased a beach house an hour outside Adelaide, intending to renovate it. However, the 1960 structure was in such bad shape that they decided to start fresh. "The concept was to replace the original beach shack in a contemporary way with more-robust materials," says their architect, Marco Spinelli. "It was important to the clients to keep the beach shack look, using simple materials while maximizing beach views, indoor-outdoor living spaces, and natural light and ventilation."

The cottage's simple, squarish footprint influenced the new two-story dwelling. Unlike its predecessor's composite cladding, however, building with poured concrete is an expensive process in Australia. "We had to use it sparingly because the budget was tight," Spinelli says. "We spent money on the concrete end walls, bringing that texture inside, and worked hard to make sure everything else was cost-effective."

The design concept evolved as two board-formed-concrete end walls on the north and south, with white mahogany and glass on the front and back of the house. "The rule was that the two end walls are solid, and everything between is lightweight glass or timber cladding," Spinelli says. After experimenting with different types of boards for the concrete form, the team settled on three different thicknesses of pine, which creates a textured surface enlivened by sunlight. After the first wall went up, the construction crew reused the form on the second concrete wall. The vertical mahogany timbers on the east and west walls are roughly the same dimensions as the boards in the formwork, so that over time the mahogany will silver, becoming one with the concrete.

Economical in style and structure, the house looks raw and natural yet sleek and seamless. On the street elevation, continuous timber cladding hides a two-car garage, while the driveway is lawn with a structural material underneath to carry the weight. "We were trying to maintain a beach shack feel; people park cars on the lawn, and it's not obvious from the street that there's a garage," Spinelli says. A boardwalk along the side leads to the main entry, where a large mahogany pivot door acts as a gateway. It conceals and secures the entrance when the owners are out of town, and stands open when they are in residence. The ground floor houses a storage room, a laundry, three bedrooms, a bath, and a rumpus room open to the back garden. Upstairs, a deep, beach-facing balcony runs the length of the house, shading the west side and making the most of entertaining space. This level contains the kitchen, dining, and living spaces, along with the main bedroom suite, a powder room, and access to the roof.

Modest interior materials—exposed concrete walls, oak joinery—look equally effortless and reflect the clients' love for midcentury design. A honey-colored sandstone wall and fireplace anchor the two levels along the stairwell—echoes of the existing low stone wall out front. In the kitchen, a two-story void opens a sight line to the front door below.

On this conservation site, the use of board-marked concrete confers long-term durability, and its surface delights the owners. "The clients tell us they can't take their hands off it; they want to feel that texture," Spinelli says. "It's such a flexible material; you are limited only by imagination and a little physics."

44 PR House

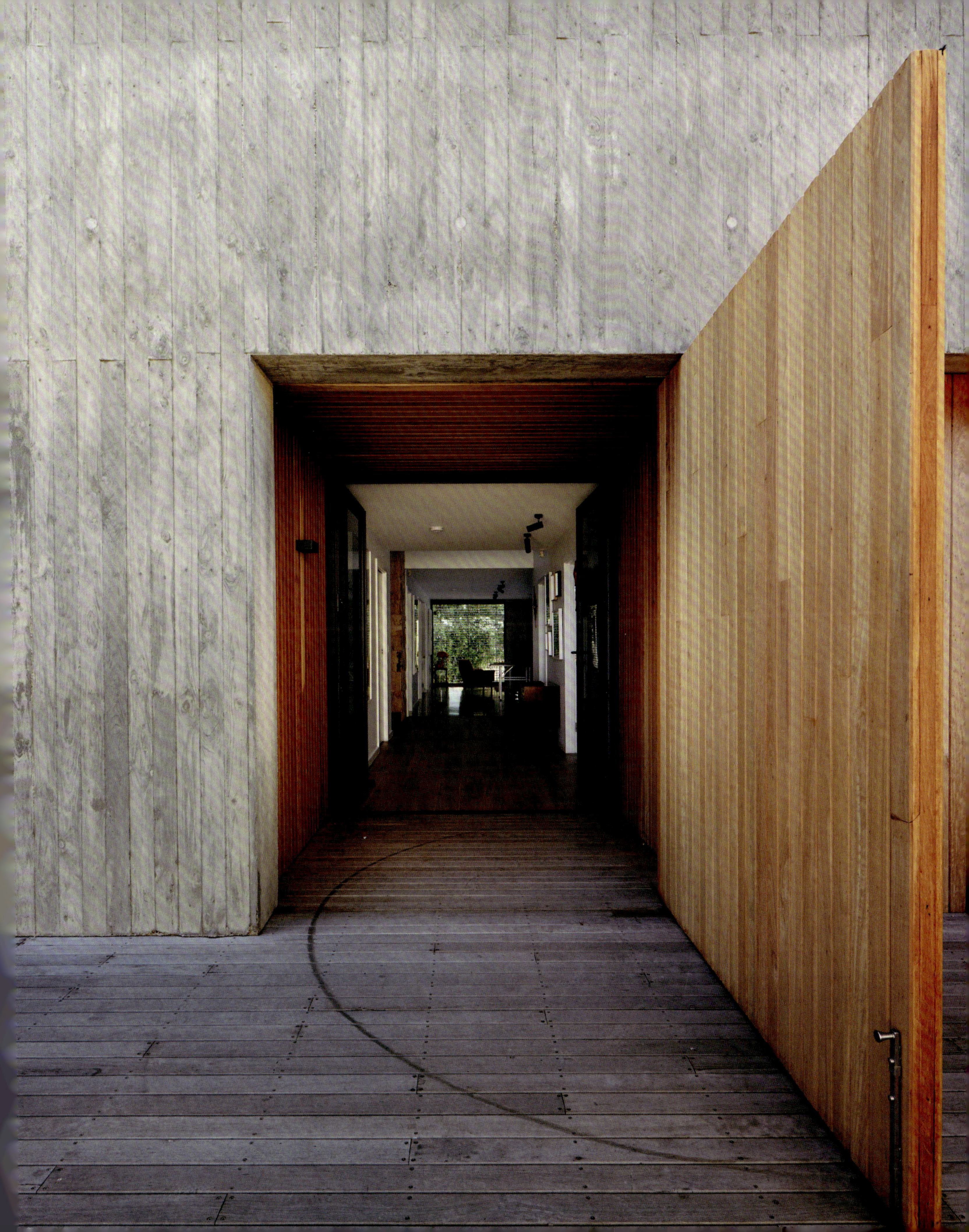

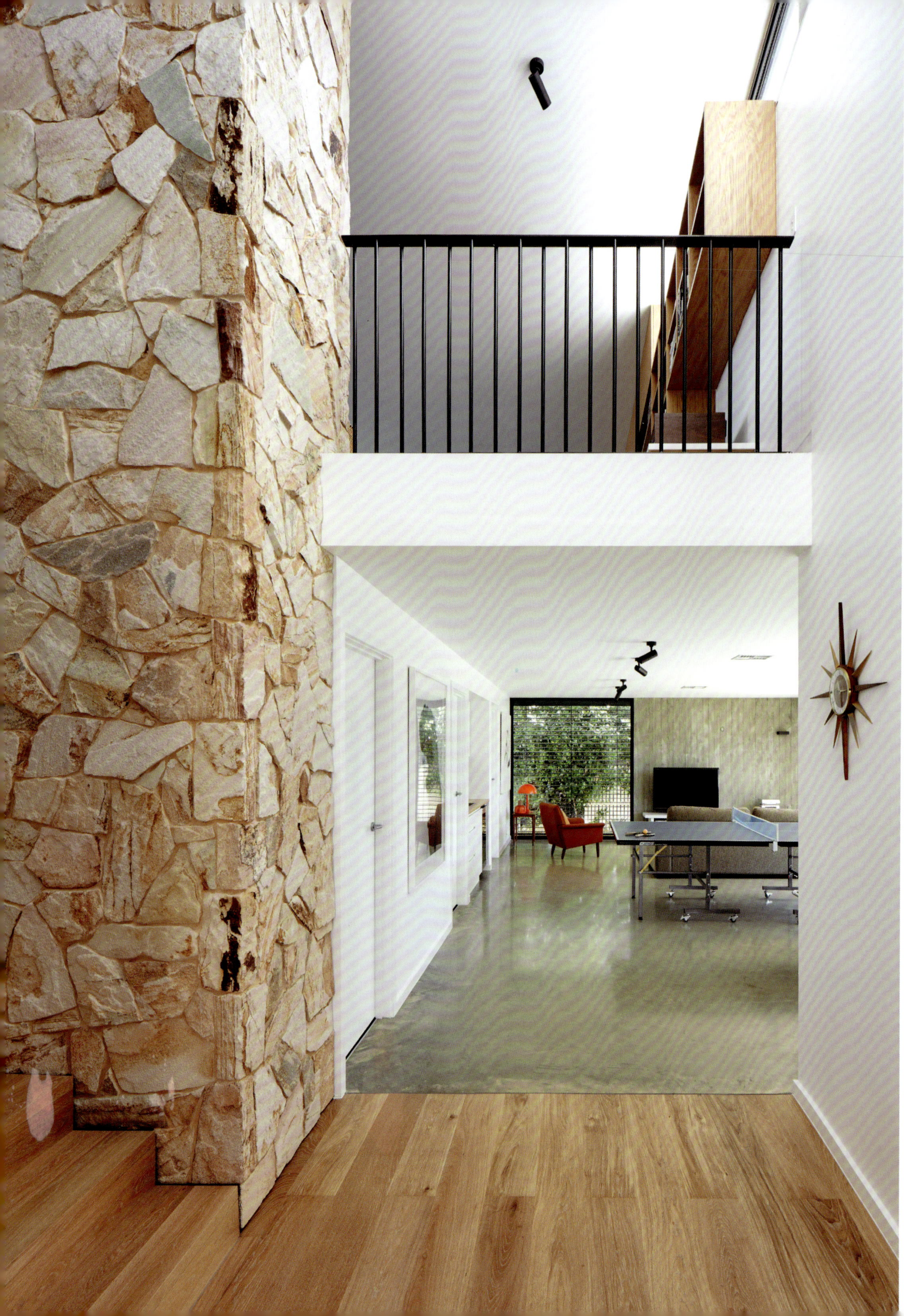

What we love about concrete is that as soon as you take the shutters [boards] off, you have instant history. The knots and imperfections are there. People are attracted to old places because they're not perfect. It's almost a surprise. You don't know what you're going to get, but I've never been disappointed.
—Marco Spinelli

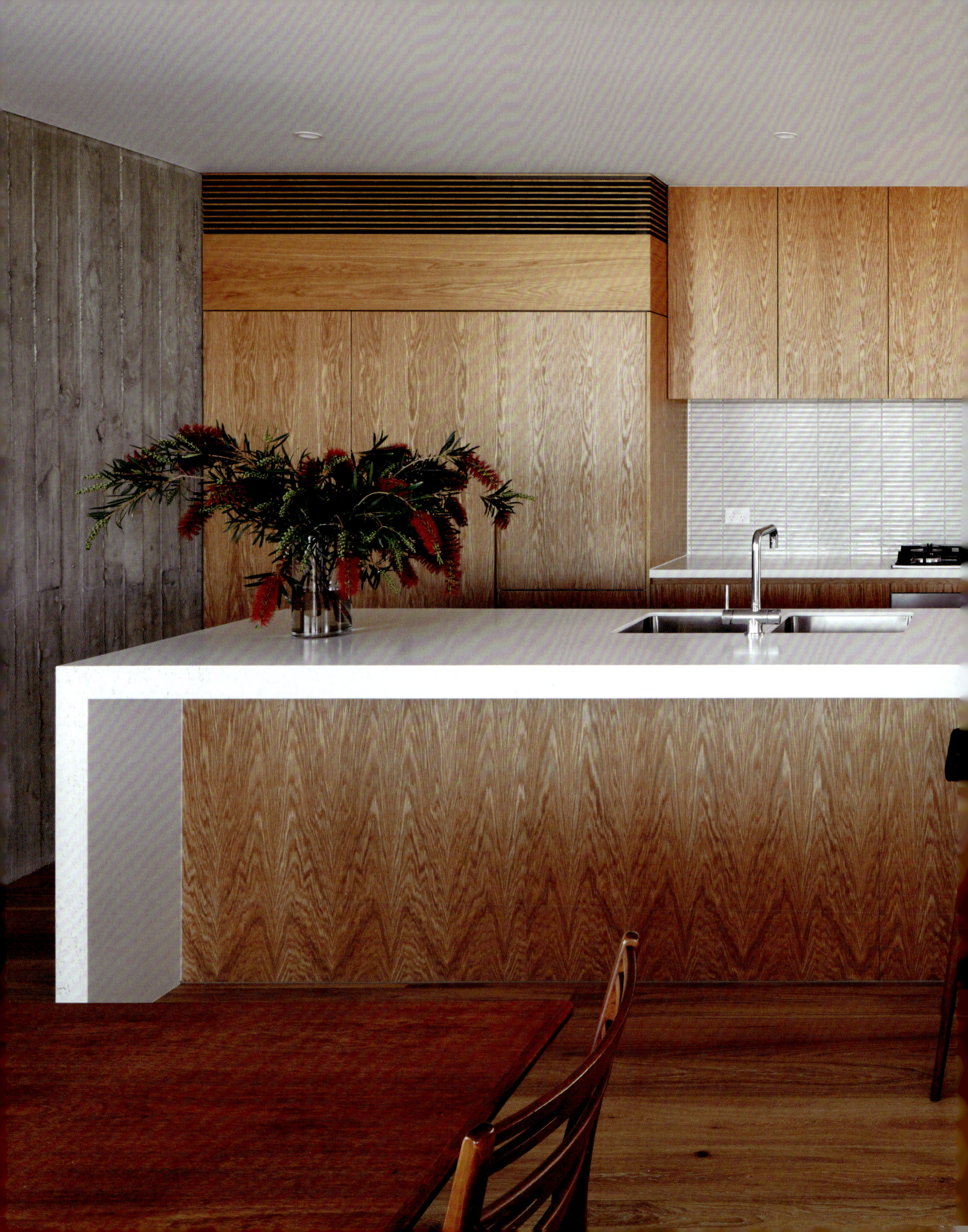

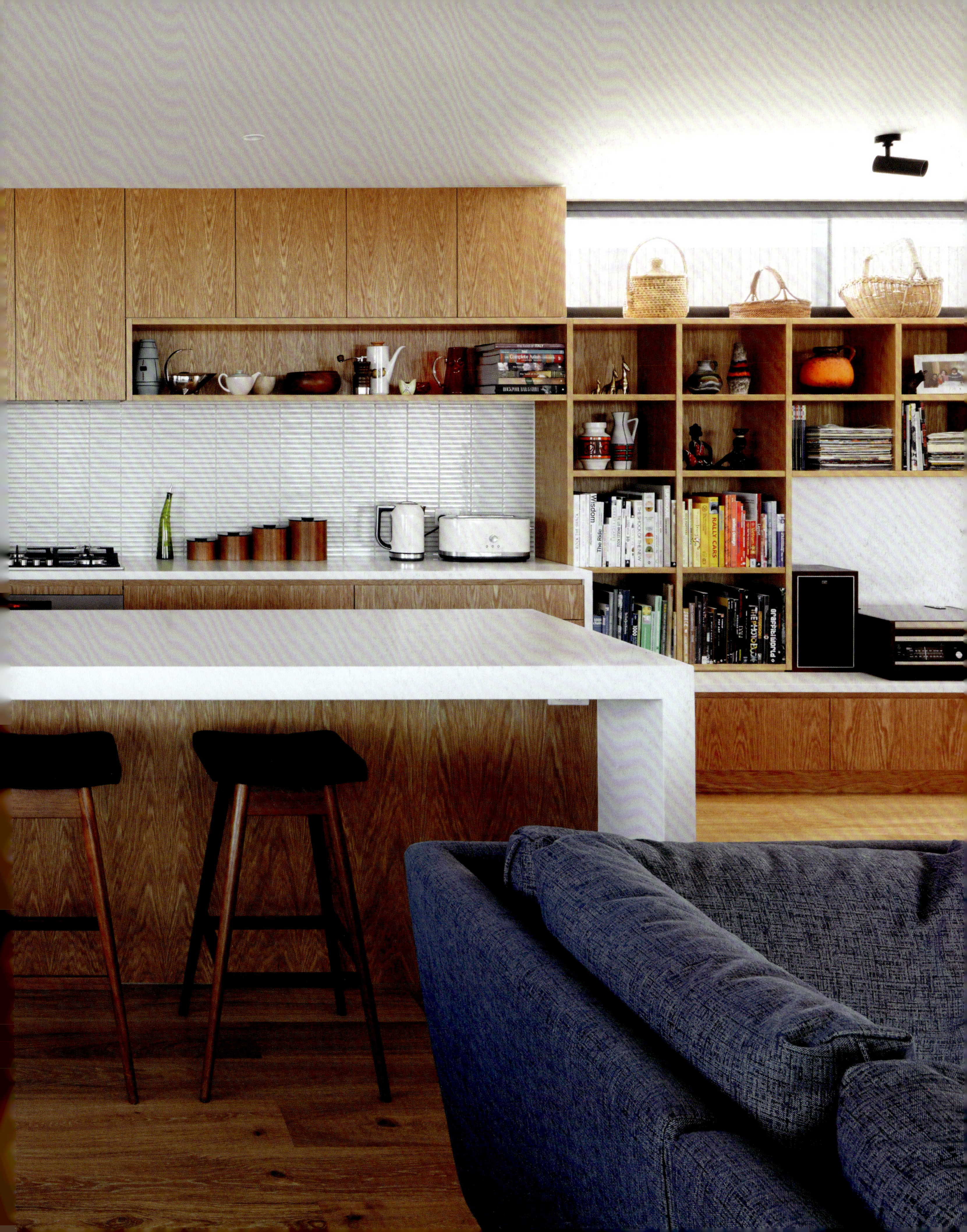
Wisdom
RALLY CARS

PR House

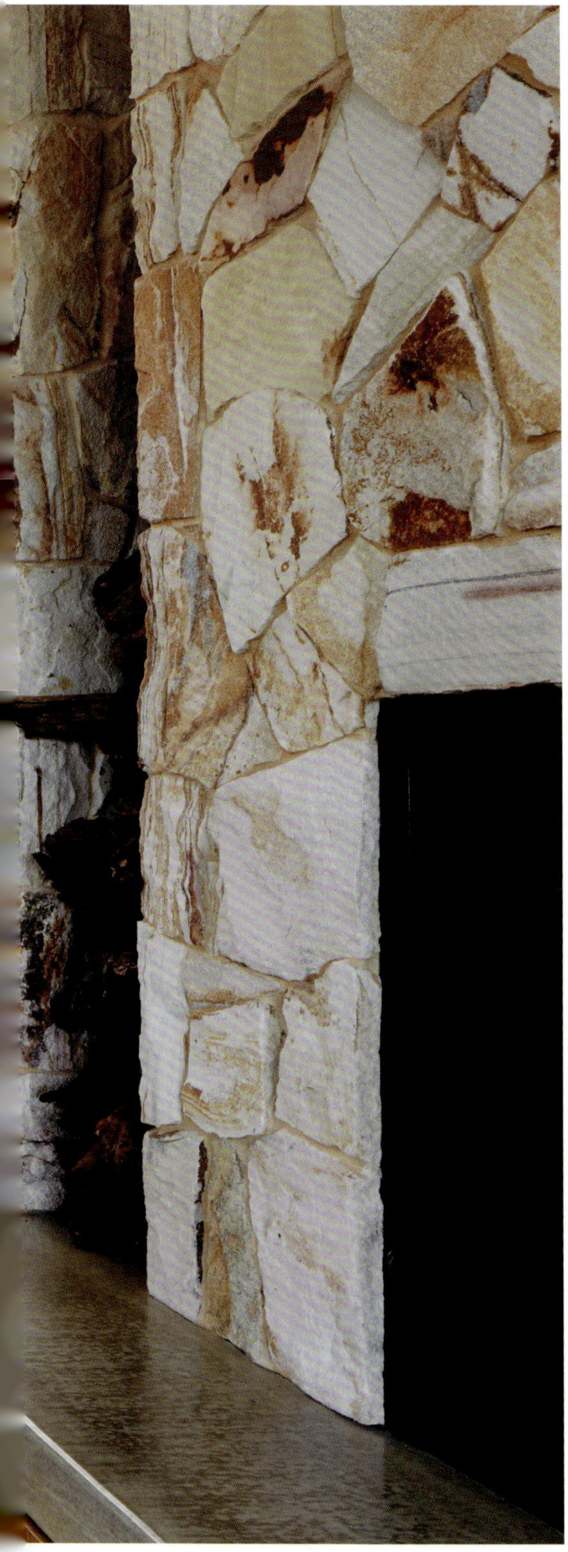

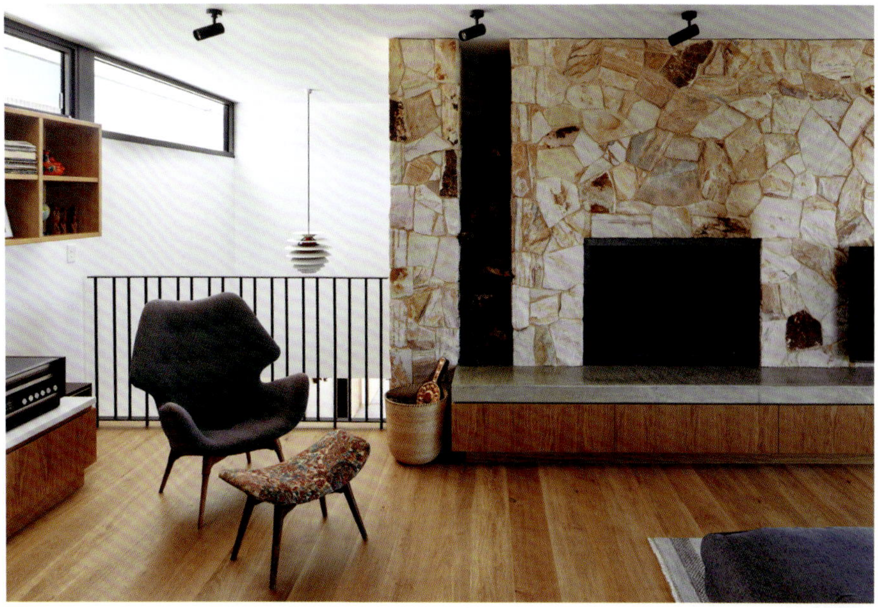

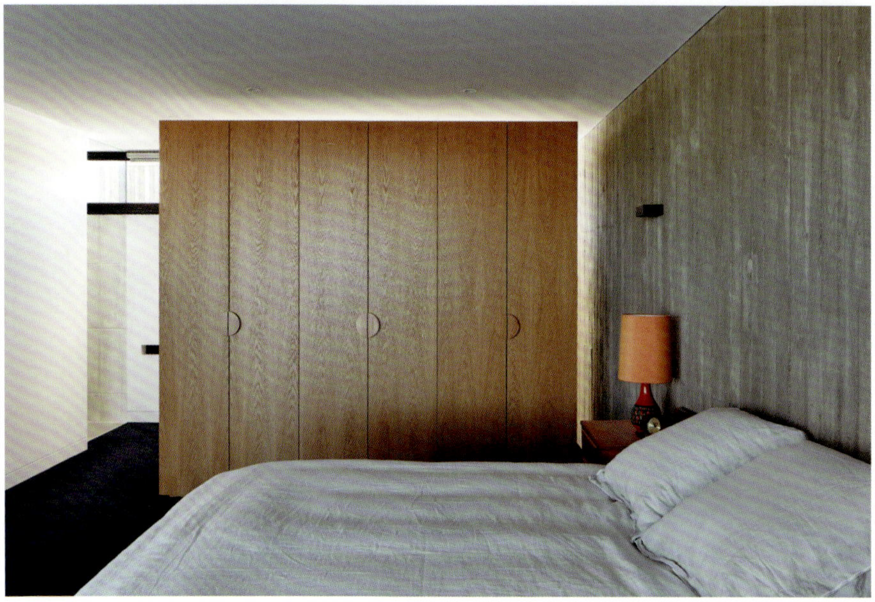

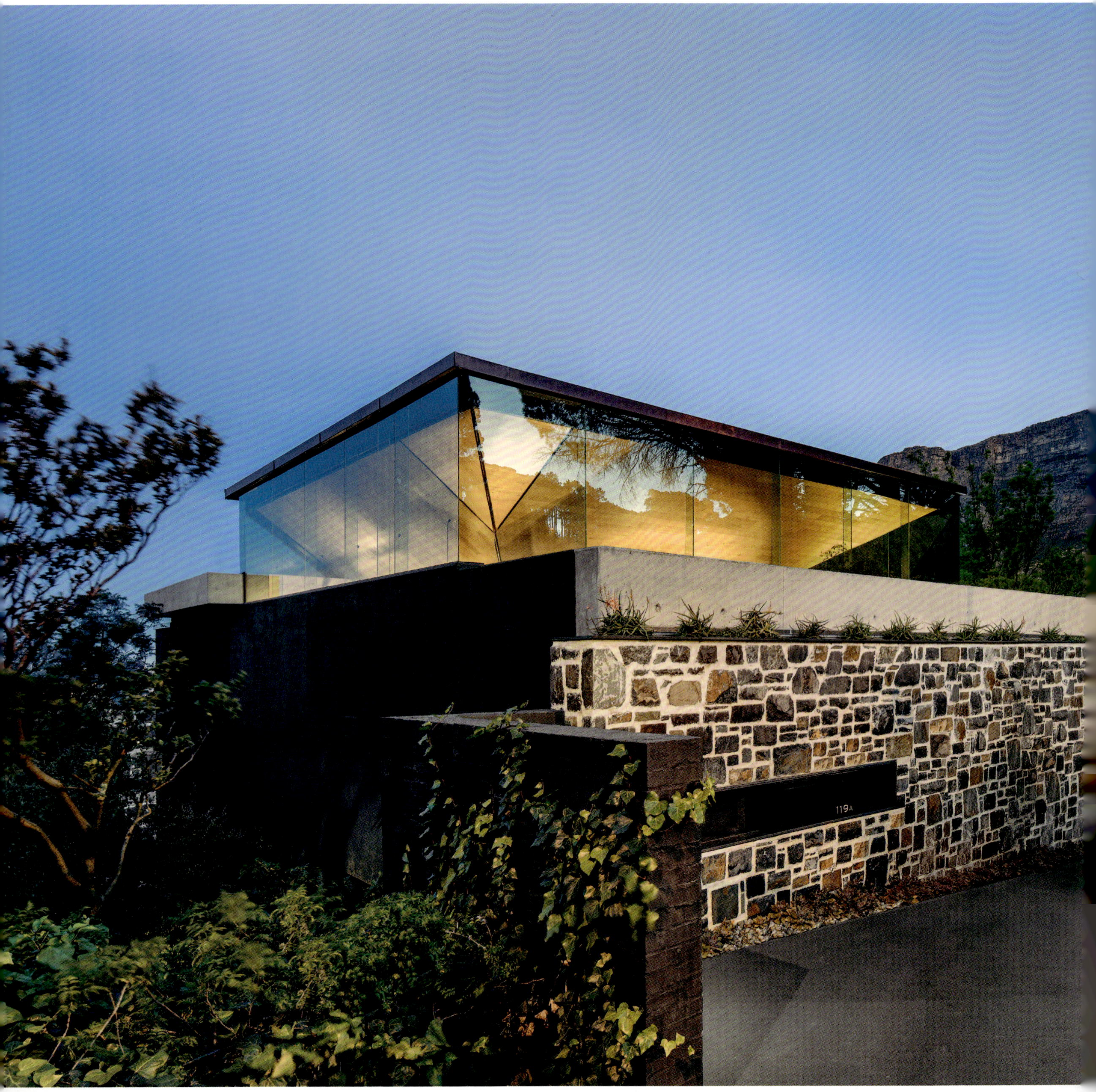
119A

Cape Town, South Africa | 2017

KLOOF119A

SAOTA

Photographs: Courtesy SAOTA and Adam Letch

The Cape Town architecture firm SAOTA has long been designing upscale work in almost every project sector around the globe. Known for dynamic buildings that are both muscular and lithe, the architects often make use of concrete's structural attributes to free up the possibilities for form, flow, and function. Rippling planes, "flying" facades, and striking silhouettes—it's all in the firm's DNA. With its deep cantilevers and long spans, principal Greg Truen's own family house is a classic example of this approach. Situated on a steep slope overlooking Cape Town, the three-level house is designed to commune intimately with its immediate surroundings and stunning views.

"The house offers an intense experience of 'dwelling between,'" commented a judge for the Cape Institute for Architecture awards. "Between the outside and in; between the nestled enclosure and expansive openness; between raw nature and the refined man[-]made."

At night, the inverted pyramid roof glows.

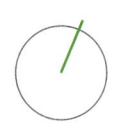

GROUND FLOOR

1 Garage
2 Staff
3 Gym
4 Laundry

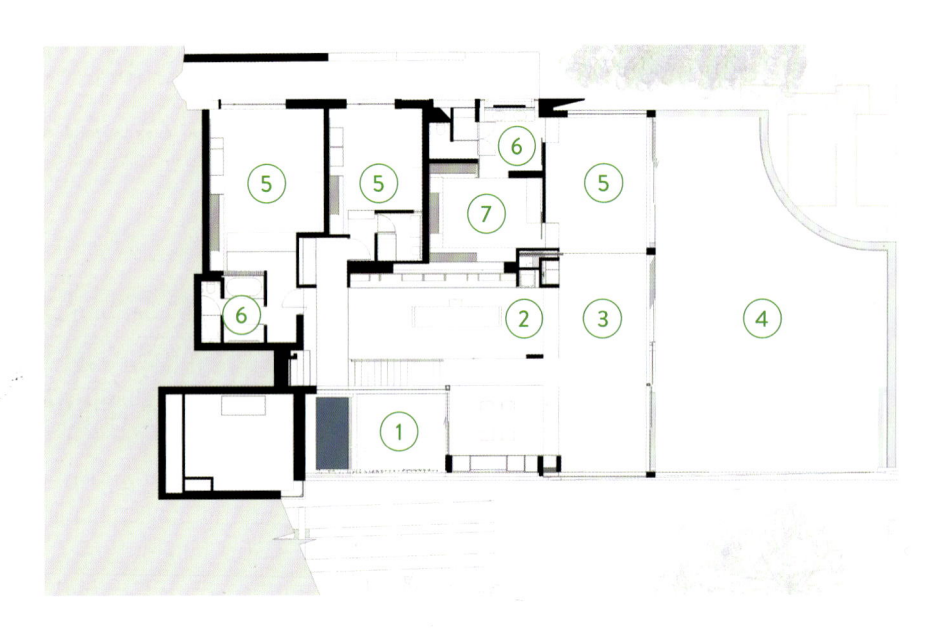

FIRST FLOOR

1 Courtyard
2 Library
3 Lounge
4 Garden
5 Bedroom
6 Bath
7 Closet

SECOND FLOOR

1 Entry
2 Studio
3 Foyer
4 Lounge
5 Garden
6 Deck
7 Living room
8 Dining room
9 Kitchen and pantry
10 Powder room
11 Study

Kloof119A • Floor Plan

Indeed, Truen and his team puzzled over how to put the 9,150-square-foot house together on the 1:4 slope, while folding in lush gardens and courtyards. They placed the living spaces and an infinity pool at the top of the house at street level. The middle floor contains three bedrooms and a library and lounge, while the lower level houses a garage, theater, gym, and guest rooms.

Dark exterior surfaces break down the house's mass and help it retreat into the background. A stone wall along the front facade evokes Cape Town's old quarries and screens the busy street. Inside the pivoting front door, visitors find themselves in a slim, liminal space, for straight ahead a green courtyard is visible through a large piece of glass. To the right, a corridor wall lined with board-formed concrete leads to the open-plan living area and its panoramic view. There, a retractable glass wall opens to the garden and an infinity pool that seems to float above the city. Here too is the house's tour de force: an inverted pyramidal roof with clerestories and folded planes that frame views of Lion's Head and Table Mountain. These windows drench the interior with light, while shifting shadows mark the march of the sun and seasons.

"By putting the living on top and having the roof opening to the sky, we made the most of the mountain views," Truen says. Below on the bedroom level, a larger walkout garden was built on the roof of the garage. To the south, a void in the floor plan carved out space for a sheltered courtyard, allowing light into rooms that would otherwise feel dim and distant. Throughout, washed oak woodwork and flamed granite floors add refined softness to the concrete, glass, and steel.

"The concrete allowed us to do a couple of things that were important," Truen says. "It allowed us to create slabs with deep planters, and the swimming pool on the top level. The roof was quite interesting because the angled elements open up to the clerestories. The beams that carry the sloping portion are formed out of concrete, with a steel beam in the middle to keep a relatively slim profile. It gives the illusion that there is no structure around the glass." Even with all the beckoning gardens, it is the roof that is the highlight of this house. At night it glows like a giant light box, giving the house an identity beyond its receding facade.

The house meets the street with a stone wall; between this wall and the house is the entrance, connected to a small courtyard (next page) that creates a "restrained and quiet" space before the dramatic views of the living areas.

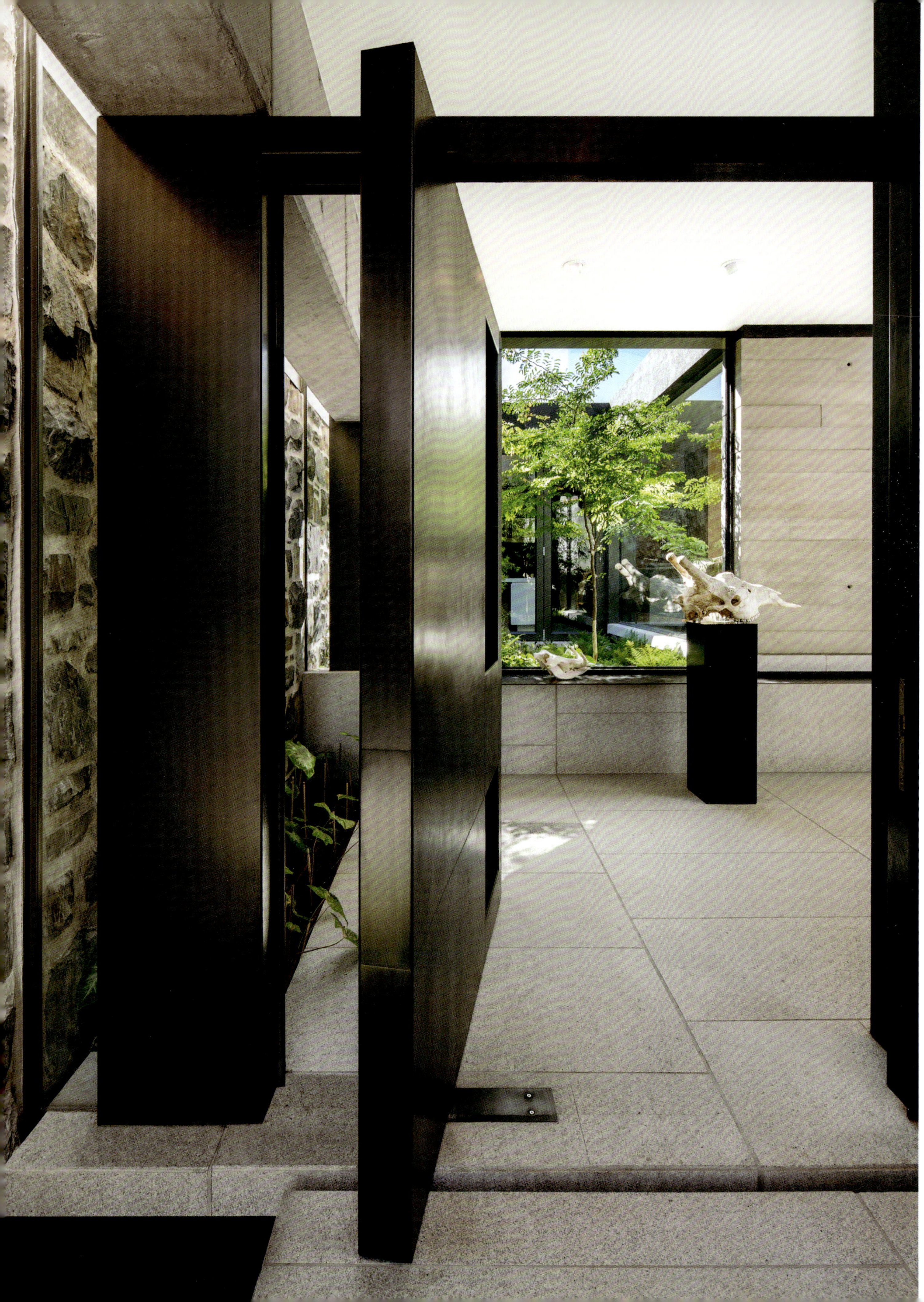

In South Africa and around the world, we use mostly concrete and masonry to accommodate deep cantilevers and long structural spans. Or we'll use concrete as a feature surface showing the board forms, or use a bush hammer to expose the aggregate.
—Greg Truen

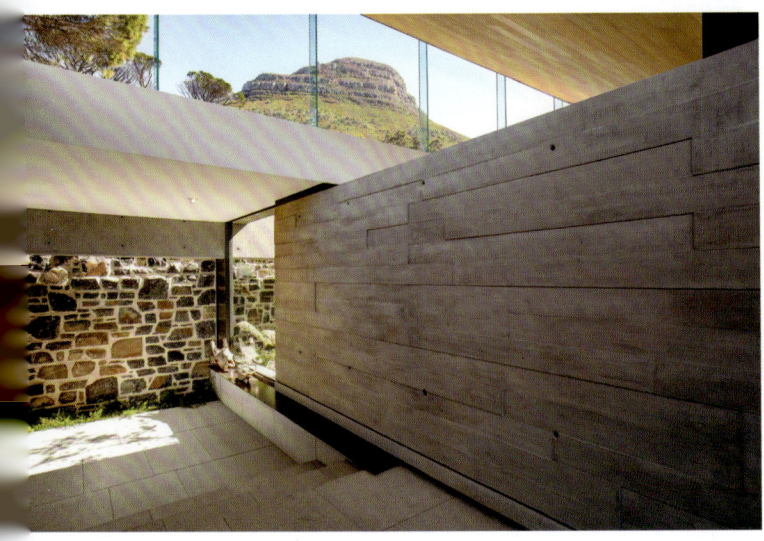

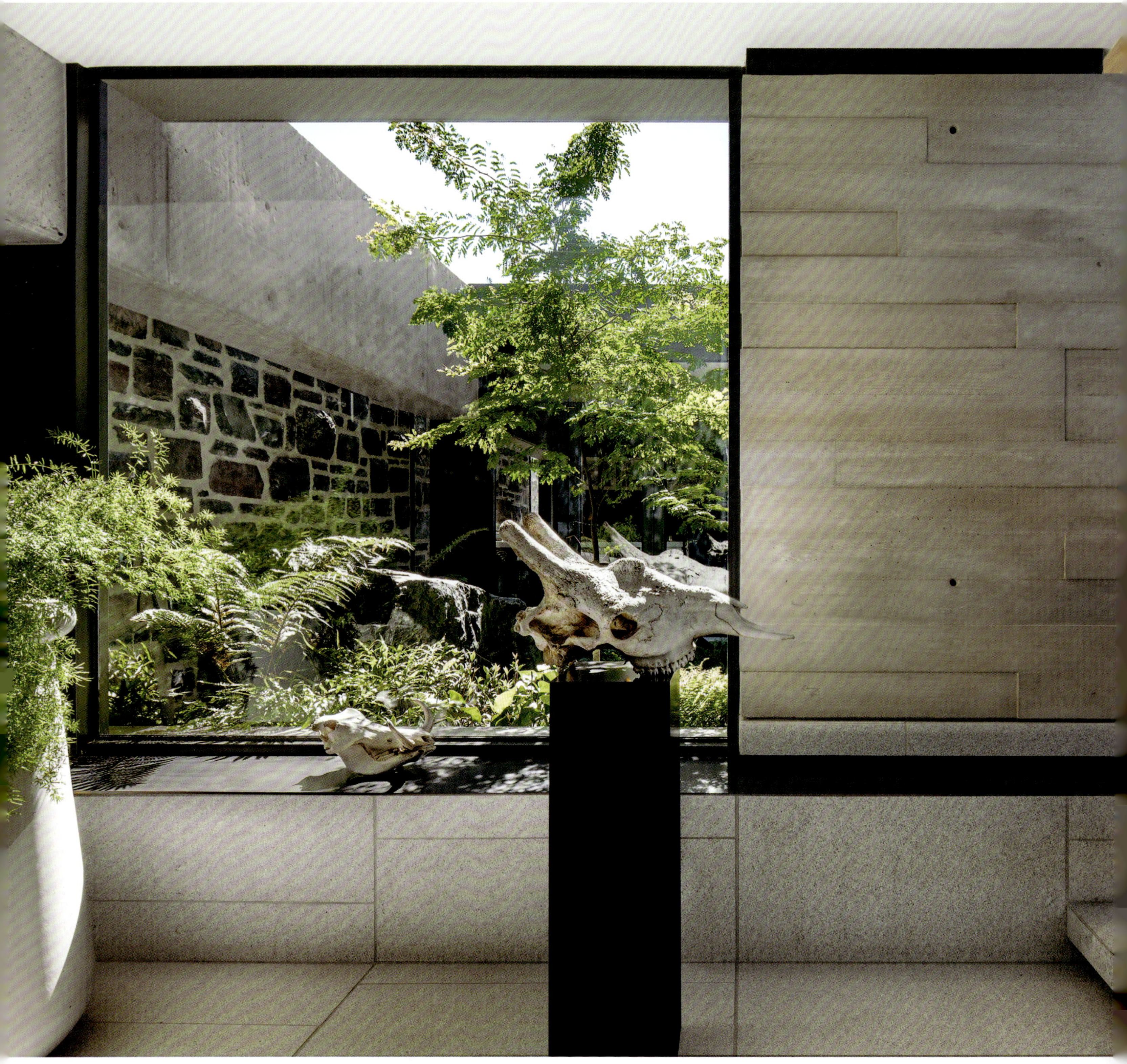

59

Kloof119A

61

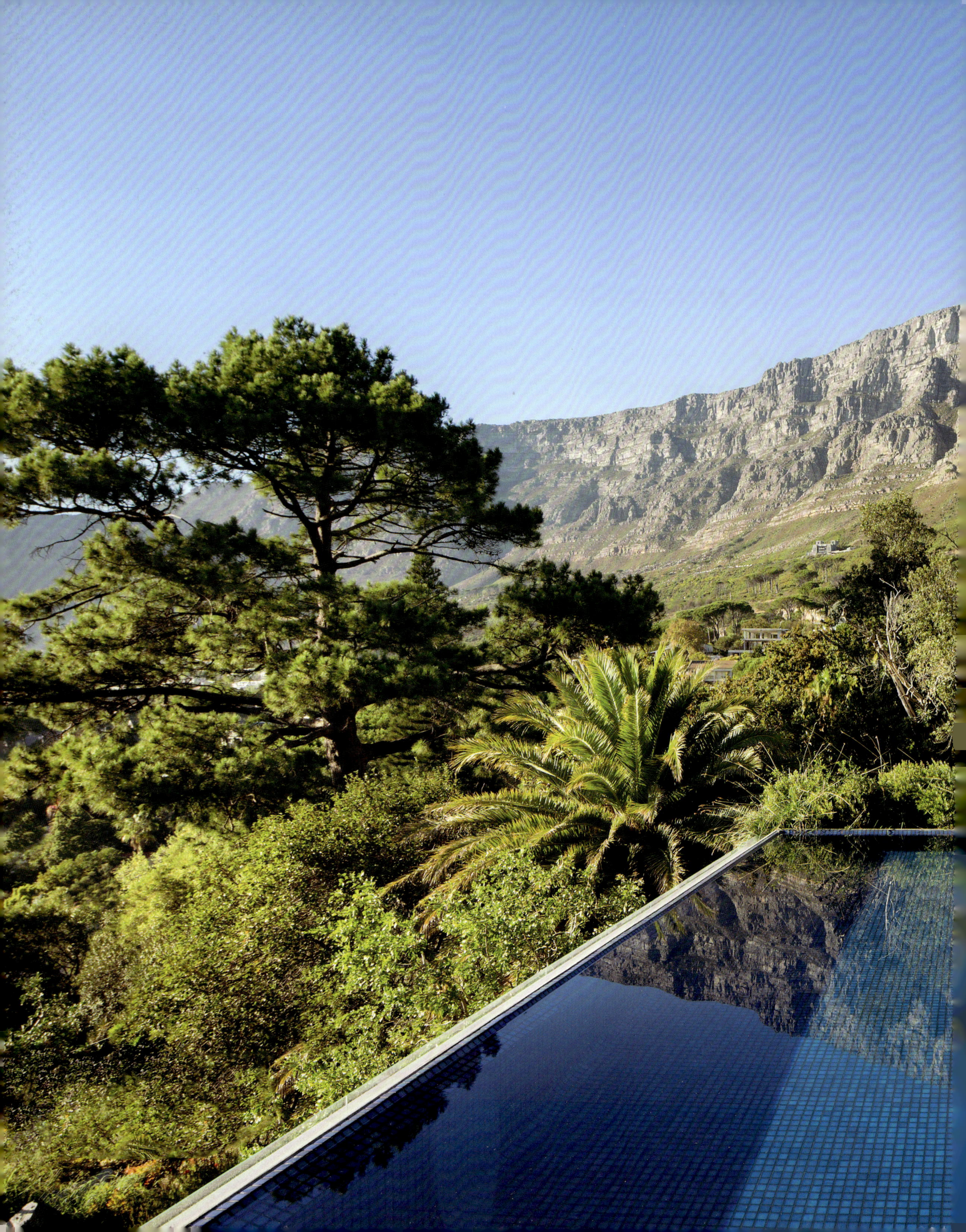

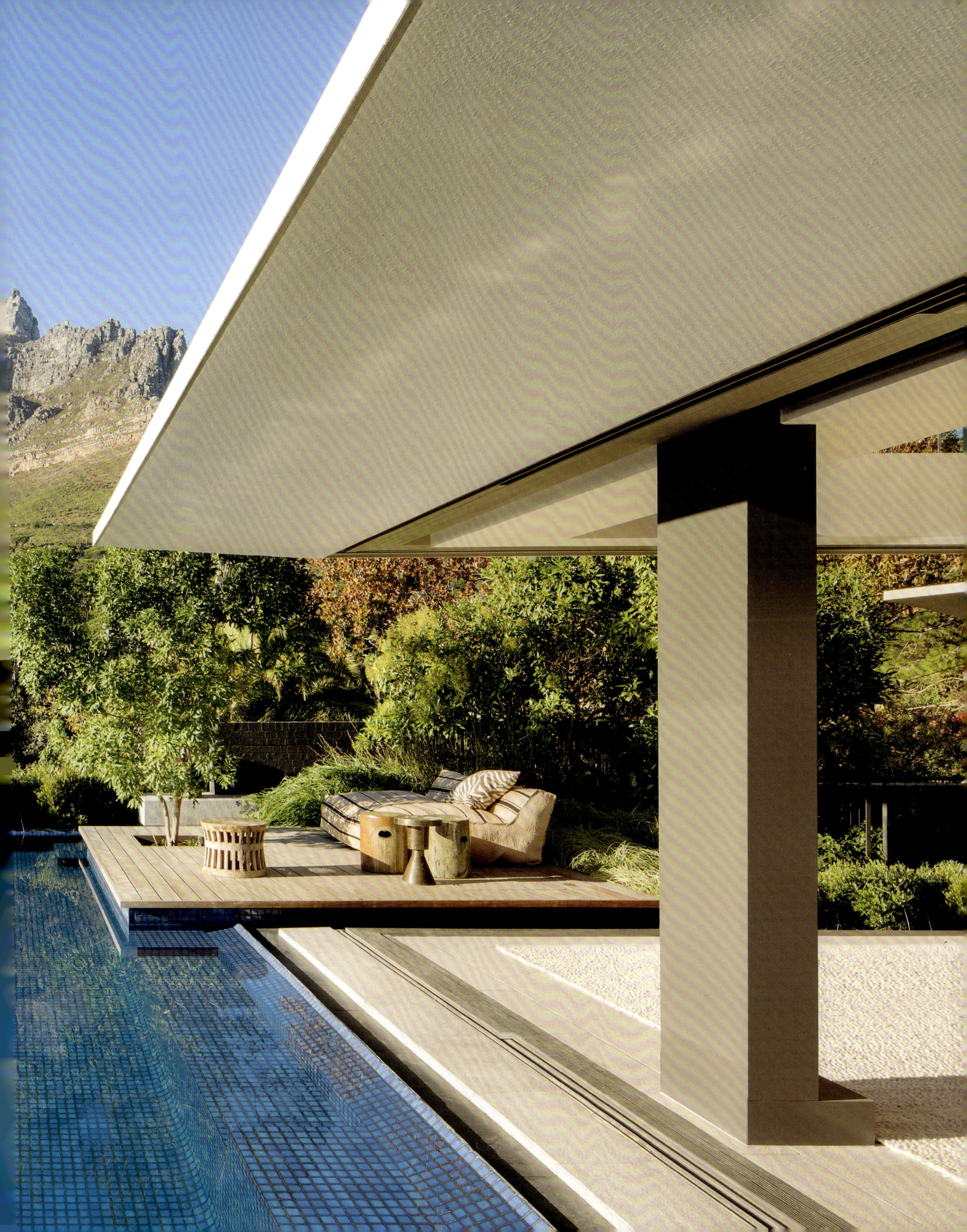

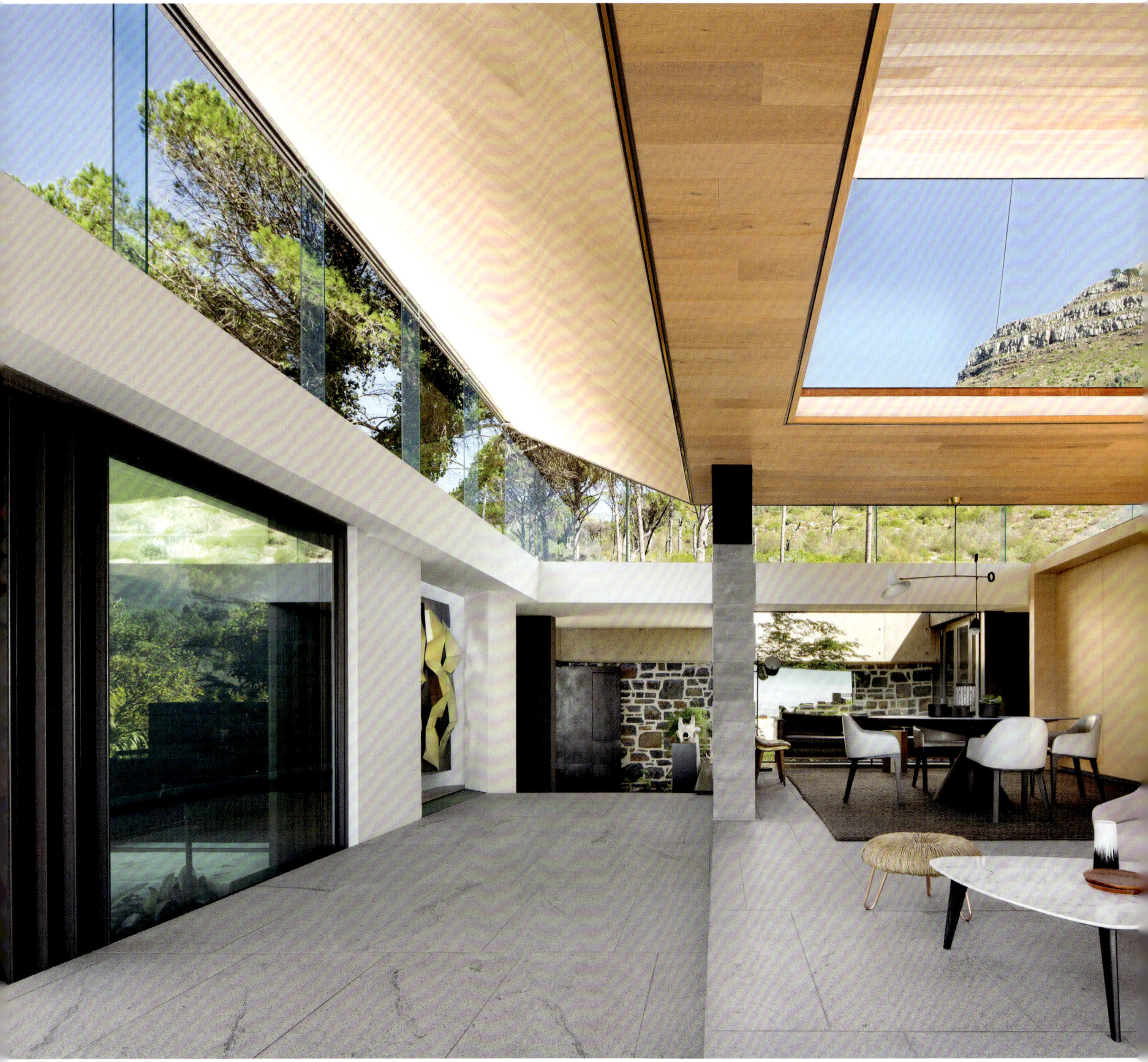

65

Kloof119A

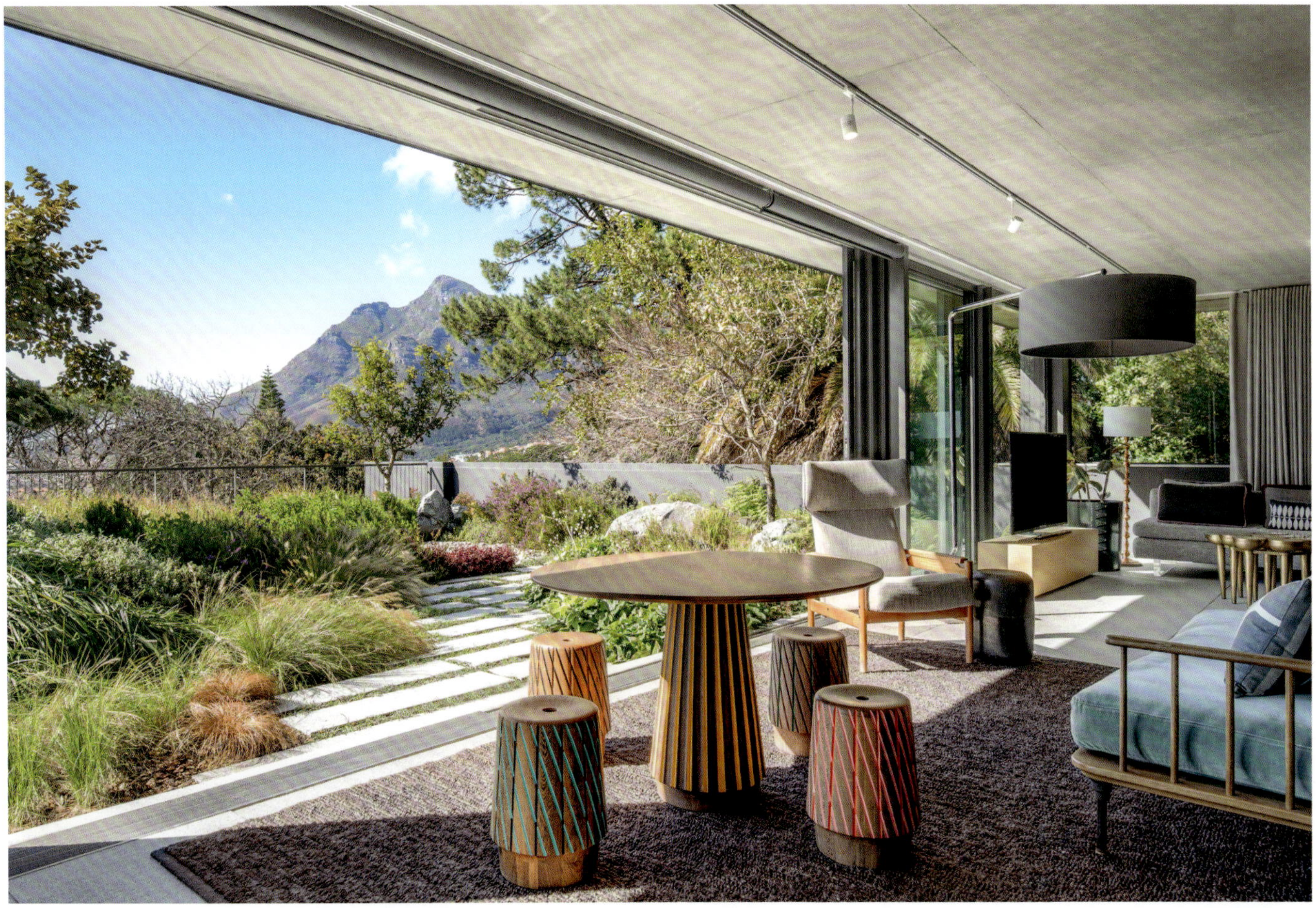

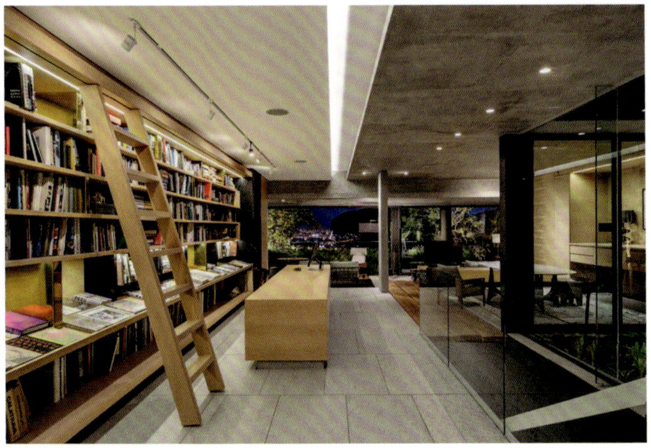

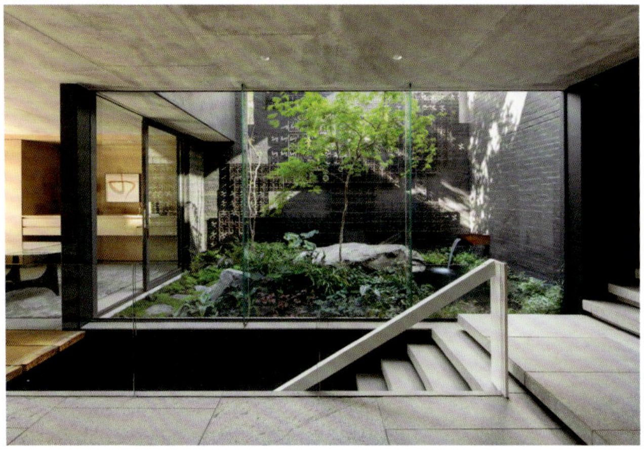

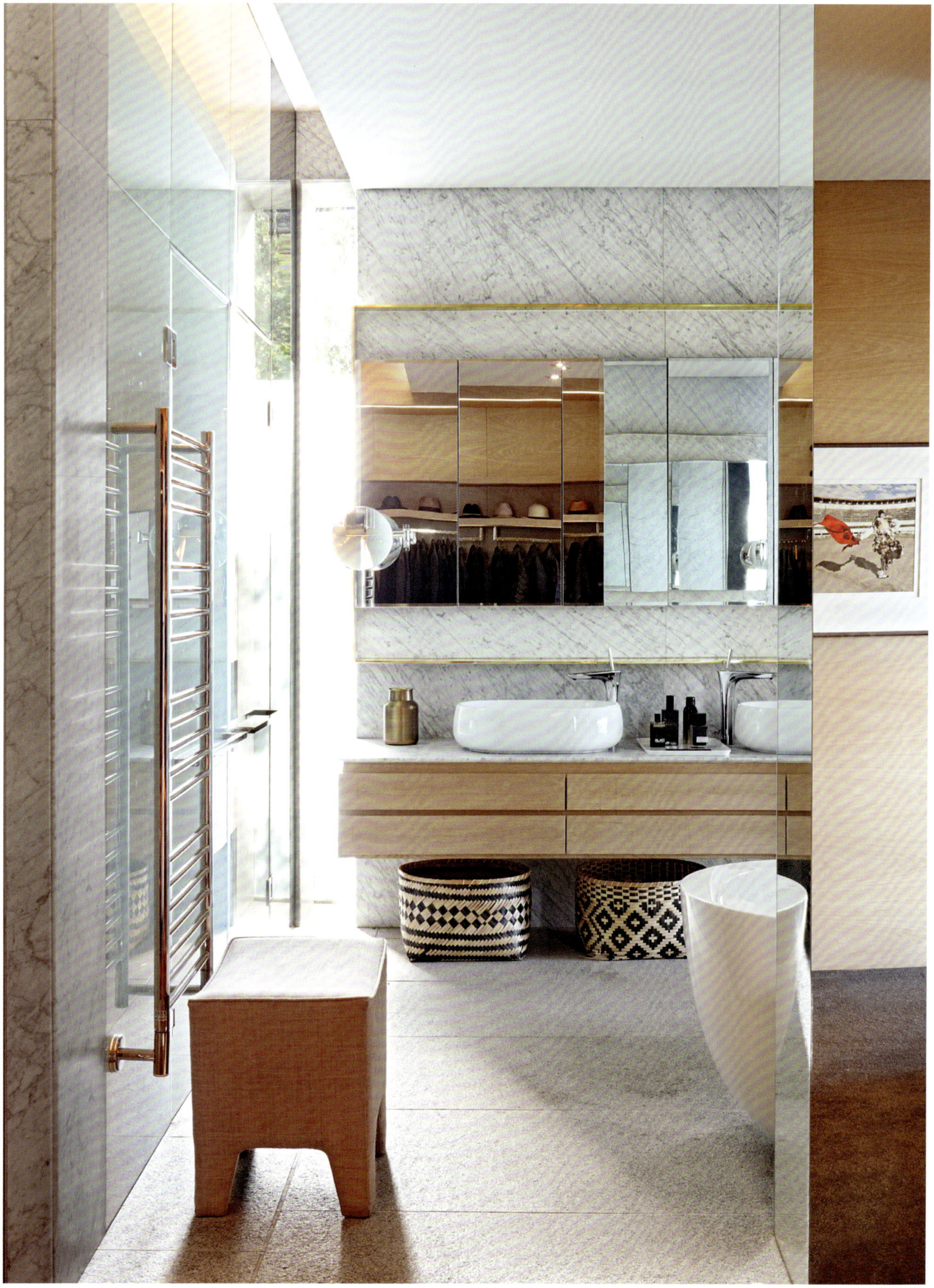

69

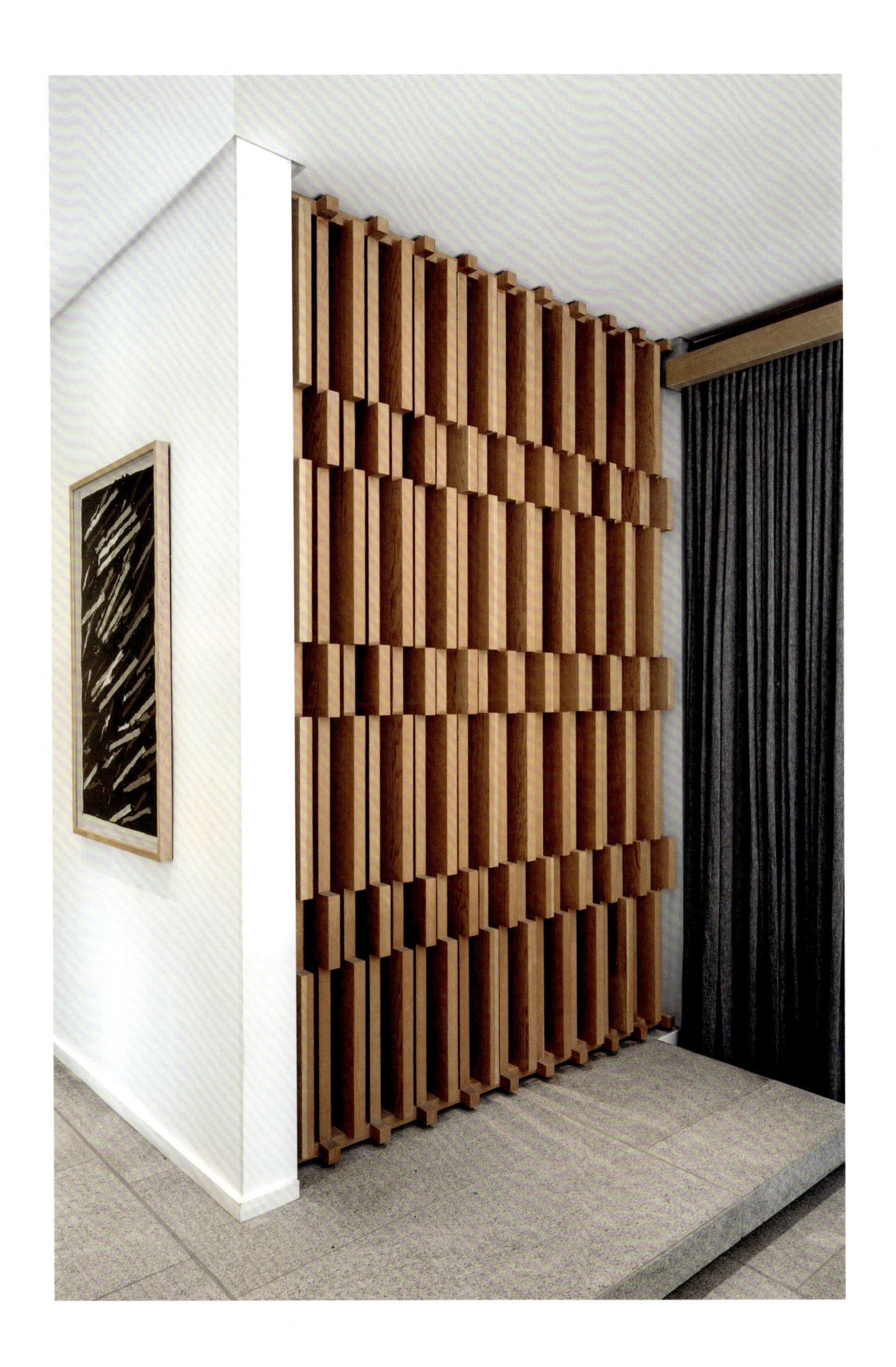

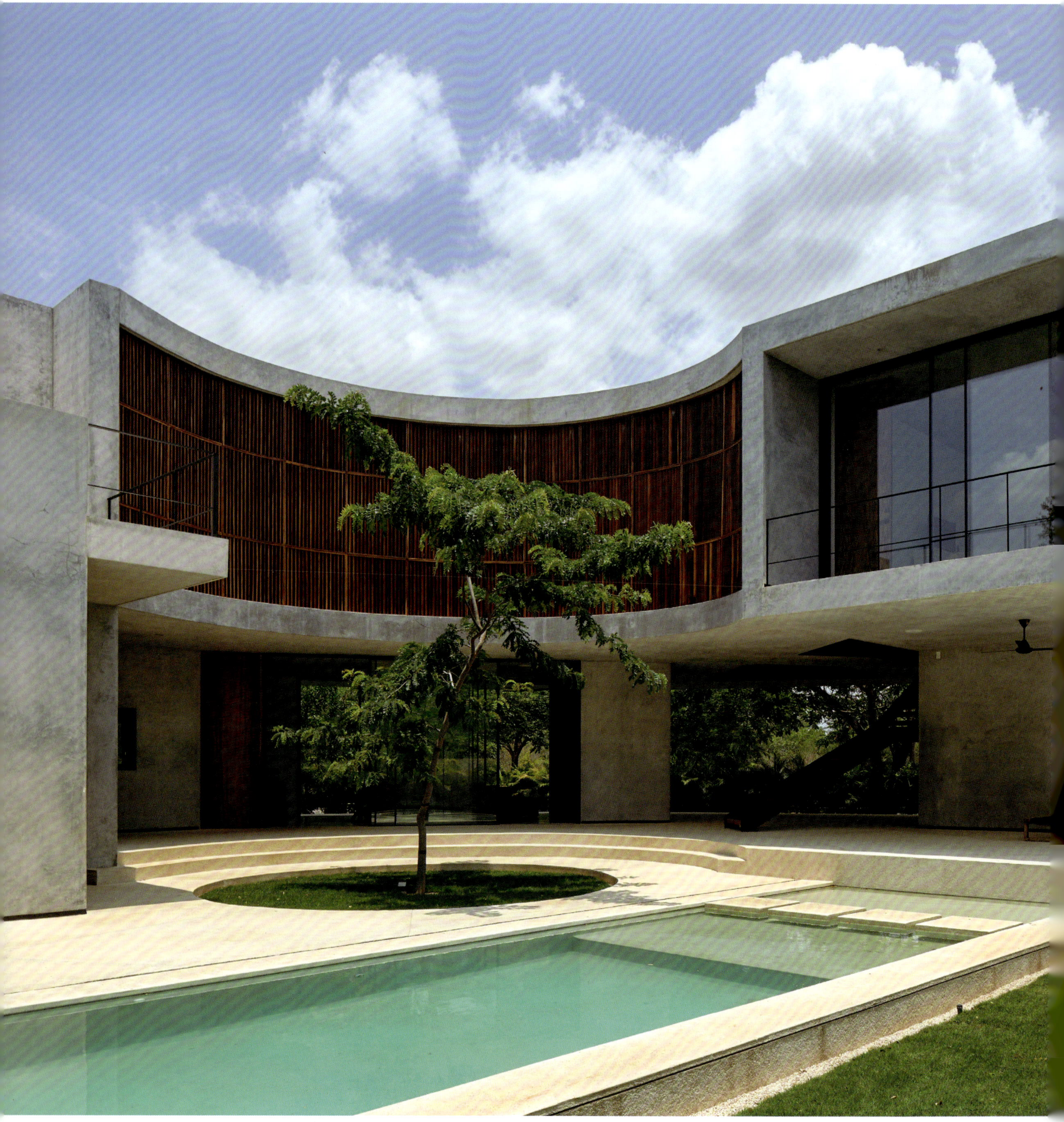

Mérida, Yucatán, Mexico | 2018

CASA MADRI

Magaldi Studio
Photographs: @Edmund Sumner

One way to minimize the scale of a large house on a corner lot is to eliminate the grand front entrance. Casa Madri makes clever use of that strategy to harmonize with its tropical surroundings. Miami-based architect Chris Magaldi designed the full-time residence for a childhood friend and his family in a gated community on Mexico's Yucatán Peninsula. Situated on an irregularly shaped corner lot, the house is 6,000 square feet, but it doesn't feel that big because of the way the indoors and outdoors are intertwined. "All the other houses are pretty enclosed, with a front gate like a regular house," Magaldi says. "I asked, 'Why not go for an open house, like a hotel, that you can enter anywhere?'"

Magaldi looked for inspiration to Mexican regionalism and Japanese simplicity, circling the domestically scaled spaces around a central courtyard. But from there the design strays from tradition. The first floor dematerializes as two independent volumes—kitchen/dining/living room and a separate office/guest room—held within a concrete terrace that traces the outer arc of the building lot.

So does the second floor. Open to the elements, it contains two detached volumes—the service quarters, two bedrooms, and a shared bath on one side of the plan, and the main bedroom suite on the other. Between them, the concrete floor follows the lower-level footprint, forming a wide curve on the outer edge, while the circular inner edge looks down on a pink-flowering specimen tree in a pool of water.

FIRST FLOOR

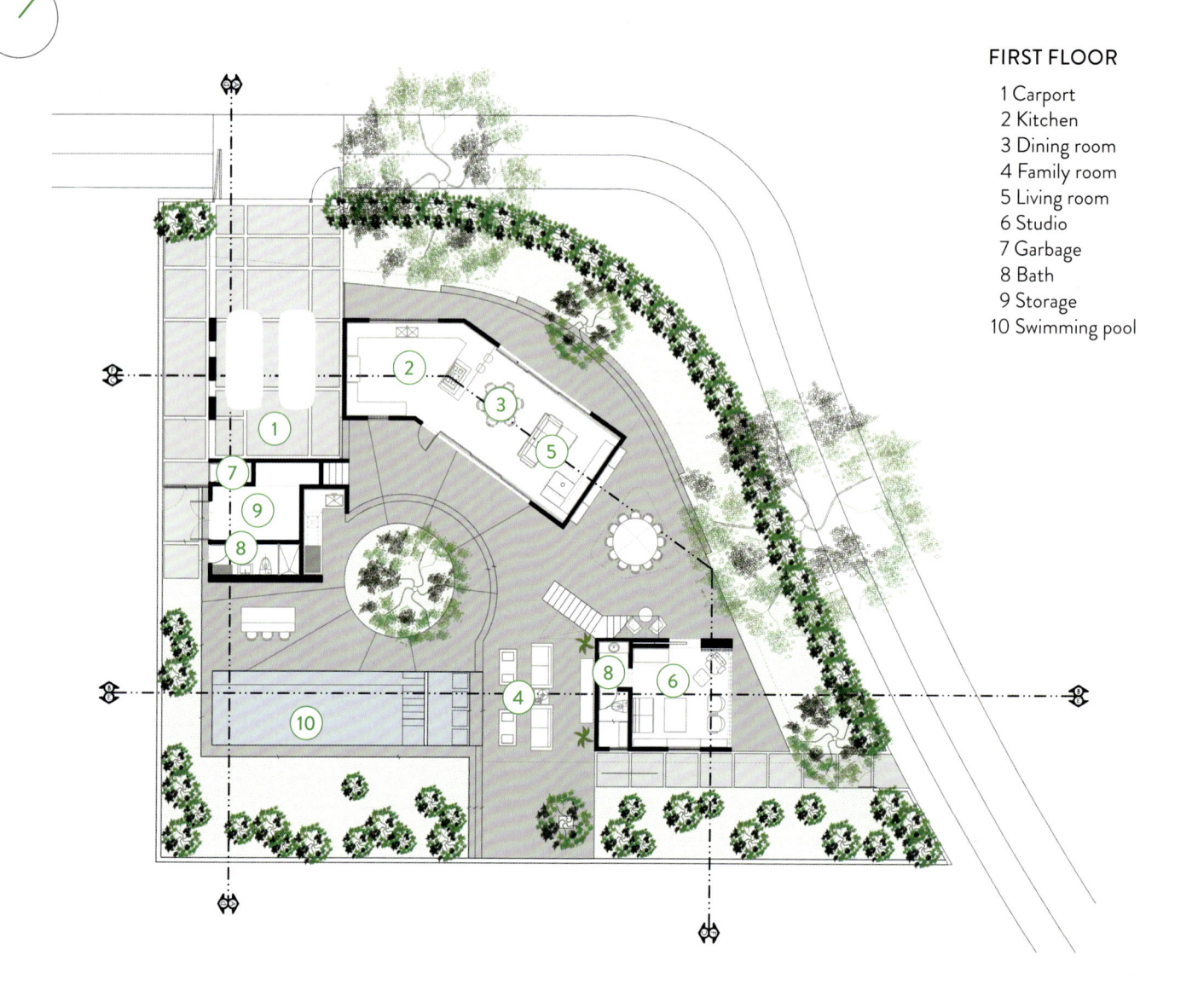

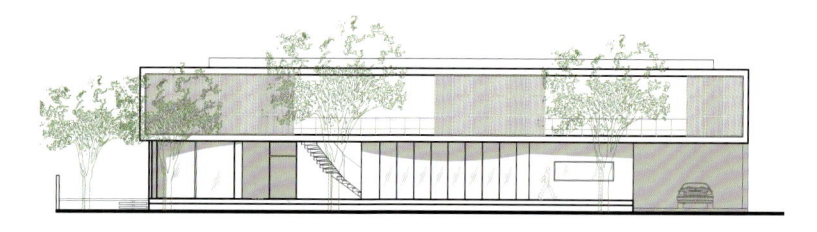

1. Carport
2. Kitchen
3. Dining room
4. Family room
5. Living room
6. Studio
7. Garbage
8. Bath
9. Storage
10. Swimming pool

NORTHEAST ELEVATION

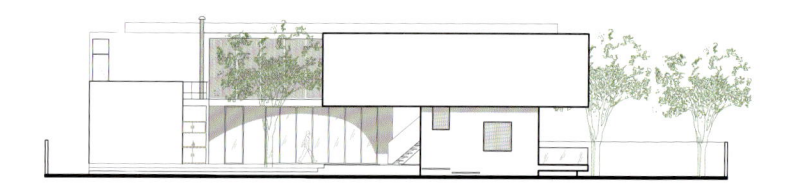

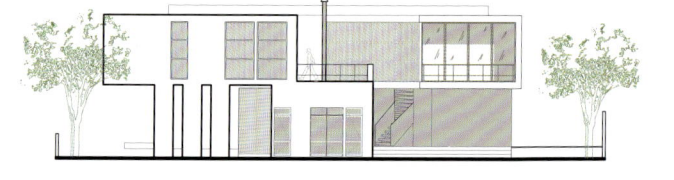

SOUTH ELEVATION

SOUTHWEST ELEVATION

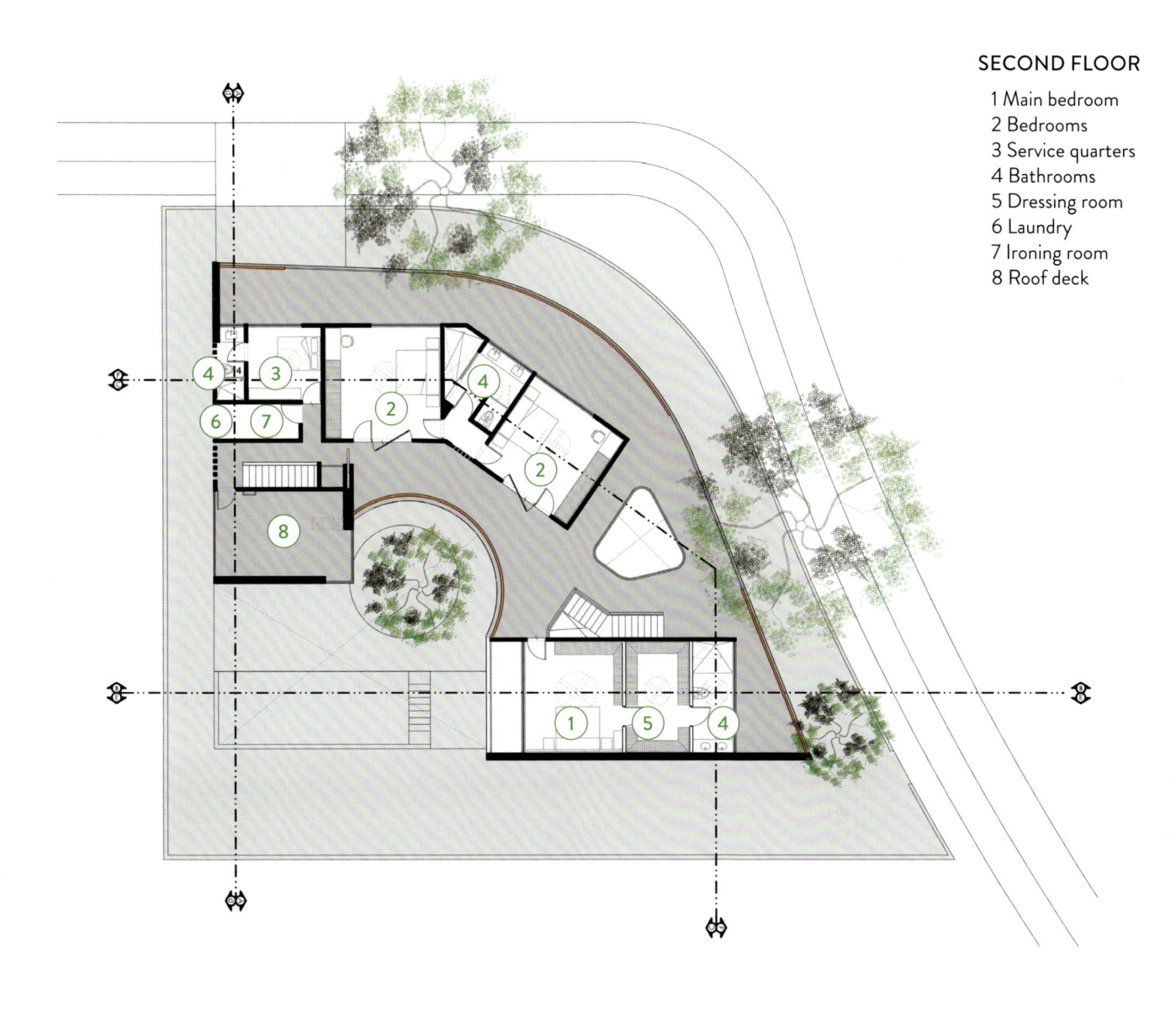

SECOND FLOOR

1 Main bedroom
2 Bedrooms
3 Service quarters
4 Bathrooms
5 Dressing room
6 Laundry
7 Ironing room
8 Roof deck

section A-A

section B-B

section C-C

section D-D

section E-E

section F-F

Casa Madri • Floor Plan

The decision to lift the bedrooms thoughtfully addressed the darker aspects of tropical life. "Because of all the animals—spiders and snakes—we wanted to go up off the ground," Migaldi says. An open stairway made of metal and parota—a hard, resinous native wood—leads directly from the courtyard to the bedroom level, which feels as though you are living in the trees. Three 16-foot-tall sections of parota slats are incorporated into the facade to control sunlight and reduce the need for air-conditioning. Near the stairway, an irregular cutout with a solid-steel rail opens another view of the courtyard below. Both it and the stairway are meant to evoke a Richard Serra sculpture, Magaldi says.

Muscular but not bulky, the home's big design moves have both a grounding and a floating effect. Massive concrete-and-steel trusses were required for the cantilevers and long spans. Inside, the concrete floors are white, finished with a wash to create a texture like leather. "The client wanted to be able to see the spiders when he walks around at night," Magaldi says of the light-colored floors. The walls are darker, and the exterior is coated with chukum, an old technique that creates a unique water-resistant surface.

Casa Madri offers an airy facade to the street, so as not to disrupt the lush setting. By so thoroughly blurring the edges between exposure and enclosure, it brings a new dimension to tropical living.

74 Casa Madri

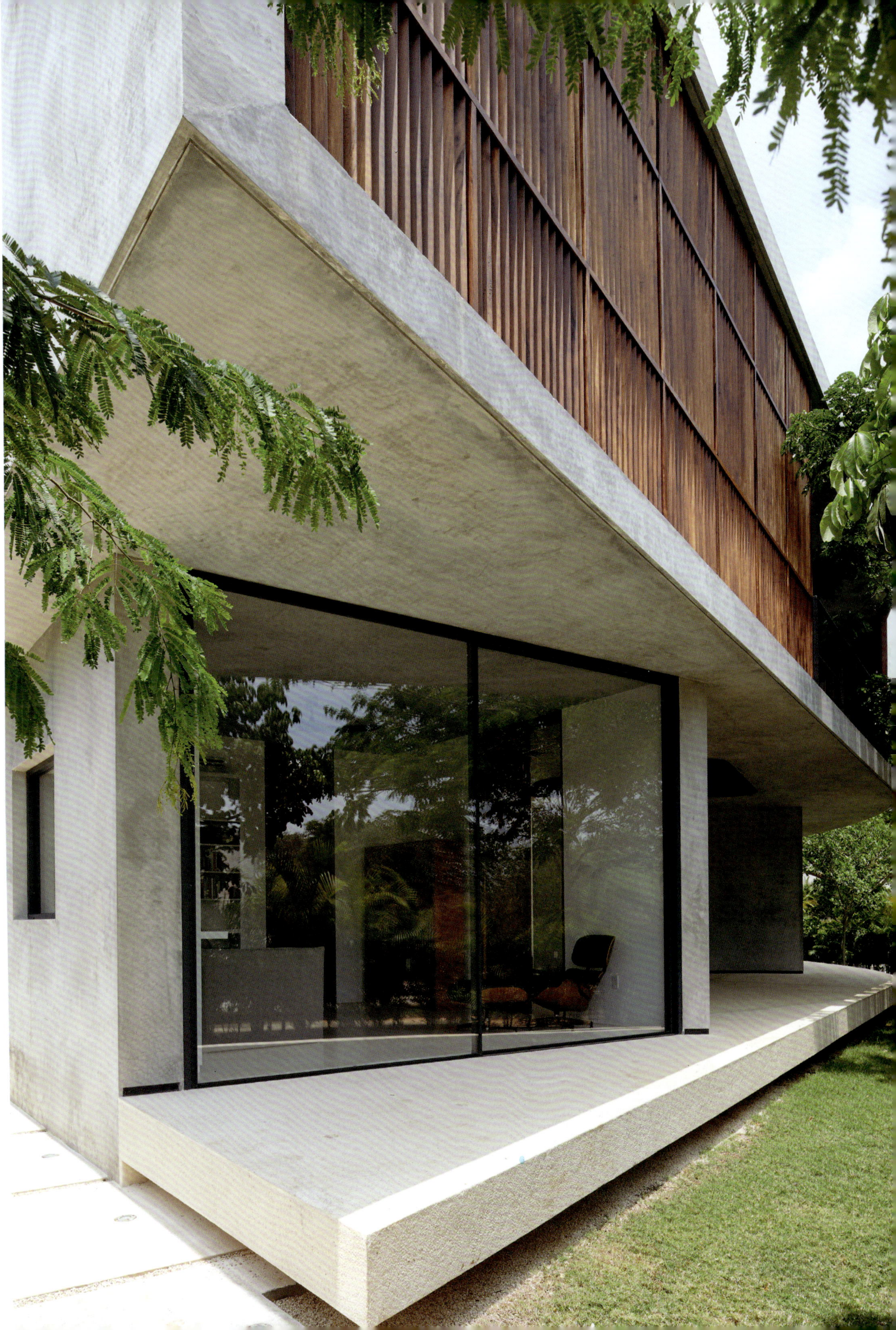

Casa Madri

The exterior is coated with chukum, an old technique that creates a unique water-resistant surface. People from the village came with the tree sap in 2-liter Coke containers and mixed it, like a honey. When it rains, the colors change. There are not just grays but pinks and other warm colors in the concrete.
—Chris Migaldi

Lifting the bedrooms on massive steel-and-concrete trusses made way for covered outdoor living and dining at ground level and allows fresh air to flow through even the enclosed public spaces when the windows and doors are open. Parota wood screens and a perimeter wall made of a tawny local stone lend warmth.

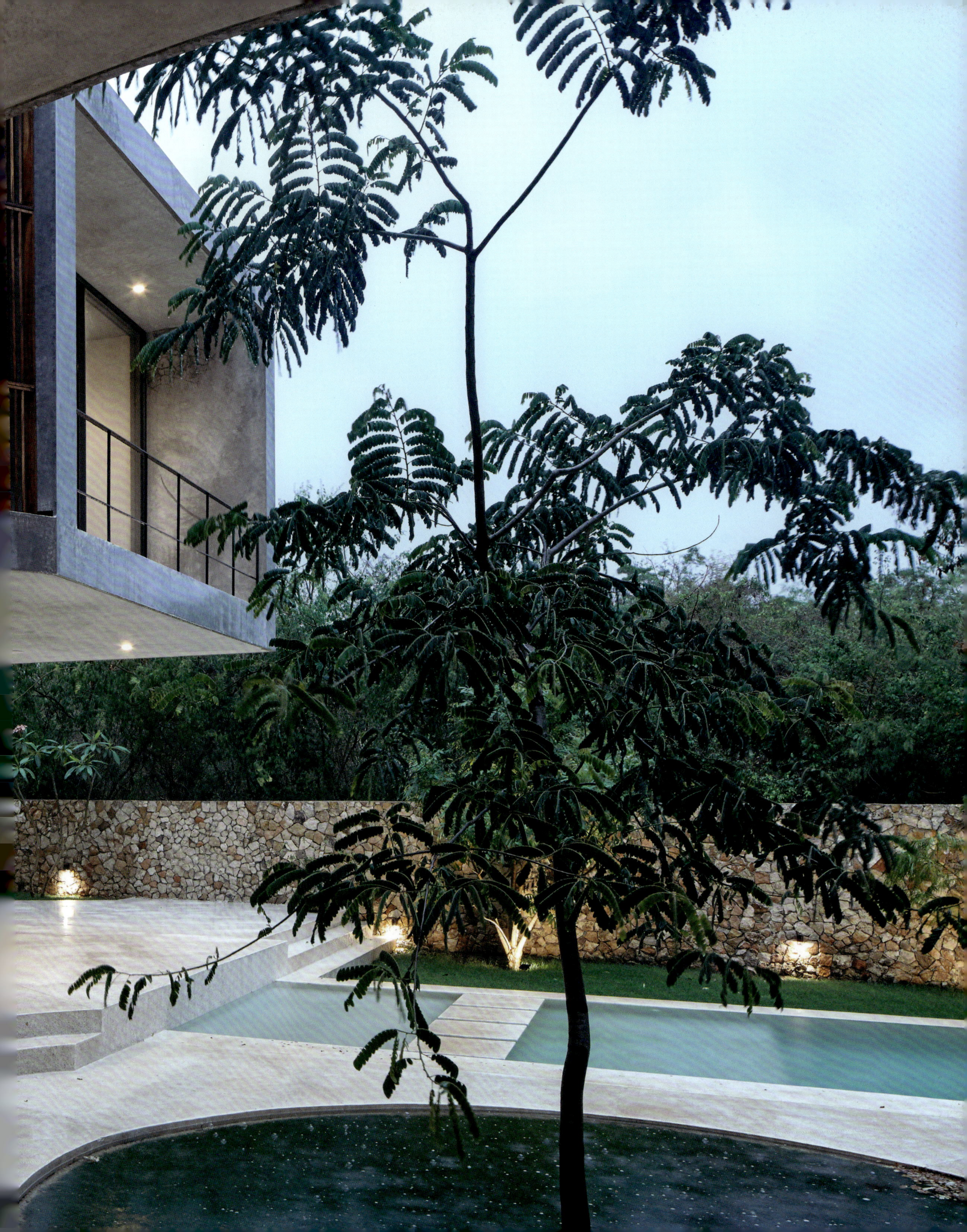

Casa Madri

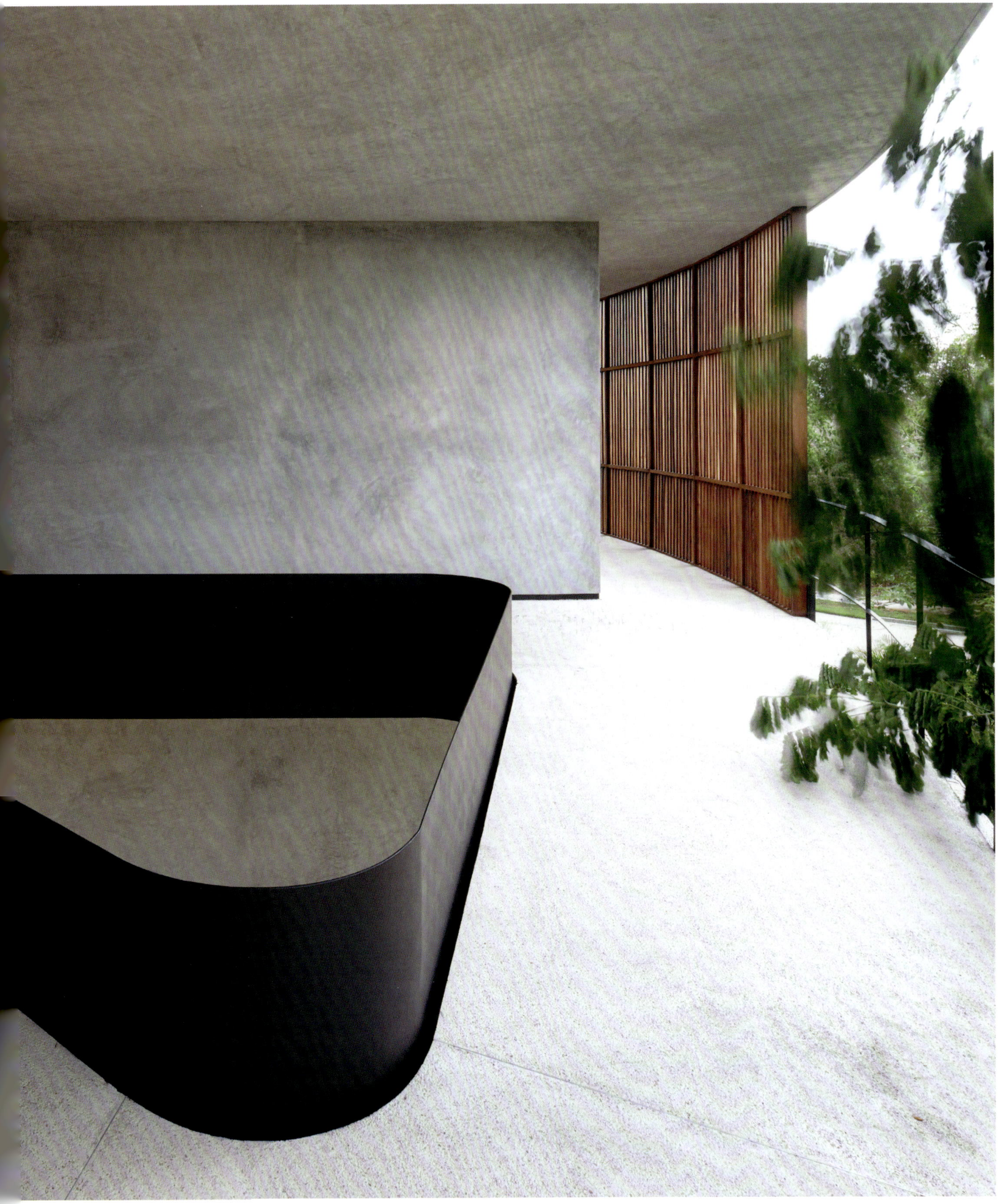

Three sections of 16-foot-tall parota screens provide shade and privacy on the second floor.

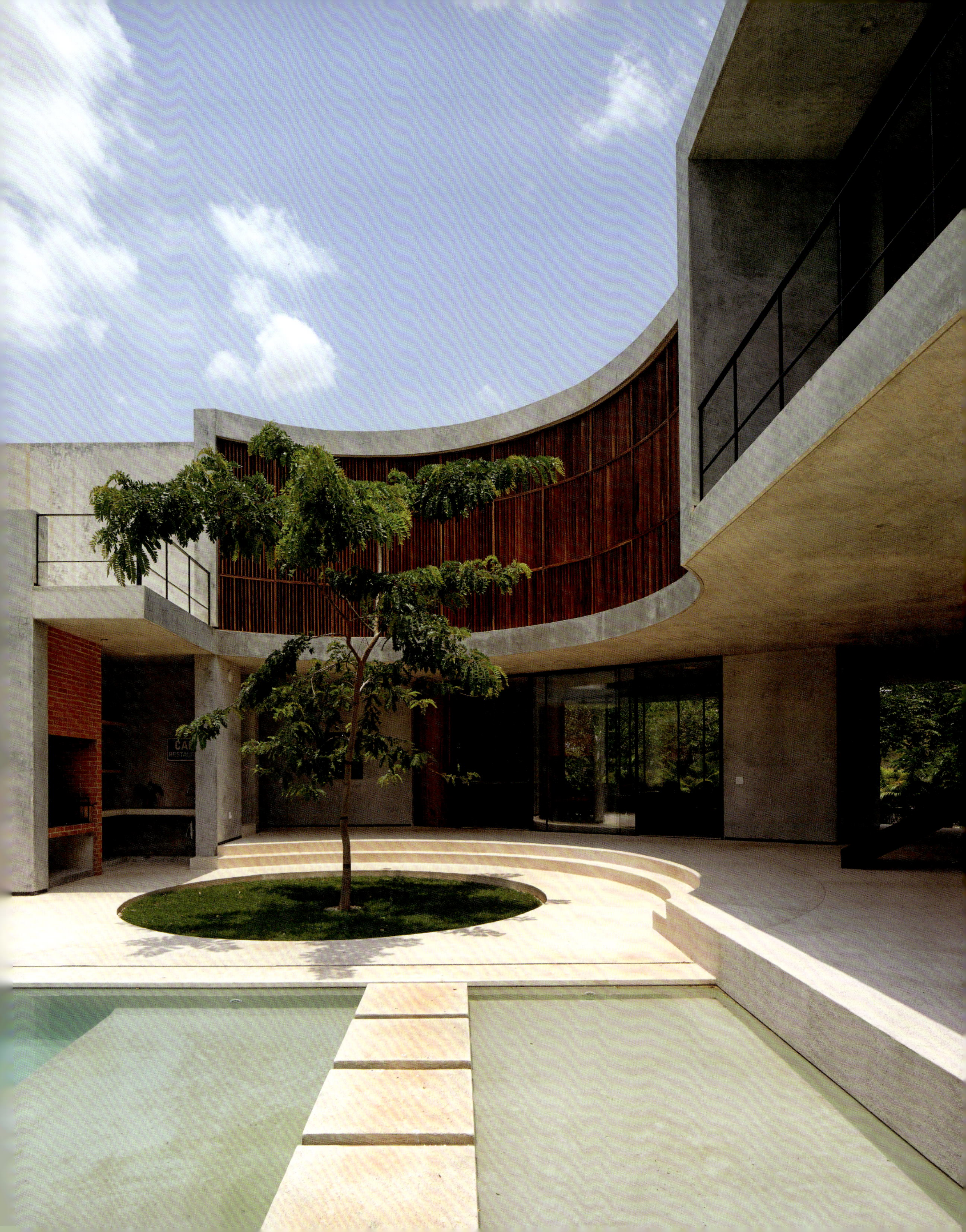

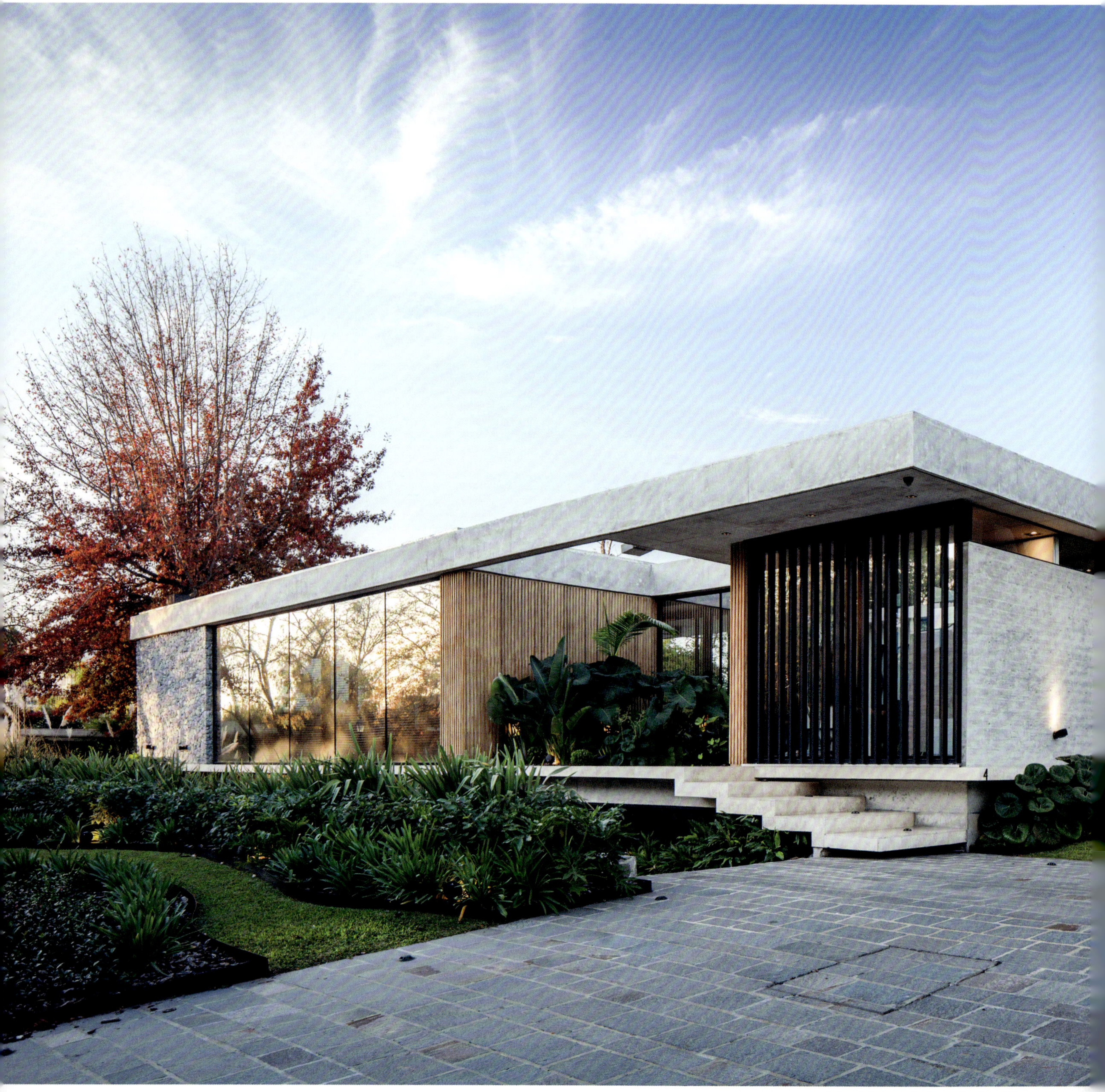

Buenos Aires, Argentina | 2019

CASA BT

Jorgelina Tortorici & Asociados Arquitectura
Photographs: Estudio Jorgelina Tortorici Arq and Nicolas Lanza Arq

Casa BT is an extraordinary example of how site-specific architecture can feel inevitable, as though the solution was obvious all along. Its refined but relaxed attitude belies the rigor of every move on this exposed lot, from the skillful layout to the harmonious balance of glass and silky concrete. The precise assemblage of these elements creates a symbiosis between the house and garden, treating exterior space as an extension of the architecture.

Located at the entrance to a private community in Adrogué, 14 miles south of Buenos Aires city limits, the 4,844-square-foot house sits on the corner of a busy street and a quiet cul de sac. Although the clients requested a single-level house with indoor-outdoor connectivity, the lot itself was fairly featureless, requiring the architecture to do all the work. "We wanted to focus on interior-exterior continuity through facades that open, slide, or are perforated," says architect Jorgelina Tortorici, "generating different filters that sift the light, control the visuals, and give depth and movement to the house."

BASEMENT

1 Garage

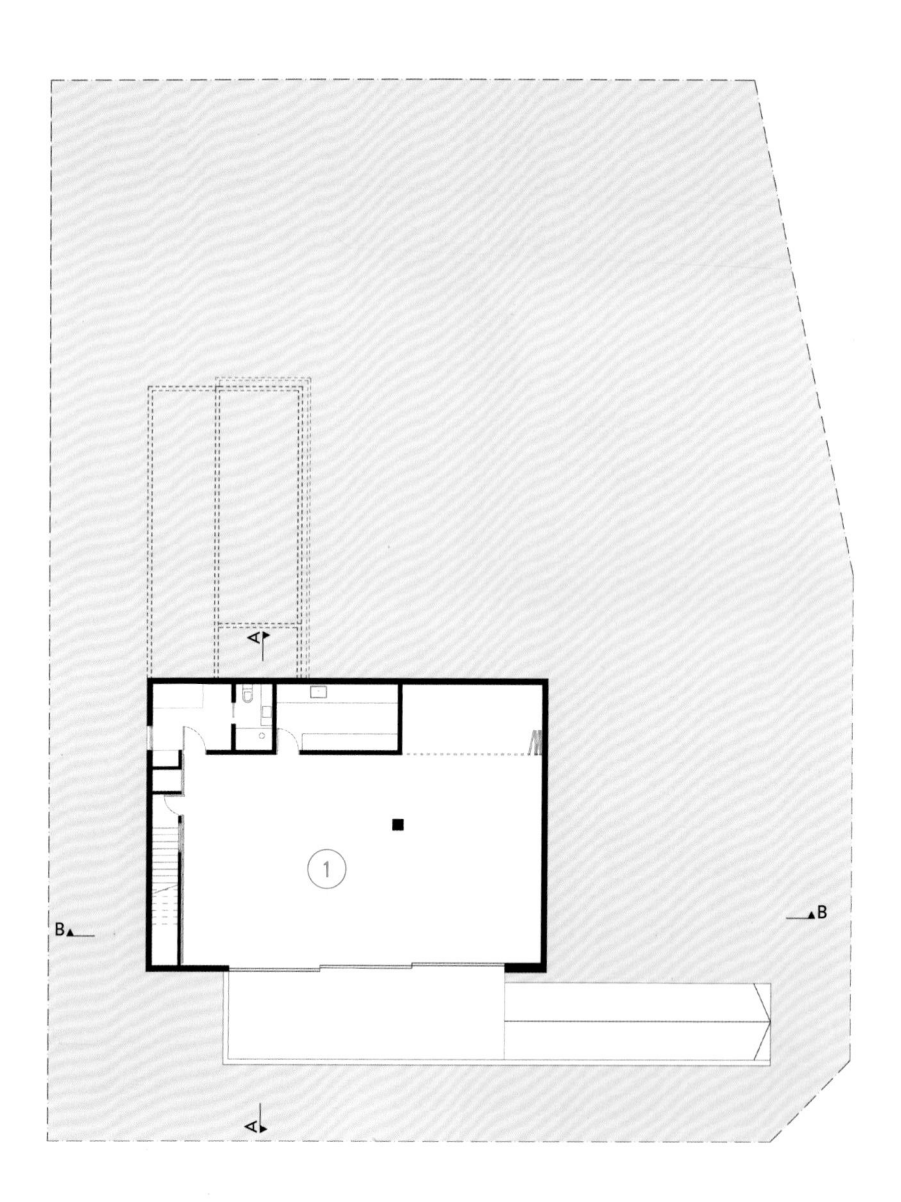

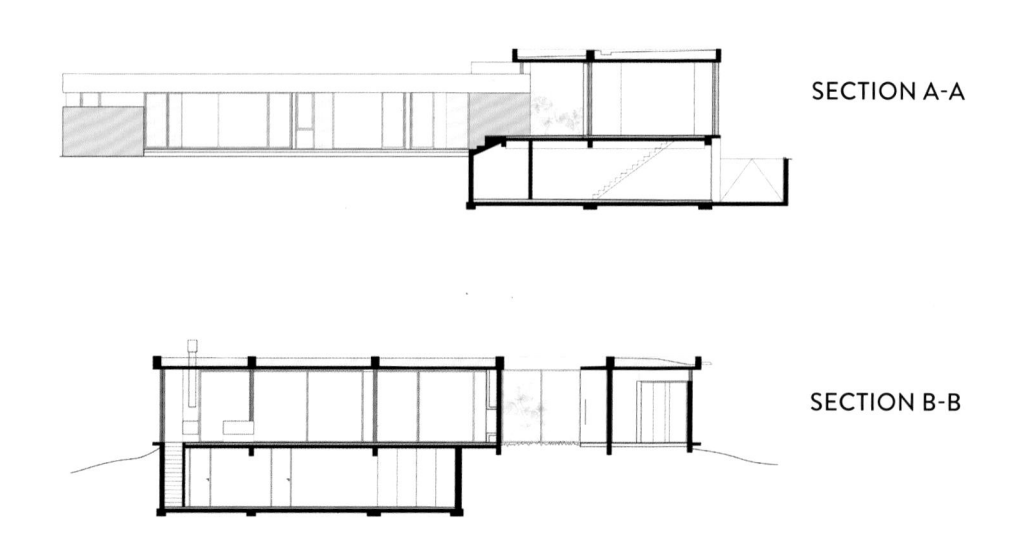

SECTION A-A

SECTION B-B

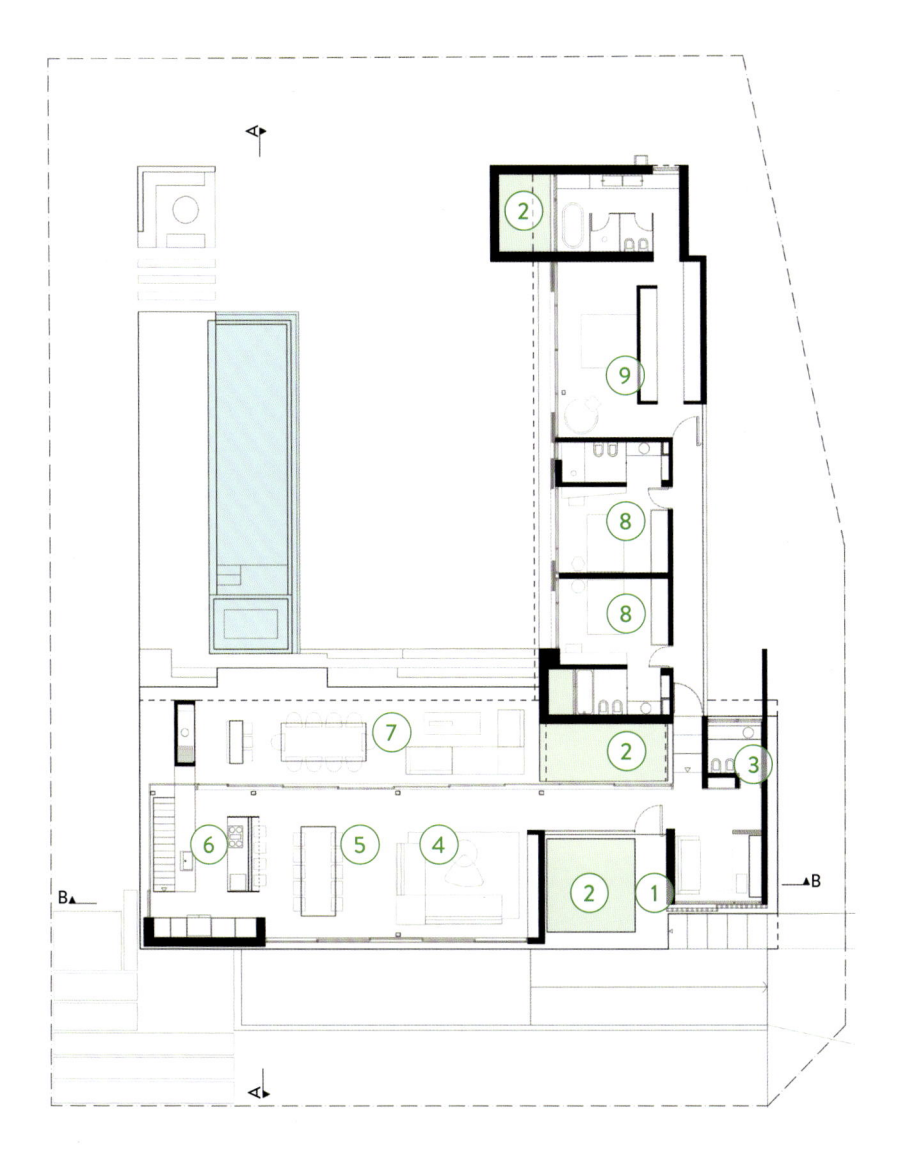

FIRST FLOOR

1 Entry
2 Garden
3 Powder room
4 Living
5 Dining
6 Kitchen
7 Outdoor terrace
8 En suite bedroom
9 Main bedroom suite

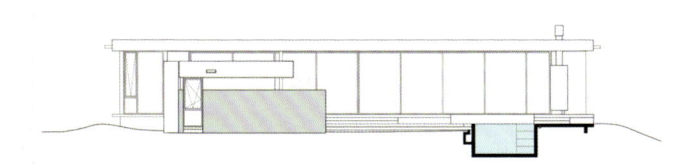

NORTH ELEVATION

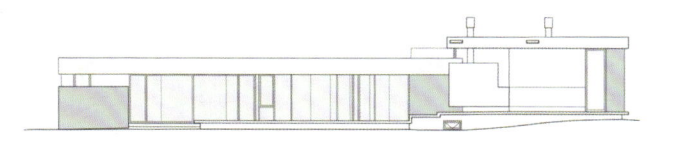

EAST ELEVATION

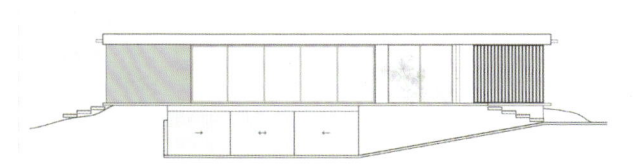

SOUTH ELEVATION

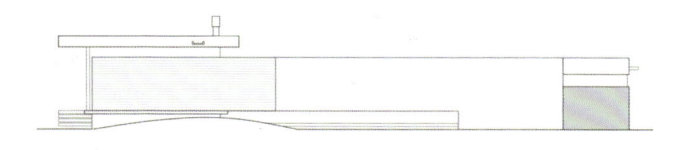

WEST ELEVATION

Casa BT • Floor Plan

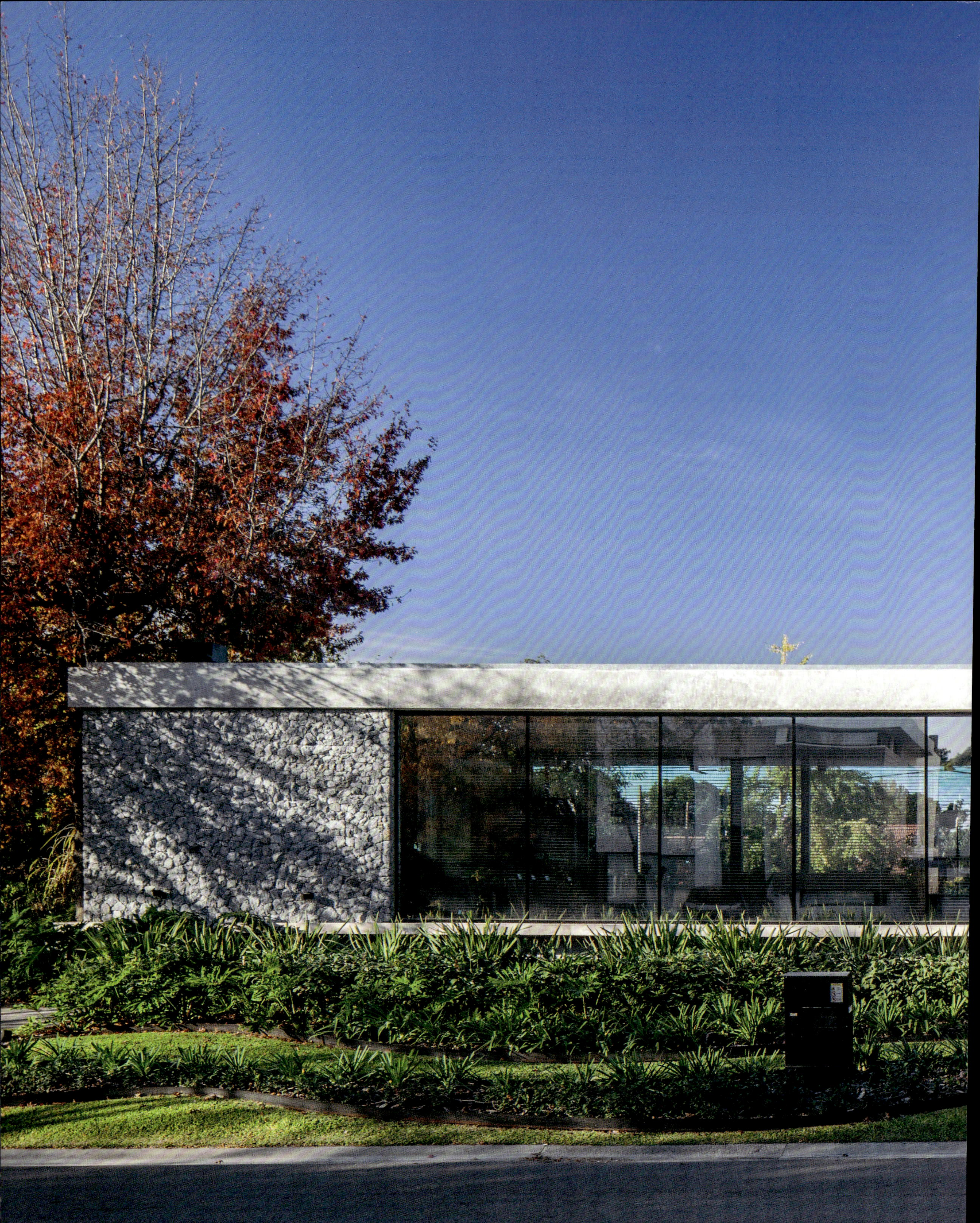

The interior-exterior continuity, a subject we wanted to focus on, was achieved through facades that open, slide, or are perforated, generating different filters that sift the light, control the visuals, and give different depths and movement to this house.
—Jorgelina Tortorici

Viewed from the road, fluid landscaping hides the entrance to the subterranean driveway at the front of the house.

She drew an L-shaped plan that focuses inward to a central garden. The bedroom wing reads as a solid concrete wall along the busy road, while the living wing forms a right angle behind it. This section sits a little higher to bury the garage below it and gain longer views toward the garden.

The house's inscrutability fades as you approach it on foot. A courtyard with tropical foliage tips you off to the entry, where the wings hinge. Inside, the foyer is caught between two planted courtyards "that provide light, vegetation, and freshness, melding the interior space with the exterior," Tortorici says. To the right and down a few steps, a long hall leads to two en suite bedrooms and the main bedroom and bath with its own private viewing garden. To the left of the foyer, a transparent spine connects the large, open living zone to a sweeping terrace and the central pool garden through full-length glass doors. Blind on the street side, the entire bedroom wing also opens to the garden through slide-and-stack glass doors. This fluid, garden-facing facade is fitted with a microperforated metal skin that filters the sun and provides security.

"Concrete is not so common here because it is very expensive and handmade," Tortorici says, "but it creates a lot of structural and spatial possibilities. There's the poetry of having liquid stone, and then with the cast you make the shape you want." The public zone's roof slab floats slightly above the foyer and, in the living zone, extends past the long glass wall to cover the outdoor terrace. On the private wing, a ground-level ribbon of glass in the monolithic exterior wall provides an unexpected source of light and an intimate encounter with nature.

It all comes off as effortless, which of course it was not. "Concrete is a structural rather than an aesthetic decision," Tortorici says. "Its construction takes a lot of time, but it is a material that represents our architecture."

92 Casa BT

93

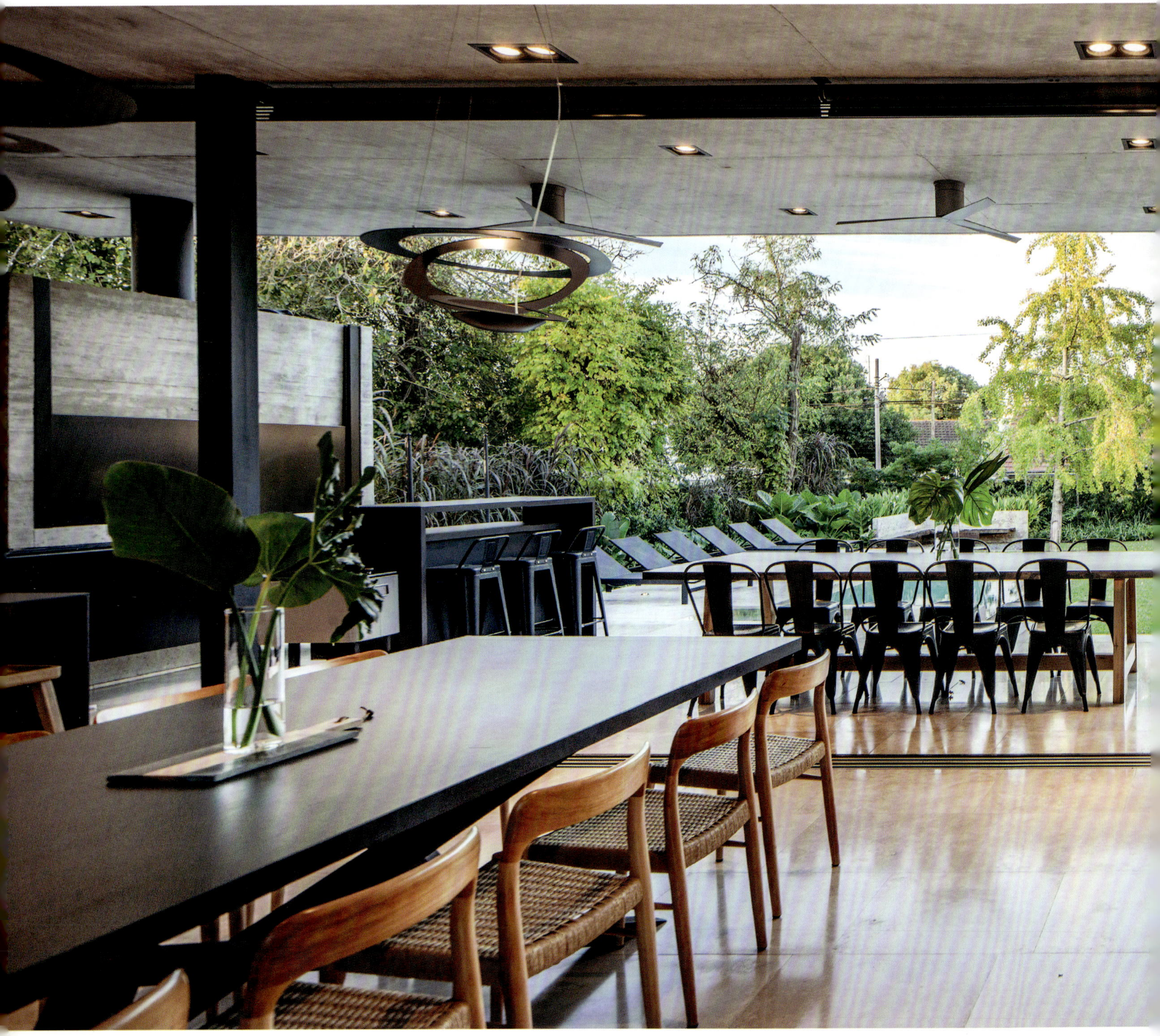

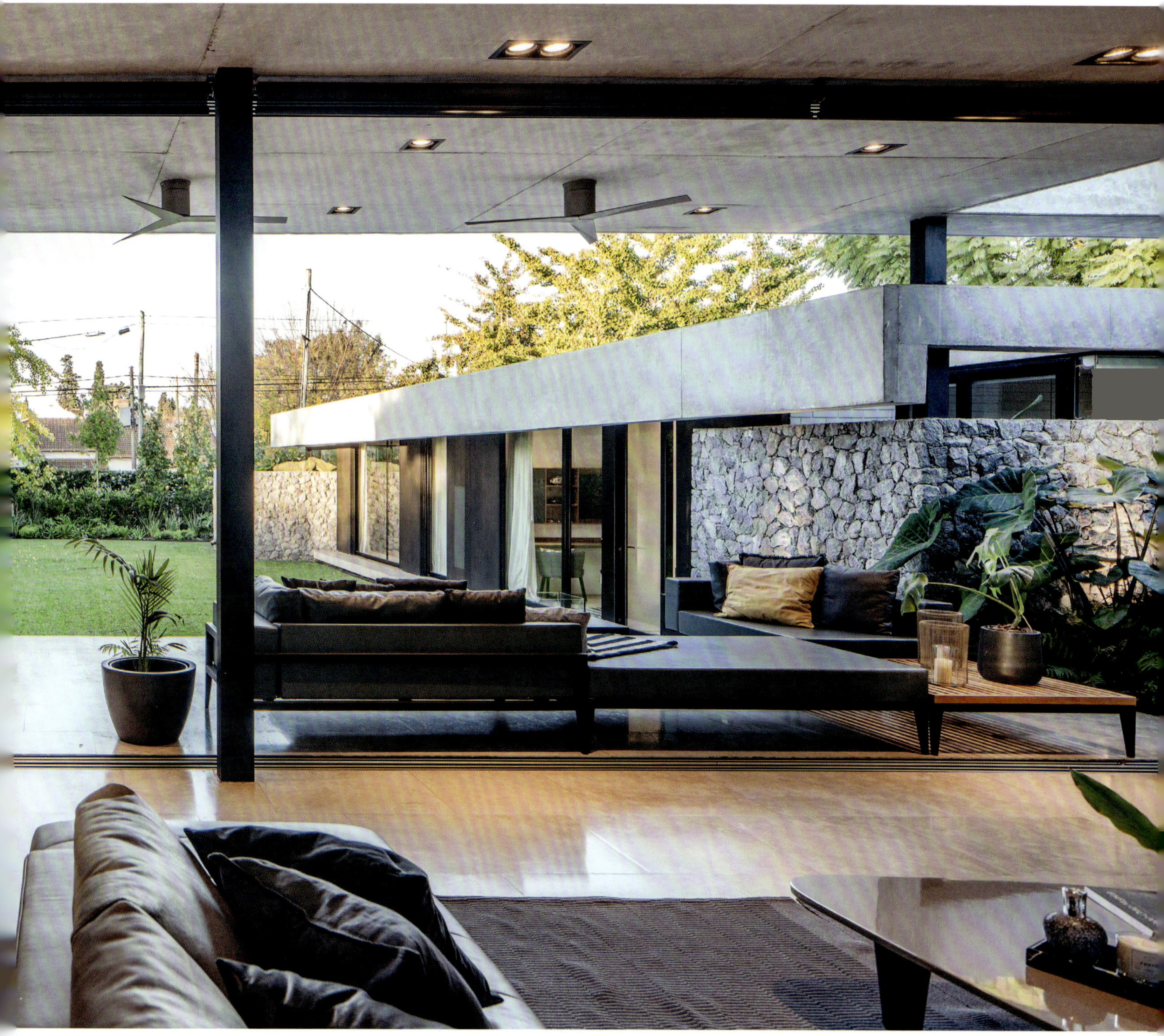

Casa BT

97

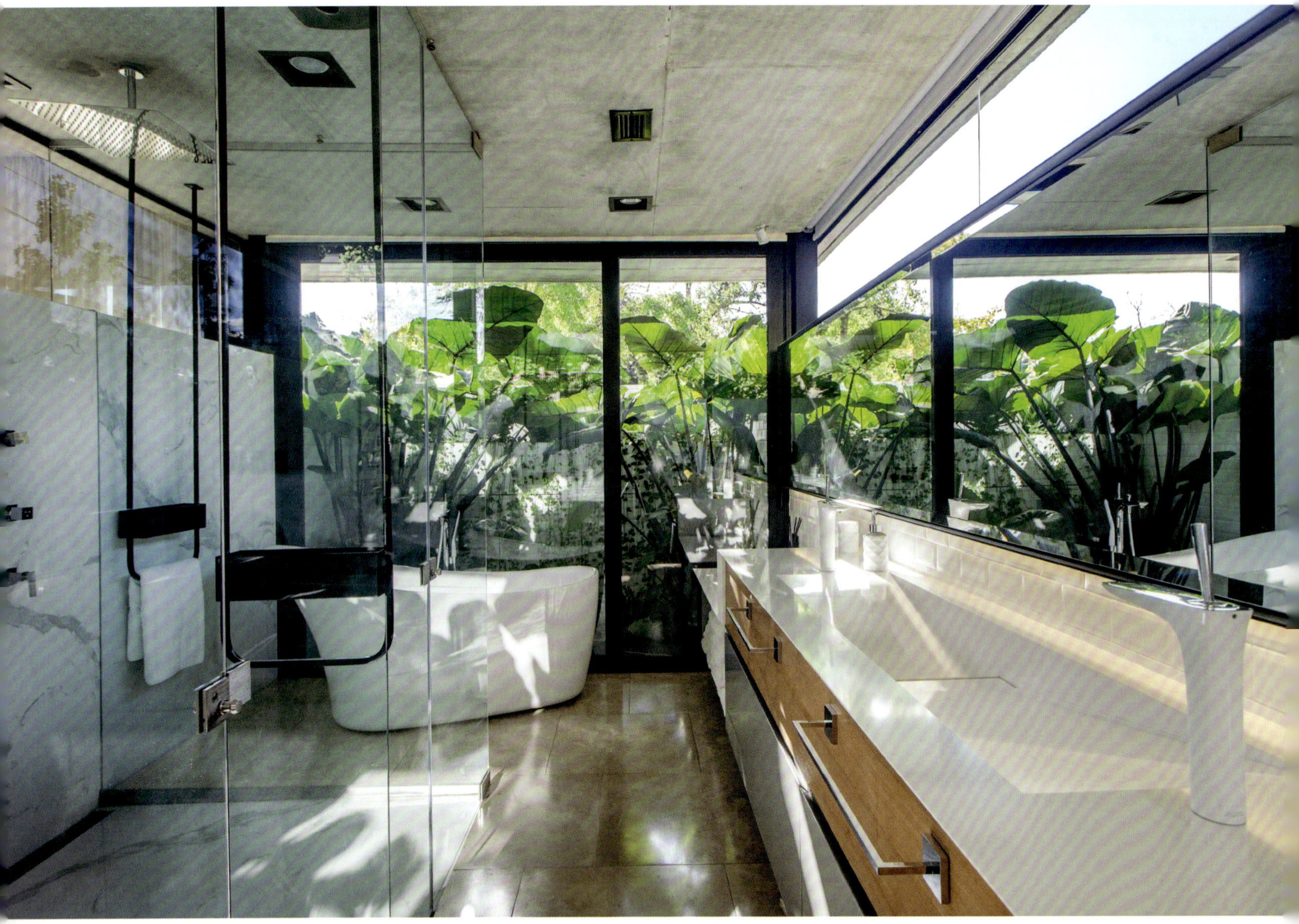

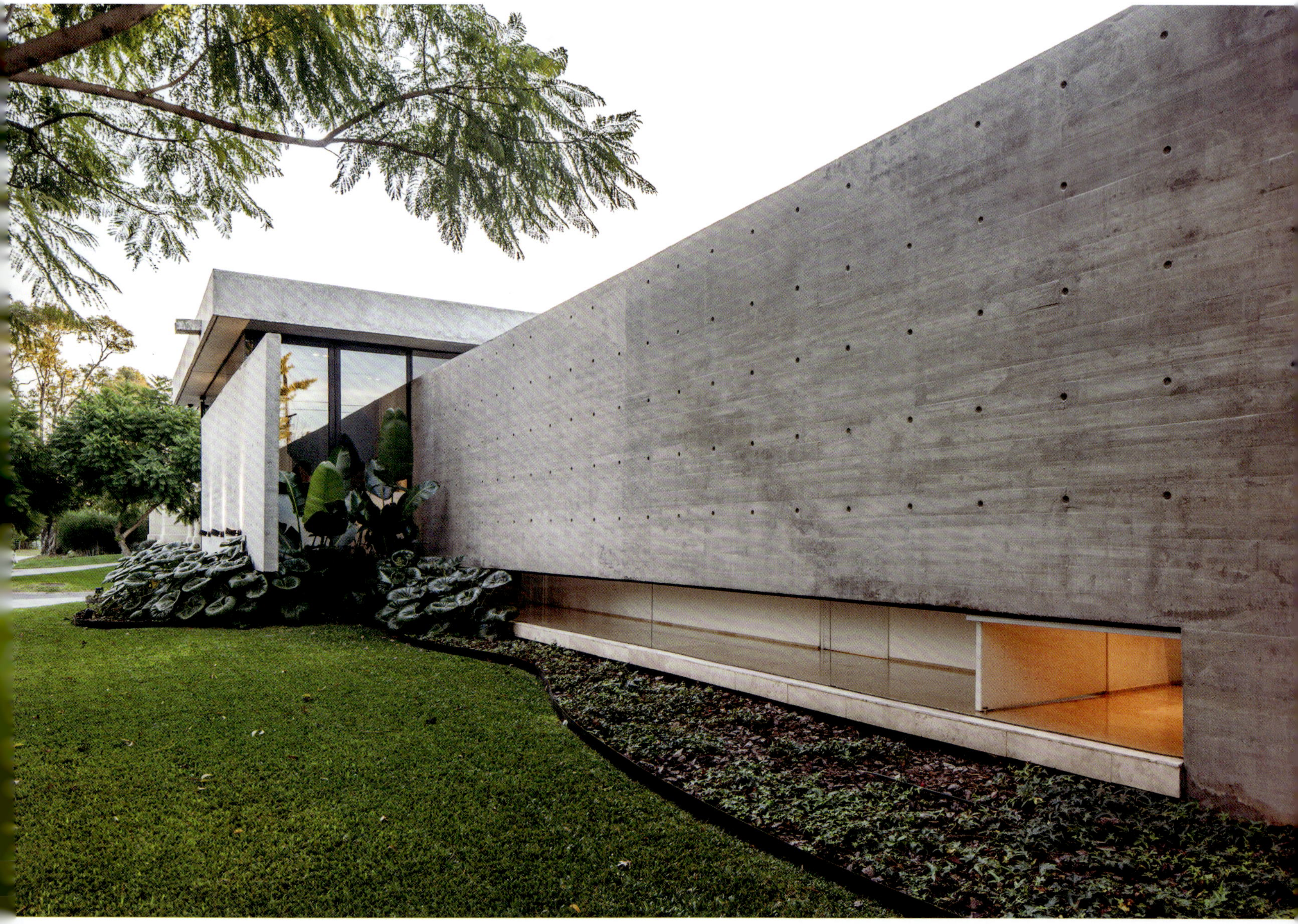

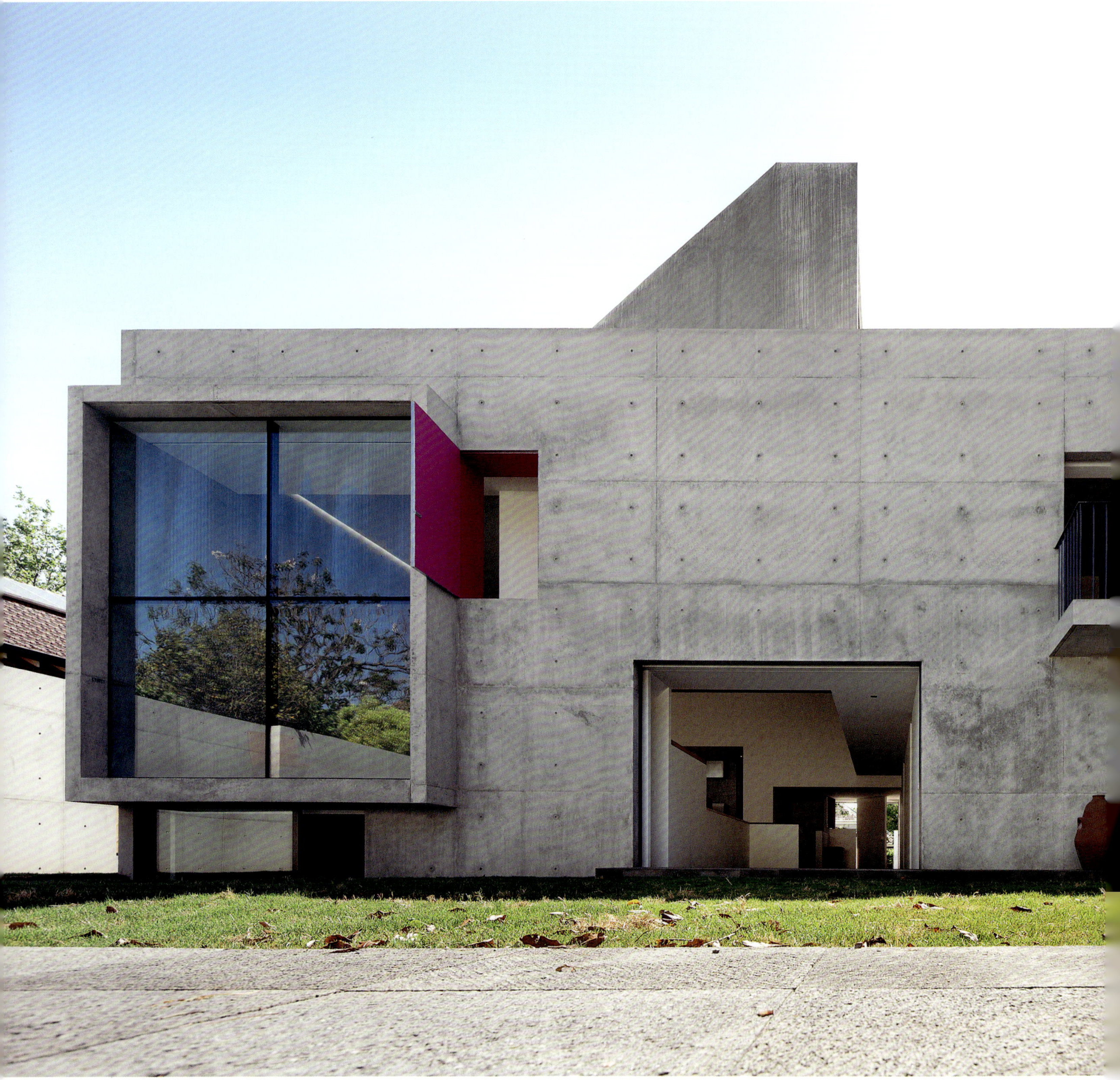

Melbourne, Australia | 2015

MEXICAN CONTEMPORARY HOUSE

Andrés Casillas de Alba and Evolva Architects
Photographs: John Golling

Dramatic yet subdued, this house is an extraordinary example of concrete's ability to express pure form. One of a handful of dwellings built outside Mexico that can be traced to the Luis Barragan school of architecture, it was designed by Andrés Casillas de Alba, who is broadly acknowledged as Barragan's only protégé. The clients, Mexicophiles and fans of Barragan's work, tracked Casillas down to design their house in Australia. Later they commissioned Melbourne-based Evolva Architects to adapt it to the country's building regulations and lifestyle. "We made adaptations to the design with the client as a go-between," says Evolva Architects principal Matthew Scully. "If we changed anything, he ran it past Andrés in Guadalajara to get his tick of approval."

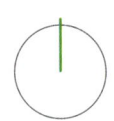

FIRST FLOOR

1 Entrance
2 Central hallway
3 Bedrooms
4 Kitchen
5 Living room

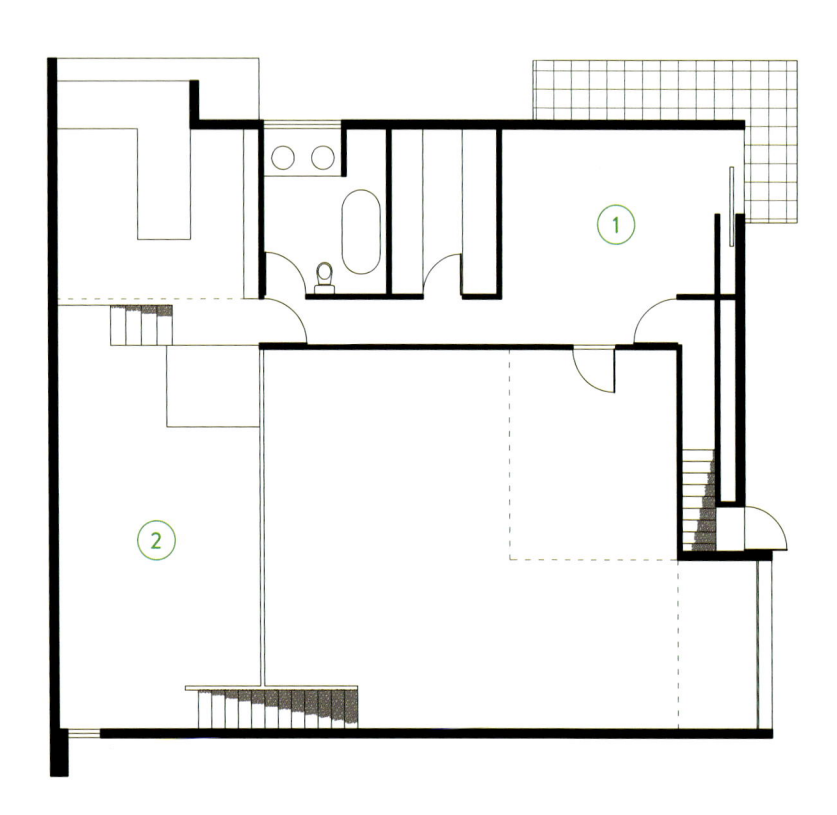

SECOND FLOOR

1 Main bedroom suite
2 Study

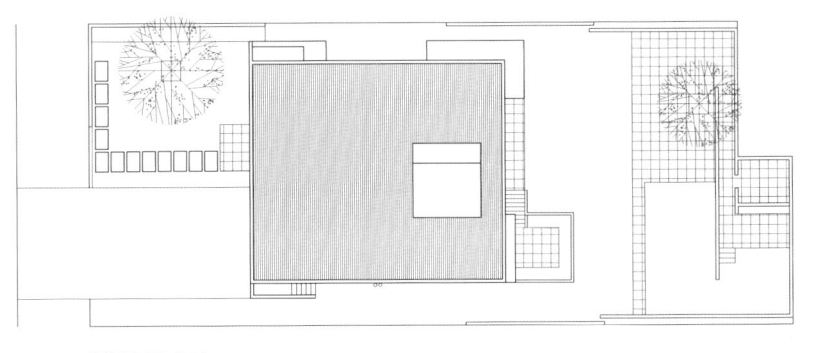

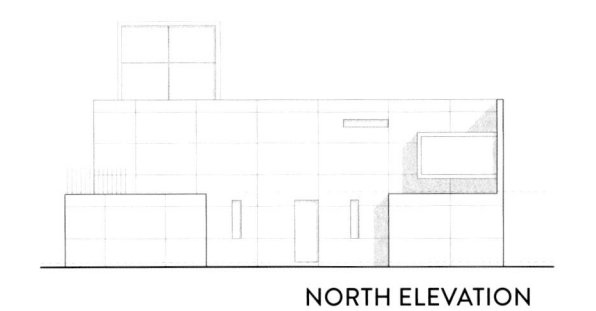

SITE PLAN

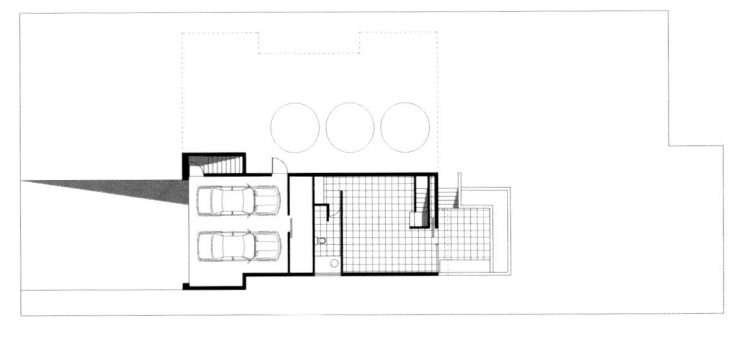

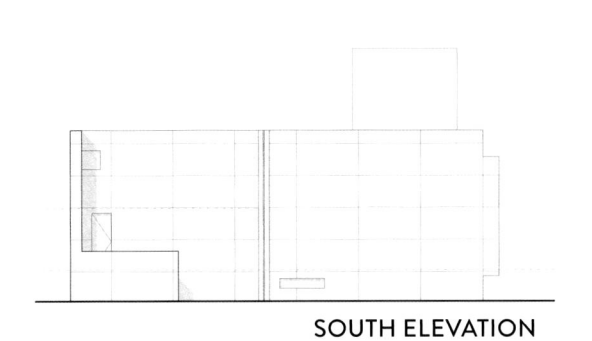

NORTH ELEVATION

BASEMENT

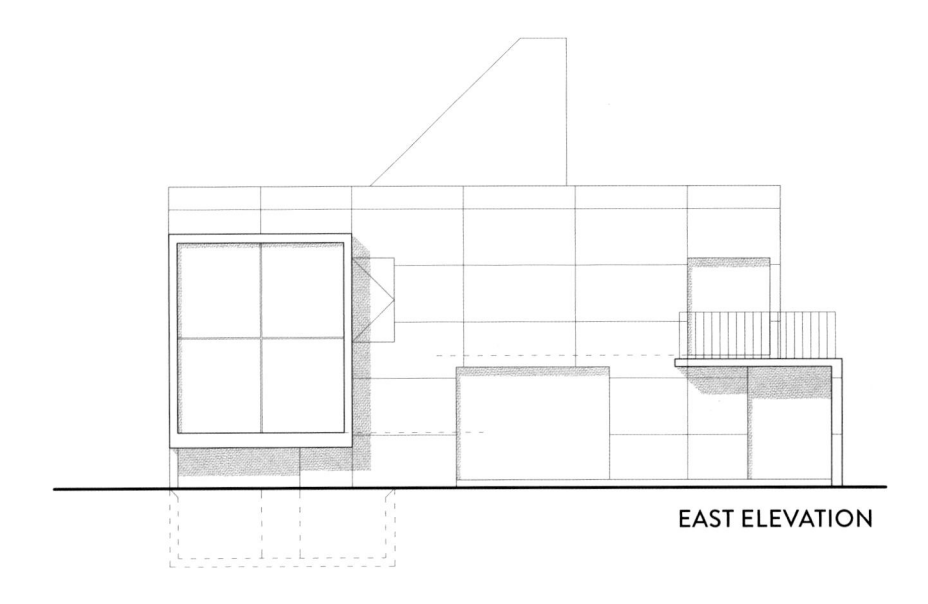

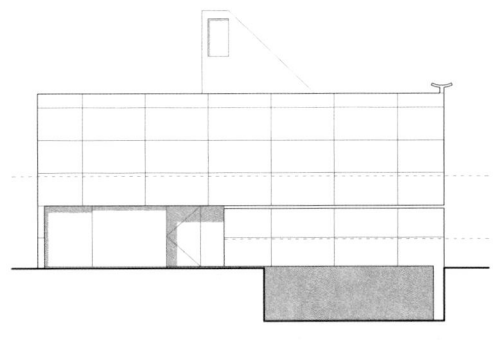

SOUTH ELEVATION

EAST ELEVATION

WEST ELEVATION

Mexican Contemporary House • Floor Plan 103

Barragan's work is a sort of pre-Hispanic interpretation of the modernist school, Scully says. While Europe modernism was about white cubes of steel and glass, Barragan's architecture is solid and heavy, reminiscent of Mayan temples. And although this house's austere, board-formed-concrete facade expresses that solidity and permanence, it is a screen for the complex spatial arrangements inside.

The inscrutable street facade is broken only by a large window on one side. Visitors arrive over stepping-stones through a front garden filled entirely with water. Inside the pivoting front door is a central circulation spine, or internal courtyard, that runs from front to back, which Casillas described as an "internal strait," Scully says. "It has an indoor-outdoor intention about it." On one side, under low ceilings, are two bedrooms. On the other, the space explodes into a triple-height living/dining/kitchen room that sits about 3 feet above the central courtyard, as though it were a stage. Dominating this space, an east-facing cruciform window casts shadows on the towering walls, while the soaring atrium clerestory shaft tracks northern light across this volume, playing up the dramatic ceiling and wall planes.

A classic Barragan move, this expansion and compression unfolds through six interlocking levels and ceiling heights. "When I was drawing it, it was kind of hard to get your head around all those interplays," Scully says. "For Andrés to have conceived of that from a desktop shows real mastery and control." There are two hidden stairs off the elevated living space—one leading to a study above the kitchen that overlooks the living area, and another to the main bedroom suite. The garage is on a lower level, which also houses a guest room with its own sunken concrete courtyard facing the pool.

The "stable doors" are another Barragan influence that came from his interest in horses. These strategically placed ventilation panels show up not only on interior walls but most notably at the back, where a "Mexican pink" door along the stairwell lends a bright pop of color to the facade when open.

Casillas had designed this as a painted, double-faced brick house, but after figuring in painting, plasterboard, and insulation, constructing it with 8-inch-thick plywood-formed concrete turned out to be less expensive. And while it doesn't have high-energy performance on paper, the client loves its thermal comfort, Scully says. "Thermal mass isn't considered in energy-rating programs. The energy rating is a blunt tool, skewed to the 95 percent of houses built with traditional materials.

In a community of mock period houses, the neighbors love the house too, according to Scully. "The form is neutral, just a rectangle, and quite enigmatic," he says. "Because of that, it doesn't jar with anything else around it. It's surprising how comfortably it rests in the streetscape."

Small shutters, like those used to ventilate stables, reference the equestrian influence in Luis Barragan's work. Here they are placed in strategic positions to create cross-ventilation and unexpected shafts of light in the monolithic building. The pink door on an internal stairway at the back of house (*next page*) pays homage to Barragan's famous Mexican pink.

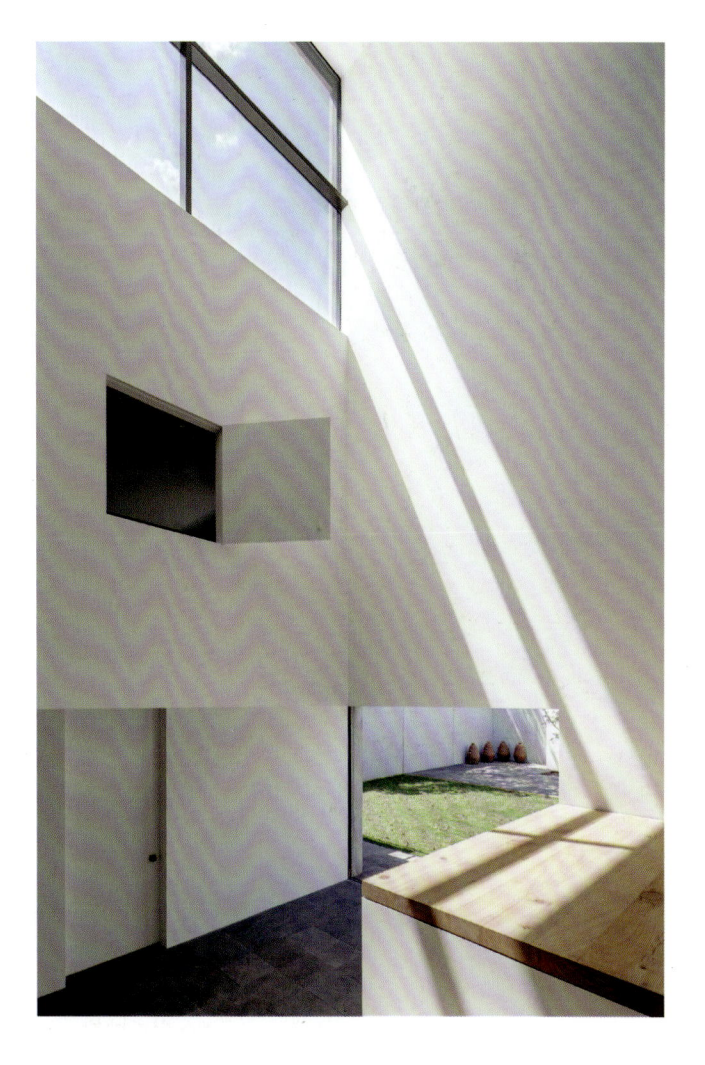

106 Mexican Contemporary House

107

Volcanic stepping-stones across the pond at the front of the house were freighted over from Mexico City. The dark floors—volcanic pavers—continue out to the rear terrace and swimming-pool concourse.

The backyard pool winds around high concrete walls—another Barragan move, which lends a monastic sense of tranquility.

108   Mexican Contemporary House

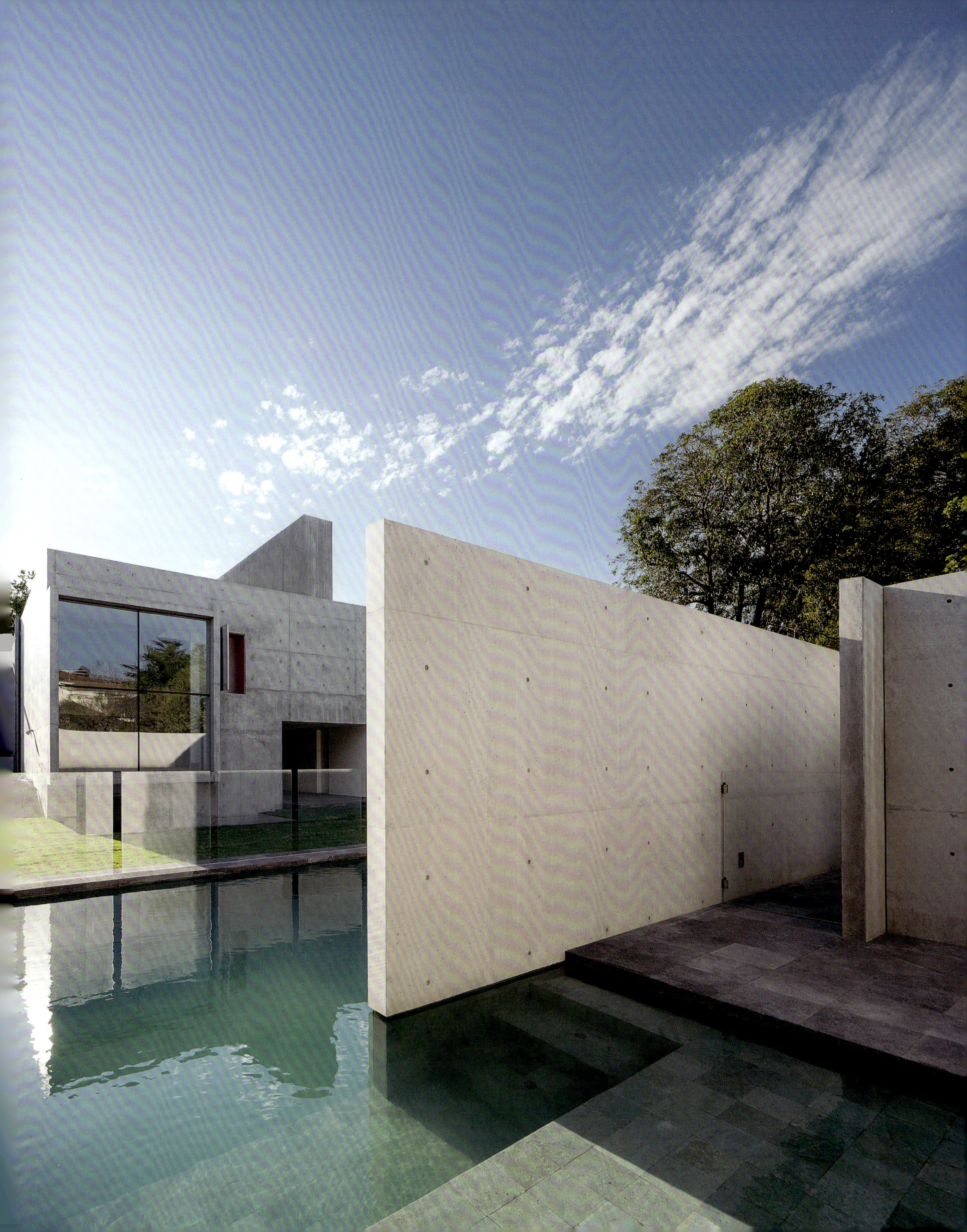

Mexican Contemporary House

Concrete is becoming more popular as a material, and what makes it interesting residentially is that it sort of becomes a material whose use is being reimagined or repurposed. Seeing it in the intimate spaces of a house adds an element of surprise. It's an honest and raw material, and off the form it has this surprise silkiness and subtleness to its surface.
—Matthew Scully

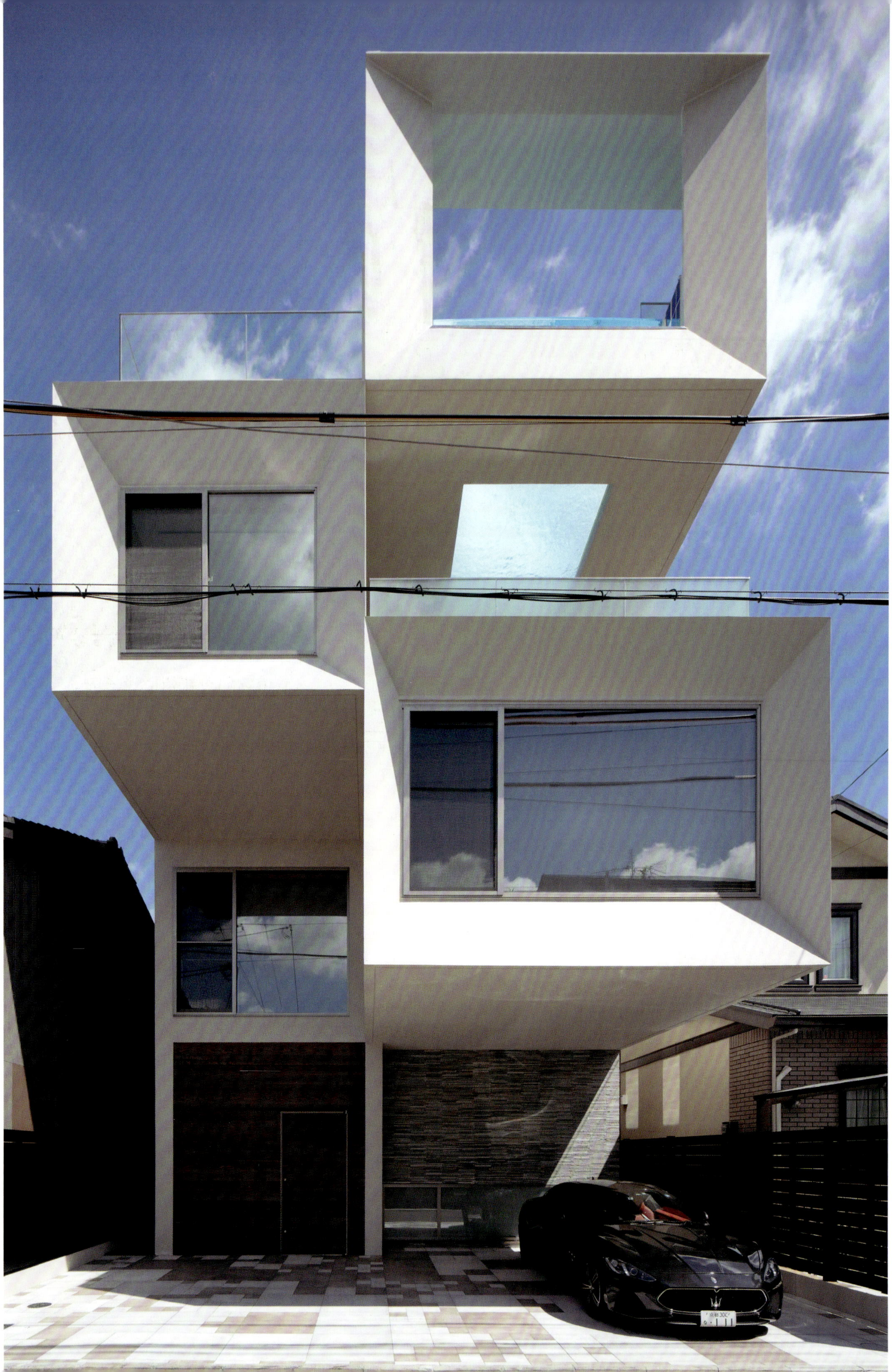

Kyoto, Japan | 2019

CONCRETE SQUARE TUBE HOUSE

Eastern Design Office
Photographs: Koichi Torimura

Anna Nakamura has always appreciated pure form: as a child she remembers being awed by the Great Seto Bridge that spans Japan's Seto Inland Sea. Now a principal at Eastern Design Office, her buildings are known for their structural gymnastics and ambitious geometries. The firm made its debut with the design of a concrete house in 2003. Later came buildings such as On the Corner, a residential complex of cut stone, concrete, and glass that comes to a startlingly sharp point on a flatiron-shaped lot; Step Tower, a stark white, ten-story apartment complex with ocean liner–like curves; and Slit House, a concrete study in figure and void that turns the concept of windows inside out.

On its urban infill lot, the 6,000-square-foot Concrete Square Tube House is a similarly robust building. There's some synchronicity in the fact that it was designed for a professional athlete, who requested training space including a gym, pool, and sauna. In a neighborhood where old wooden houses stand shoulder to shoulder with modern apartment houses, the four-story tower takes in views of a mountain range to the north and west, and the cityscape to the south and east.

From the street it appears as a pile of staggered concrete tubes; they cantilever to create a covered entryway and outdoor terraces on the top two floors. Below grade are a powder room, gym, and wine room. The entrance level contains a bedroom, followed by three bedrooms and a balcony on the second floor, and living spaces and a balcony on the third floor. On the roof is the swimming pool, bookended on the front elevation

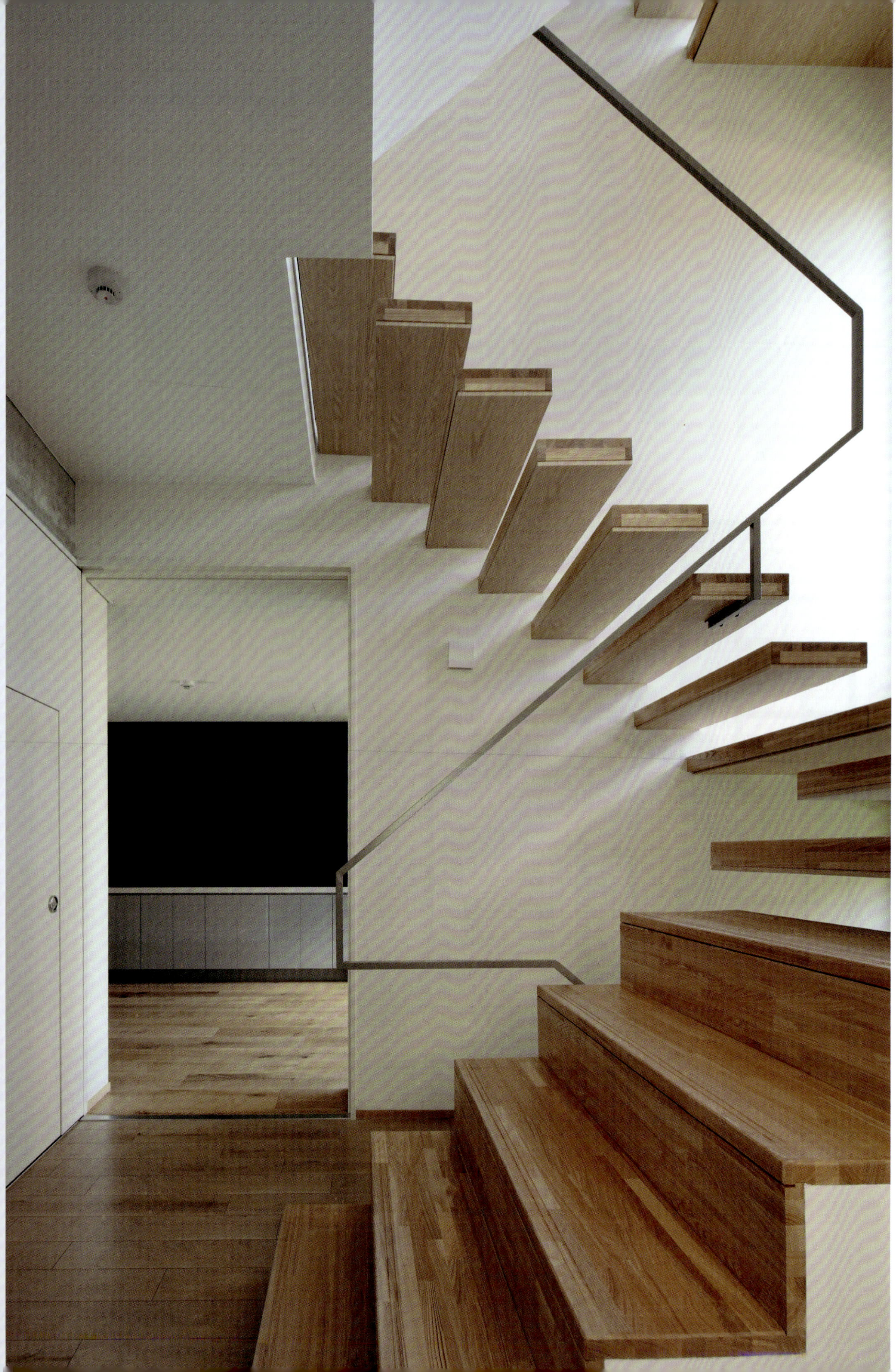

by a square aperture that frames the city views. A stairwell at the back of the house connects the levels.

"We wanted something very dynamic, and for that, our choice was concrete or steel," says Nakamura. "For the pool, you can't use a steel structure because it moves too much. Concrete is heavy and it shuts out the sounds from outside."

The interior is austere, in traditional Japanese fashion. Plaster walls and wood finishes are a womb-like antidote to the hard exterior, and there are few windows on the sides, to screen close neighbors. "Normally in Japanese houses you don't want to see each other," Nakamura says. Natural light flows in through terrace openings at the front and back of the building, but the most spectacular daylighting strategy is the pair of large skylights in the third-floor ceiling—directly under the rooftop swimming pool. They scoop light—and a bottom-of-the-pool view of lap swimmers—into the living room and adjacent terrace. Watery reflections and flickering light animate the interior, changing from hour to hour and season to season.

"Pure structural form is the reason I'm an architect," Nakamura says. That serves her clients well in dense cities such as Kyoto, where ingenuity makes possible artfully designed buildings that acknowledge the natural world.

118 Concrete Square Tube House

We wanted something very dynamic, and for that, our choice was concrete or steel. For the pool, you can't use a steel structure because it moves too much. Concrete is heavy and it shuts out the sounds from outside.
—Anna Nakamura

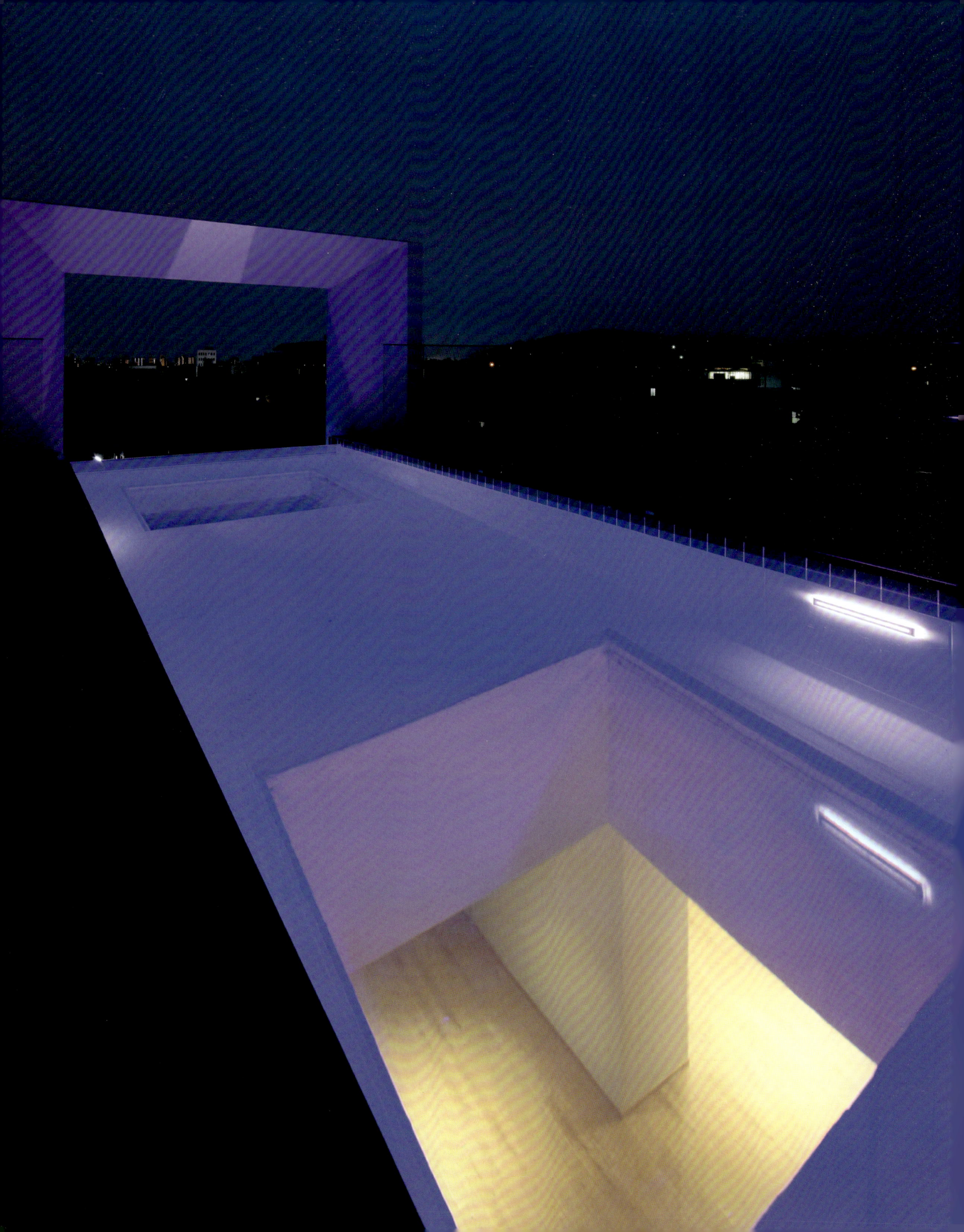

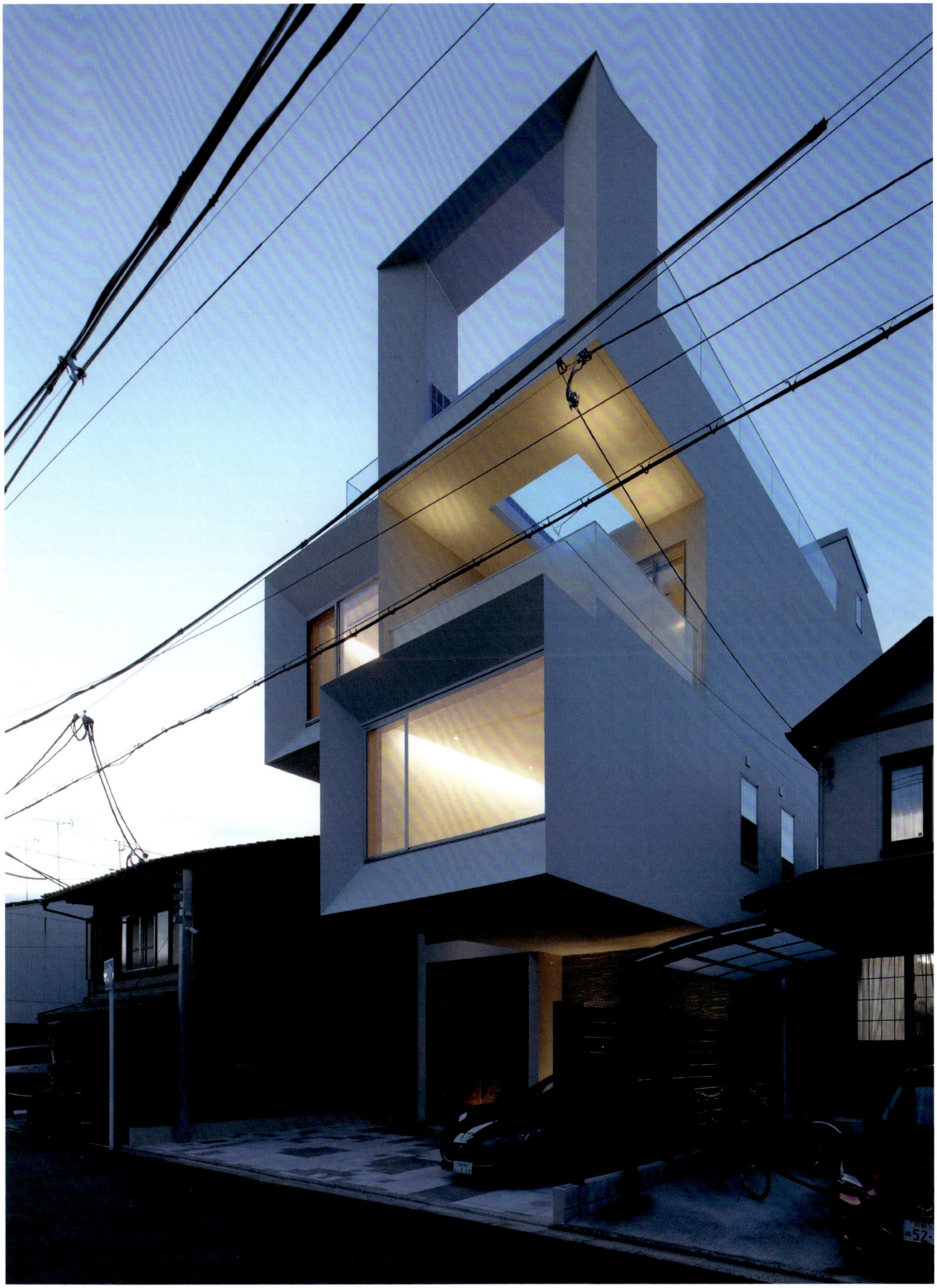

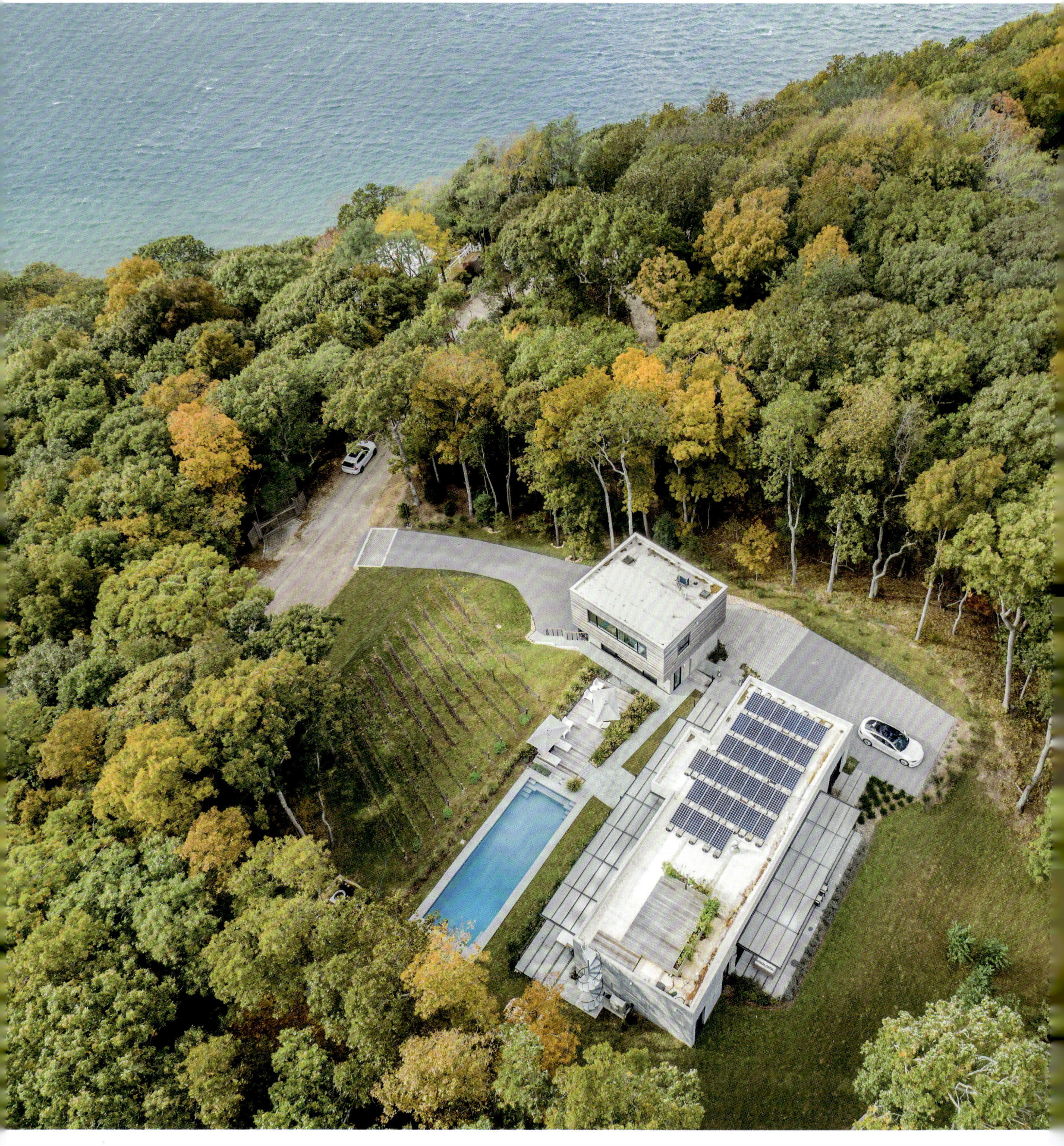

Long Island, New York | 2018

ECO HOUSE

Atelier Vibeke Lichten

Photographs: Evan Joseph

When Danish-born architect Vibeke Lichten was designing her family's weekend home on Shelter Island, she was determined to avoid fossil fuels. Durability, low maintenance, and speedy construction were top priorities too. Poured-in-place concrete ticked all of those boxes, allowing the 2,015-square-foot house and a 1,380-square-foot pool/guesthouse to be occupied less than a year after construction began.

Perched 138 feet above the Peconic River, the two buildings were deftly shoehorned into the middle of a trapezoidal, 1-acre lot to preserve setbacks and views to the water below. While board-formed concrete requires a substantial up-front investment, Lichten, who is also a developer, was frugal with the material. The building was designed as a simple rectangle, and its depth was determined by the dimensions of two modest guest bedrooms placed side by side. Oriented north–south, the home's simple plan is optimized for privacy. With the guest rooms at one end of the house and the main bedroom at the other, a central kitchen/living/dining space becomes the gathering place.

Rooftop solar panels supply all of the house's electricity needs and send it back to the grid when no one is there. A spiral stair leads to the roof garden from the main bedroom. The pool house is rotated slightly to open the view from the main house.

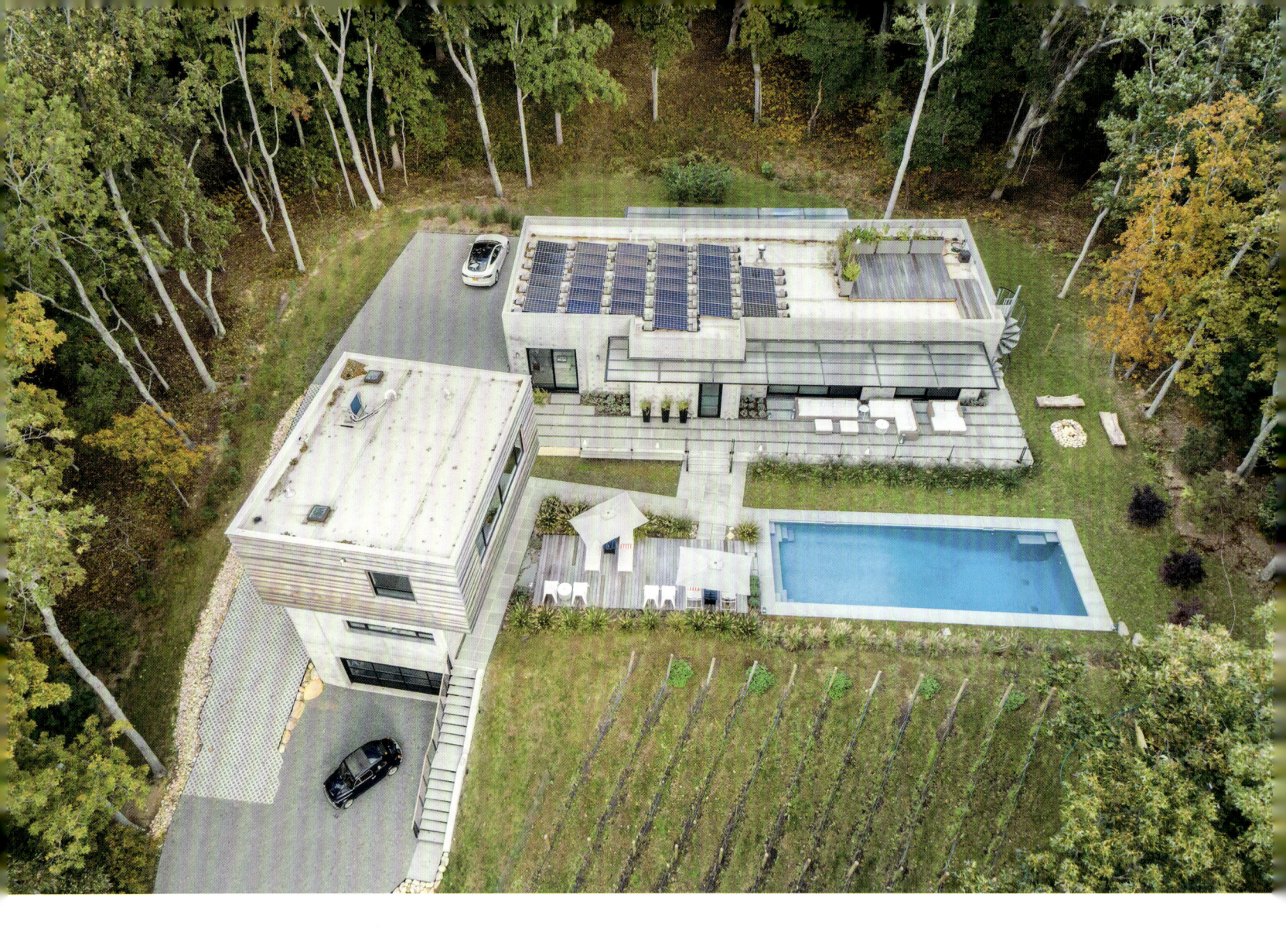

The only bump-out in the bar-shaped footprint is the entryway, which pierces through a 12-foot-deep porch canopy that runs the length of the house, facing the pool and eastern view. The cantilevered-steel canopy is repeated on the back, too, "like little wings on both sides of the house," Lichten says. "I didn't want columns, like a southern look." The visible part of a V-shaped steel structure embedded in the concrete walls, these minimalist wings support ¼-inch-thick wire glass that shades the east and west terraces. "Concrete let us do that in an elegant way," Lichten says. "There is no big beam carrying the cantilever. It looks simple but is elaborately engineered." The protective canopies are high enough that in winter, the low sun warms the 8-inch-thick concrete floors inside the house, helping to maintain a temperature of about 65 degrees without turning on the heat when weather conditions are optimal.

Paradoxically, a material that many perceive as cold makes for a cozy, quiet interior. Exterior walls range from 16 to 18 inches thick and contain, from the outside in, 2 inches of rockwool, a 6-inch air space, a second rockwool layer, and then drywall. A concrete wall in the living room was left unfinished. "In Denmark we have a long tradition of making things cold and warm at the same time," Lichten says. "I like using rough and smooth, handmade next to something cold. A conversation happens that warms it up."

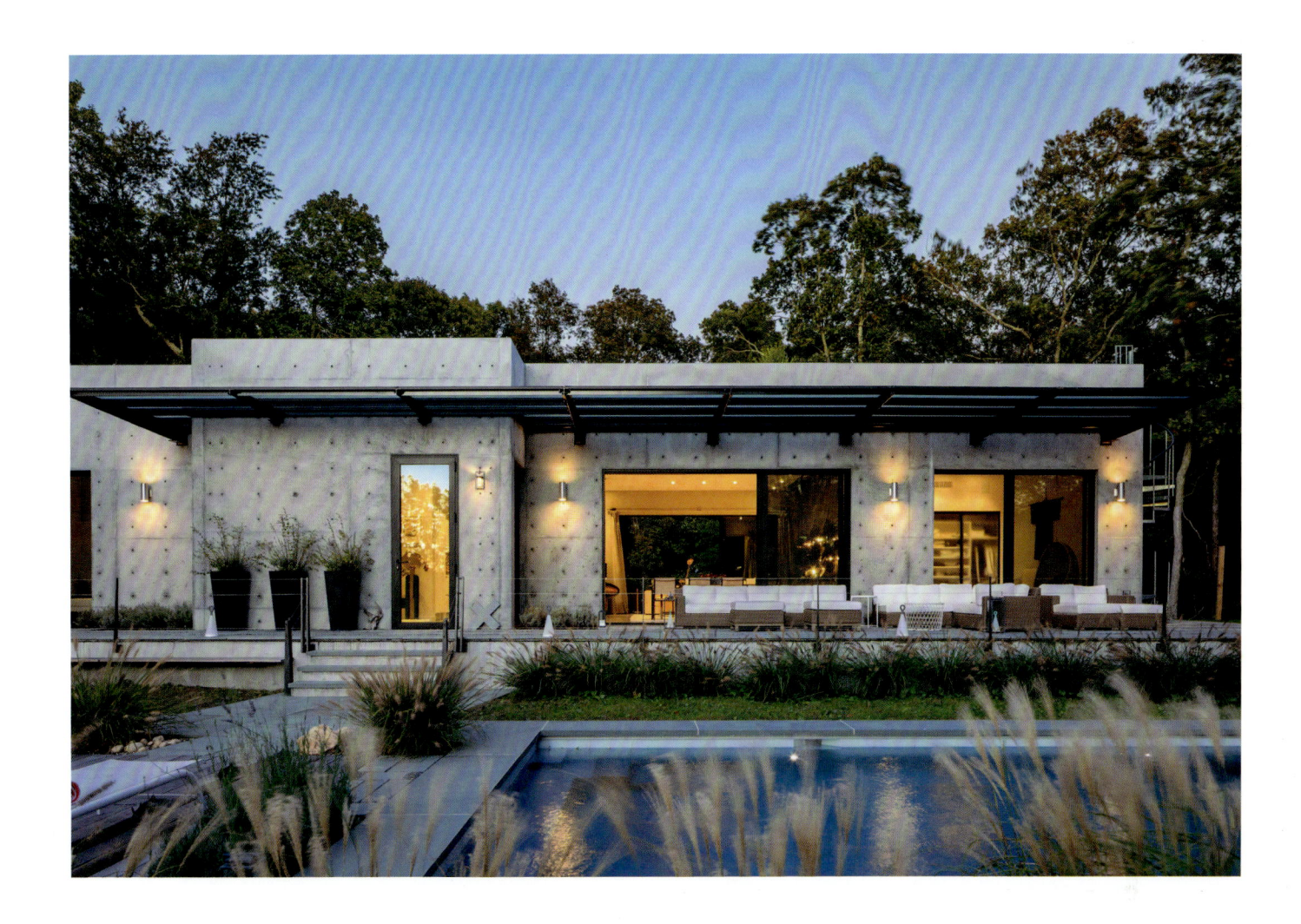

The interior palette reinforces that warmth with wood furniture accents, textured gray kitchen and bath tiles, white matte cabinetry, and a honed, flamed-granite kitchen counter that resembles travertine. When the couple entertains, guests spill out to the pool terrace planted with billowy grasses. Across the patio, a pool house tucked into the slope contains a living room and kitchenette, full bath, and sauna on the pool level; a garage below; and two bedrooms and two baths on the cantilevered second floor. "Concrete is a universal language, with similar techniques in forming the material," Lichten says. On this coastal site it takes the form of a modern, easy-living house that will last far into the future.

A recent addition, the studio sits on a concrete pedestal that allows the wood-framed upper portion to cantilever over the sloping terrain.

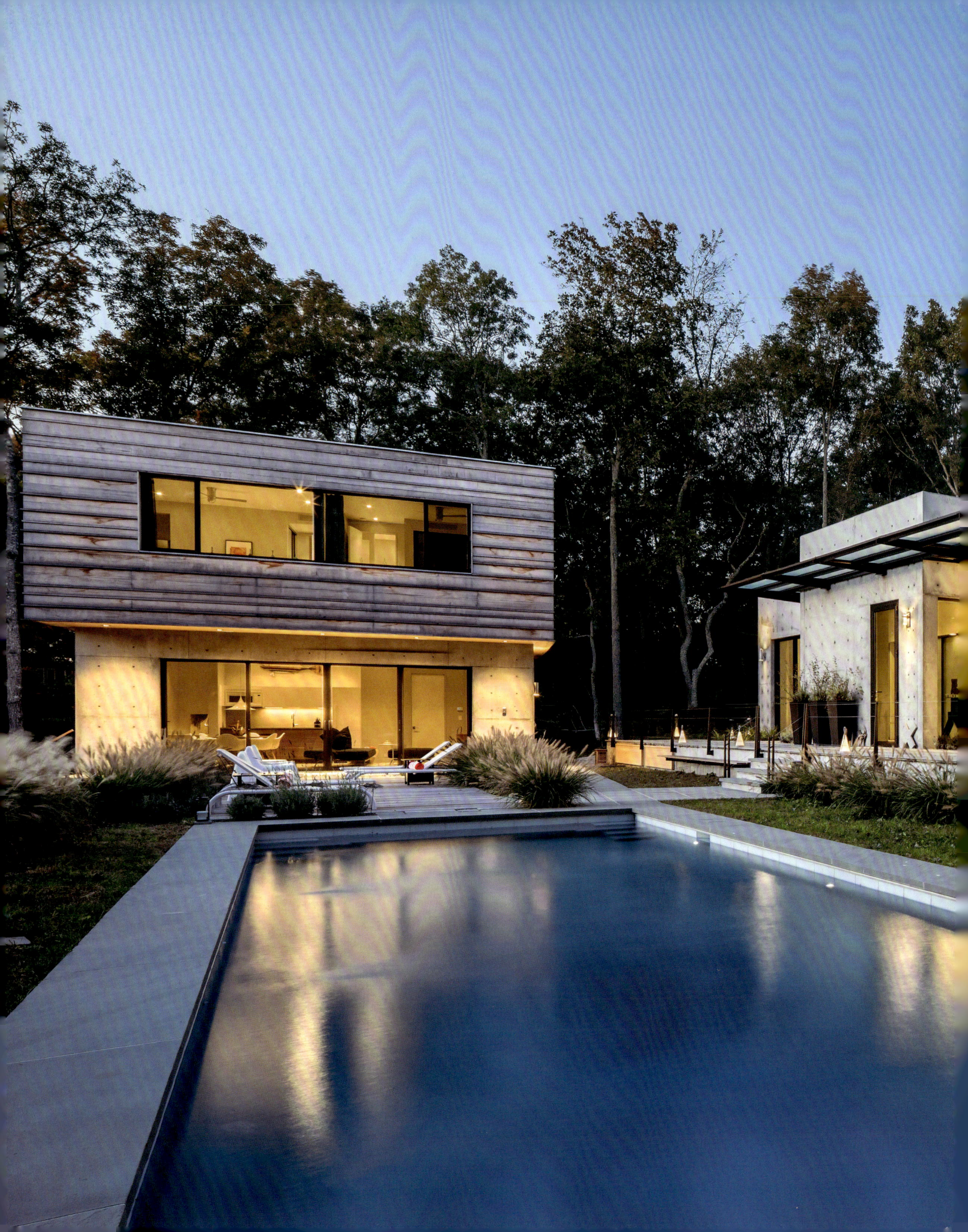

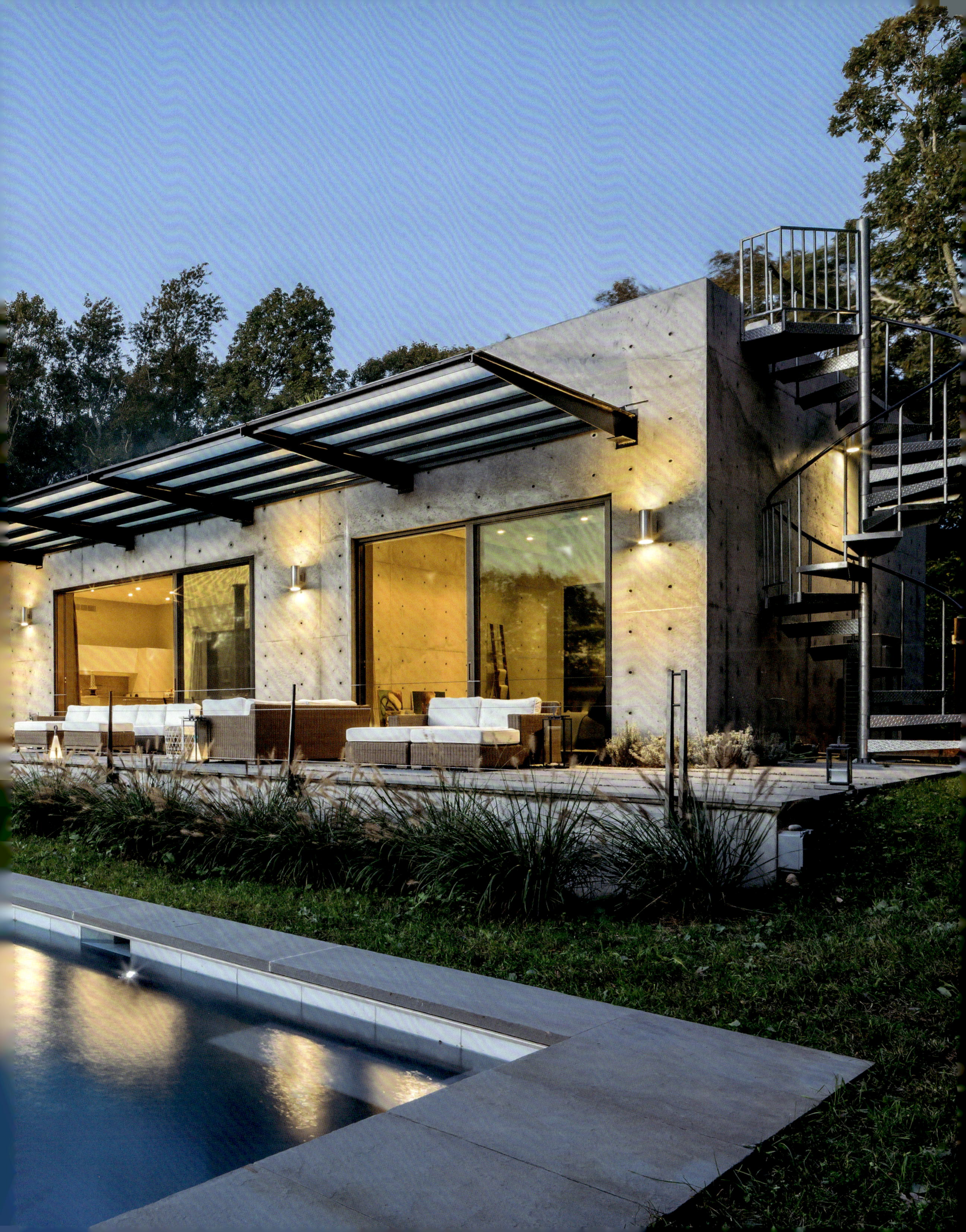

Eco House

In the living room, a striking concrete wall holds three glass vitrines displaying a collection of turned wood pieces. Glass pendulums lower the vitrines for access.

If everything is well planned and well organized, concrete is a quick way to build. It's good for places with a short season.
—Vibeke Lichten

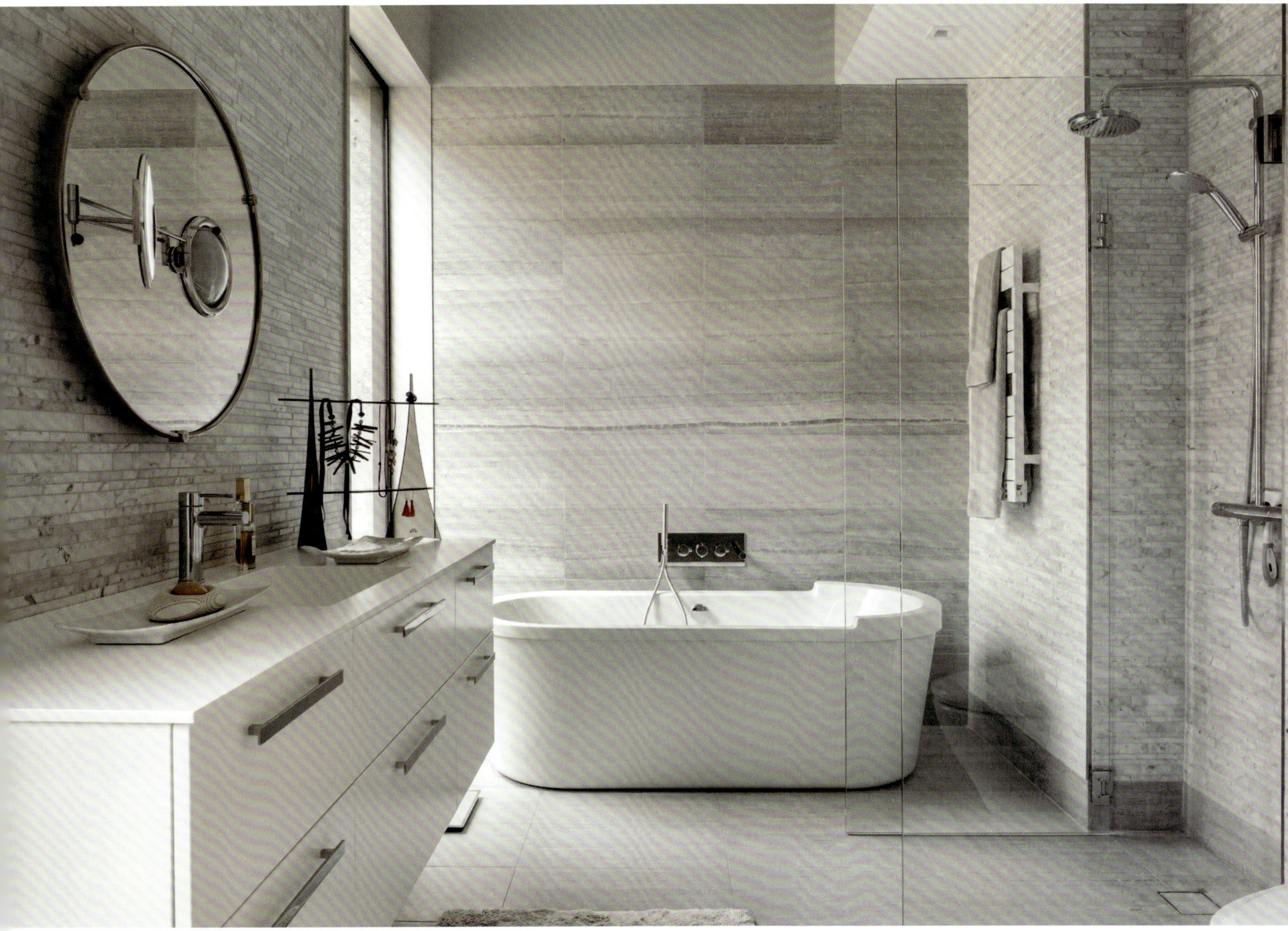

134 Eco House

Above and top: A pool house tucked into the slope contains a garage on the lower level, and a living room with kitchenette, full bath, and sauna on the pool level.

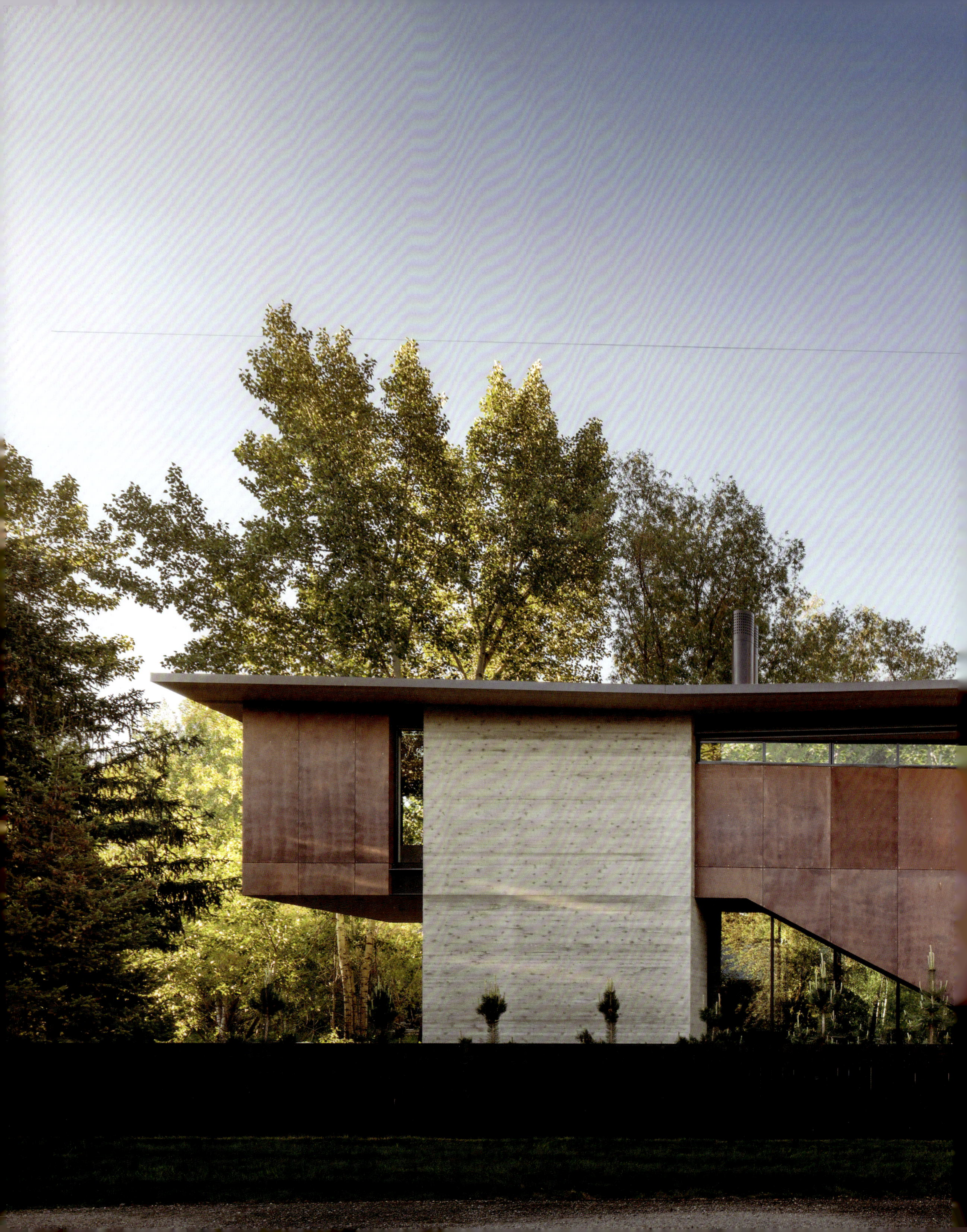

Ketchum, Idaho | 2017

RIVER HOUSE

Olson Kundig Architects
Photographs: Nic Lehoux and Adam Letch

For this second home on a riverbank in Ketchum, Idaho, the client mandate was both clear and wildly open: they wanted a house that would embrace the landscape and nurture a fifty-fifty relationship between the inside and outside. Architect Tom Kundig, who is known for designing houses firmly embedded in big landscapes, gave them exactly what they wanted. Situated on a shallow, 60-foot-wide slot of land between a neighborhood road and a forested riverbank, the house nimbly negotiates the two opposing sides. Its concrete and weathering steel front facade provides privacy, "punctuated by moments of transparency," Kundig says, while the back opens almost entirely to the natural landscape, extending the livable space outdoors to the Big Wood River.

Also known for his expressive, honest use of materials, Kundig chose concrete and weathering steel for the exterior because they're resilient in this demanding environment; over time, they will develop a patina in tune with the surrounding birch and ash trees. Under a lightly swooping roofline, the steel sections reflect what's going on inside. "The areas clad in steel panels highlight specific design moves, like the feature staircase and cantilevered guest suite, with clerestory windows to bring more natural daylight into the interior," he says. "The wood under the overhangs is tongue and groove cedar, which matches the interior ceilings and again underscores the ease of transition between inside and outside."

The areas clad in steel panels highlight specific design moves, like the feature staircase and cantilevered guest suite. The wood under the overhangs is tongue and groove cedar, which matches the interior ceilings and underscores the ease of transition between inside and outside.
—Tom Kundig

Roughly L shaped, the house is organized lengthwise along a steel stairwell and a glassy spine that gives you the sense of walking through the landscape. The short end of the L contains the main living spaces and garage; the spine, with floor-to-ceiling glass on both sides, forms the long side of the L and connects the foyer to a library at the opposite end of the house. This move created a three-sided rear courtyard that spills out from the living spaces. Upstairs, the main bedroom suite sits atop the public spaces, and a guest bedroom and bath down the hall cantilevers over the library. The main bedroom's rear glass wall opens entirely to a large deck. In turn, this extension creates a sheltered porch outside the living room, whose full-length pocketing glass wall also provides unfettered access to the terrace and riverbank.

Hand-operable partitions of one sort or another turn up in every Kundig-designed house. "There are many movable elements in River House that allow the client and her guests to move seamlessly between indoors and outdoors," Kundig says. For example,

River House has two of his trademark gizmos: a corner guillotine window in the kitchen that opens to a walk-up bar; and a custom rolling garage door. "Kinetic architecture is important to me because I believe buildings should be adjusted and changed by the people who use them," he says. "These manual devices allow people to activate the building directly, which connects them to their home and, by extension, the surrounding natural context."

It was also important to the client that materials used throughout the home be durable and easy to maintain. Kitchen cabinets are made from stained white oak veneer, and countertops are black granite. These materials provide a warm, neutral backdrop to the colors of the landscape.

In addition to the visual connections between inside and outside, large, operable windows and ceiling fans provide natural ventilation, and the mature trees passively cool the home in warm weather. To support the river ecosystem, the design team added native, drought-tolerant, and wetlands-appropriate plants.

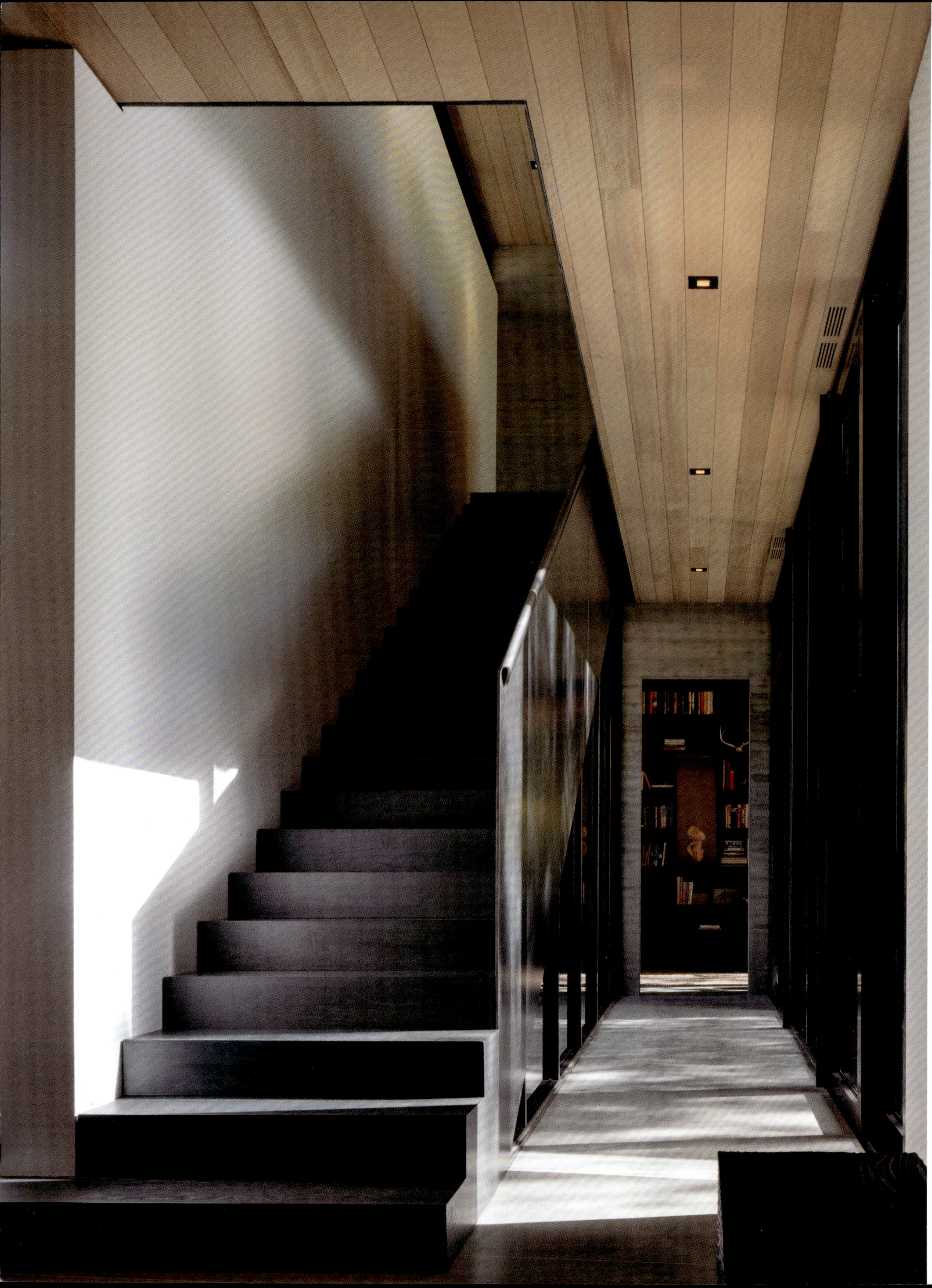

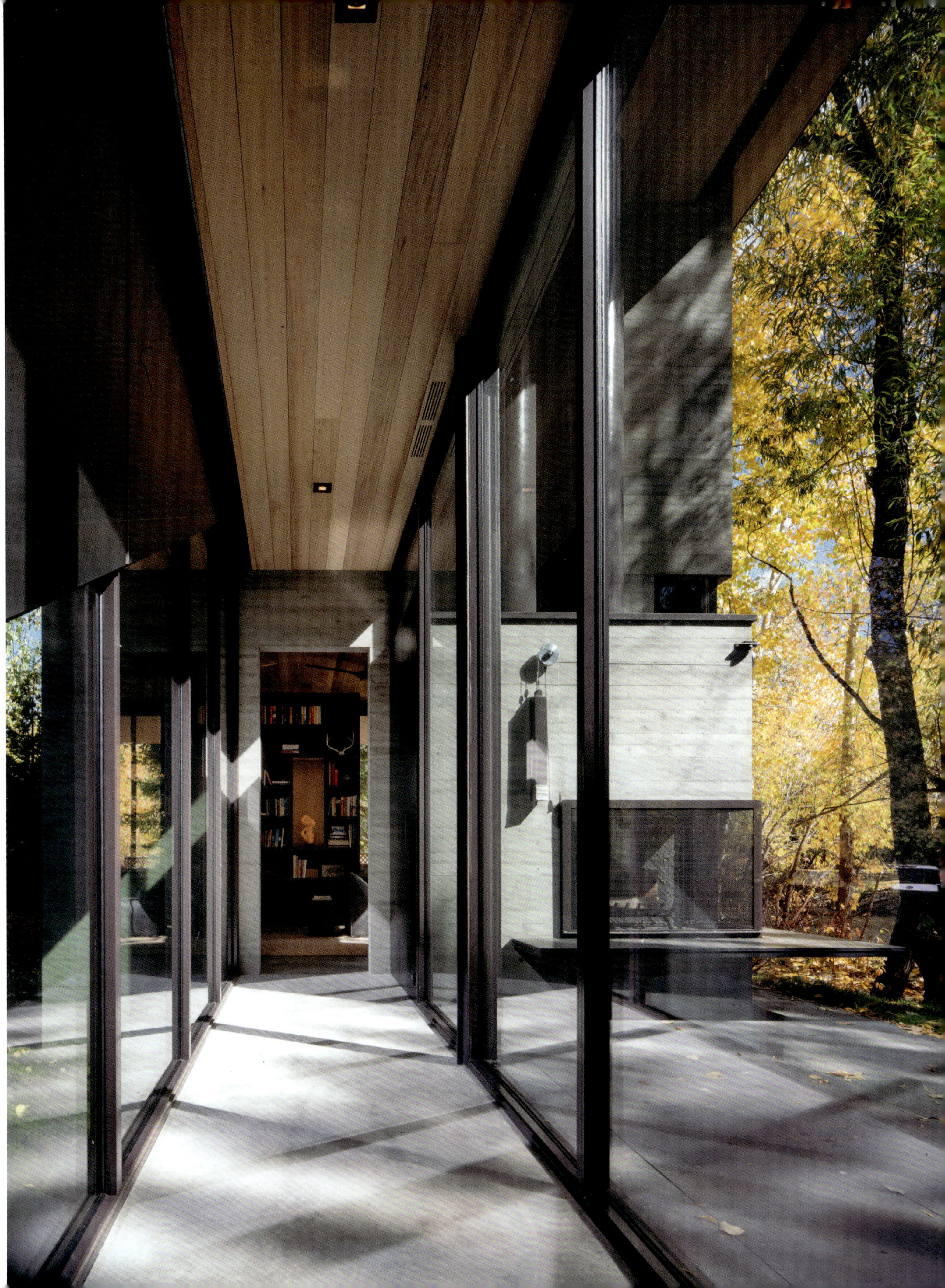

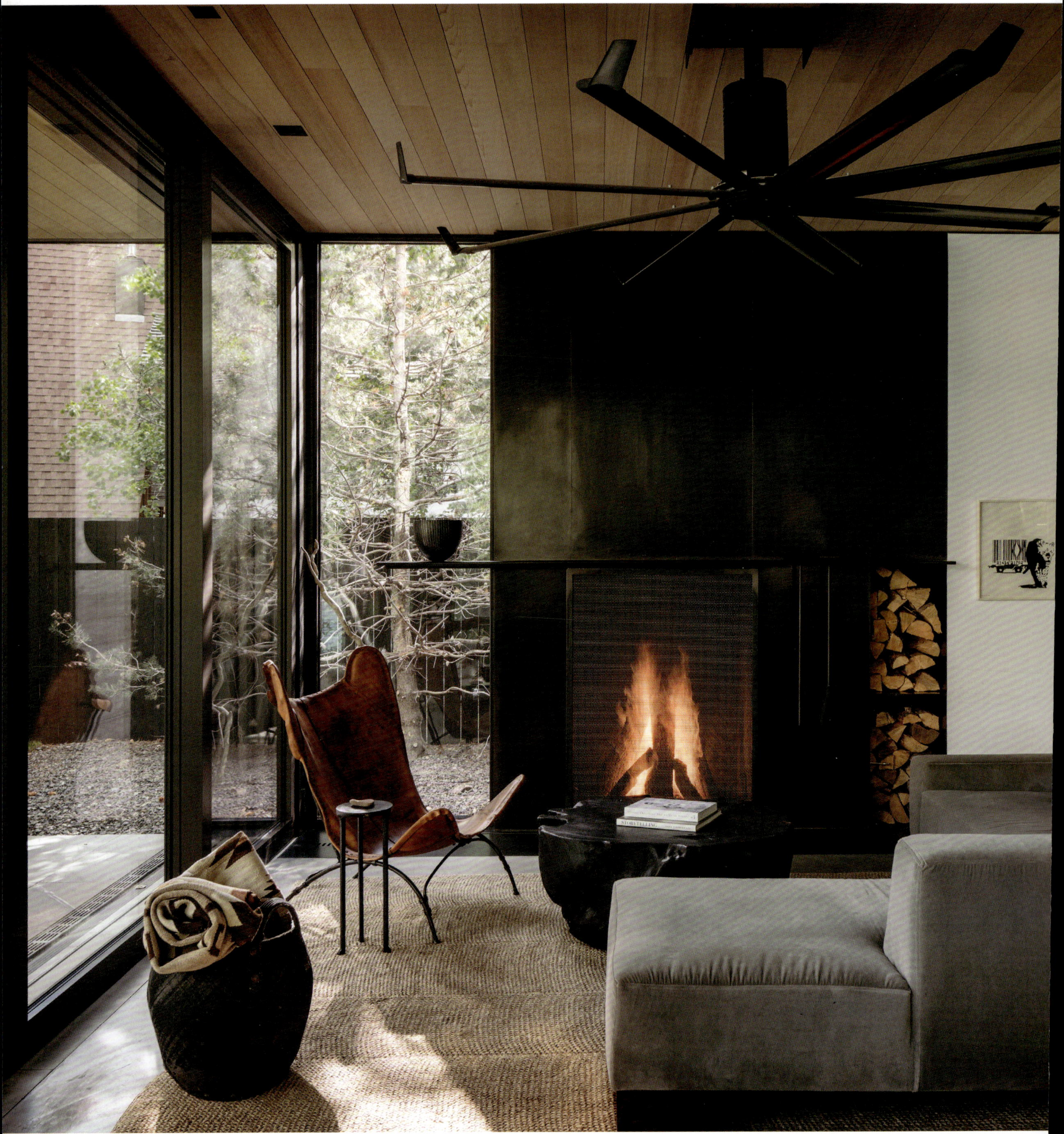

145

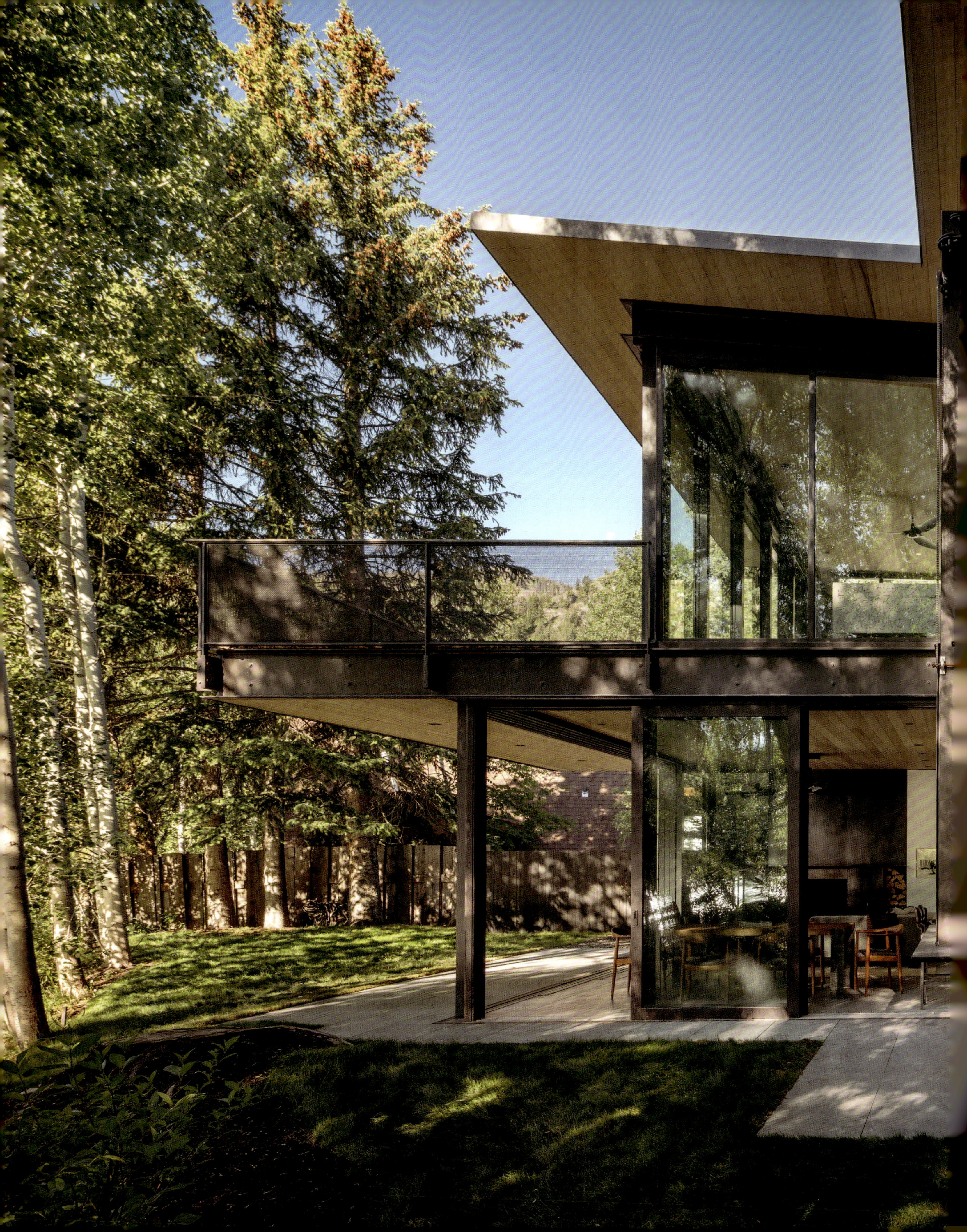

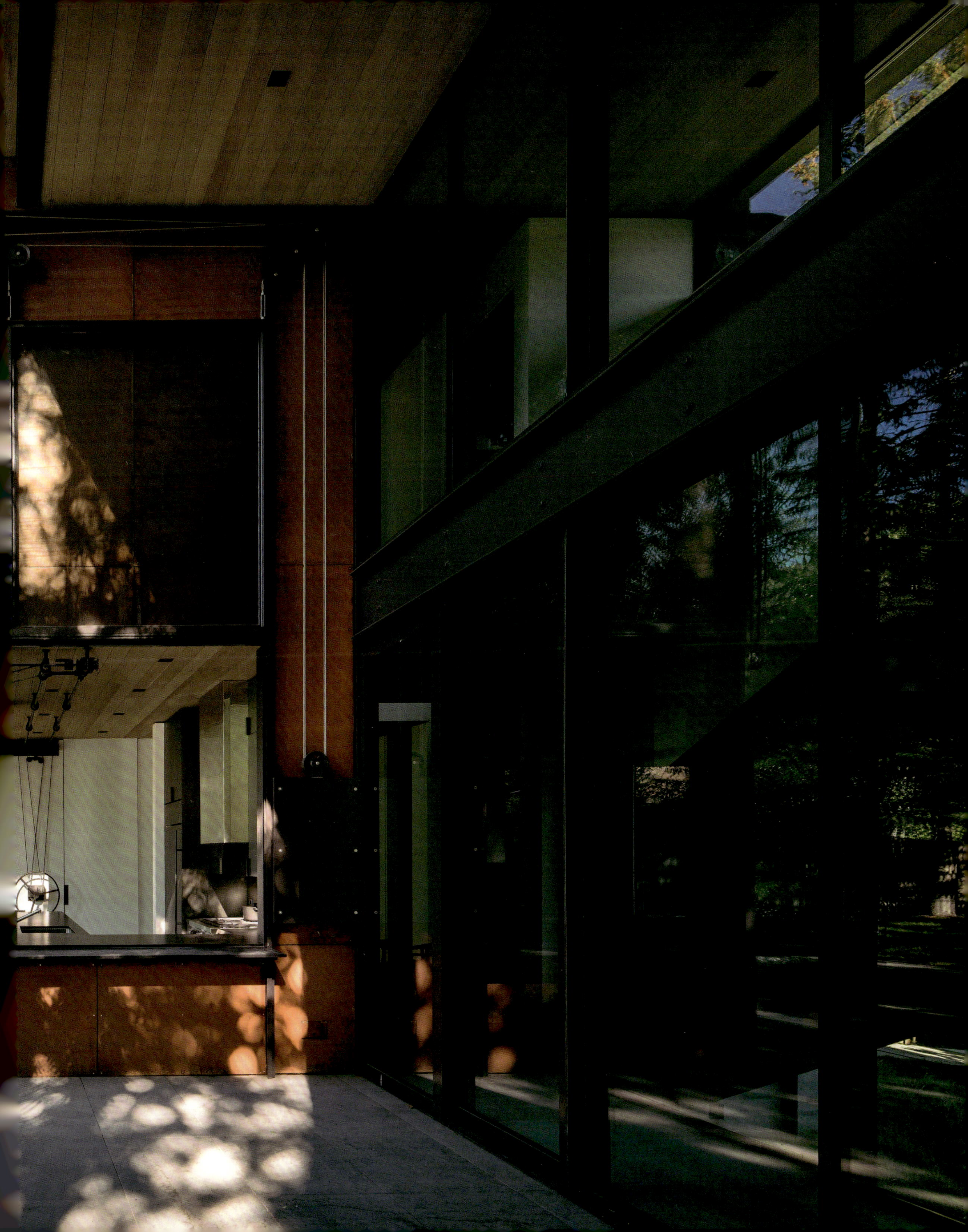

148 *River House*

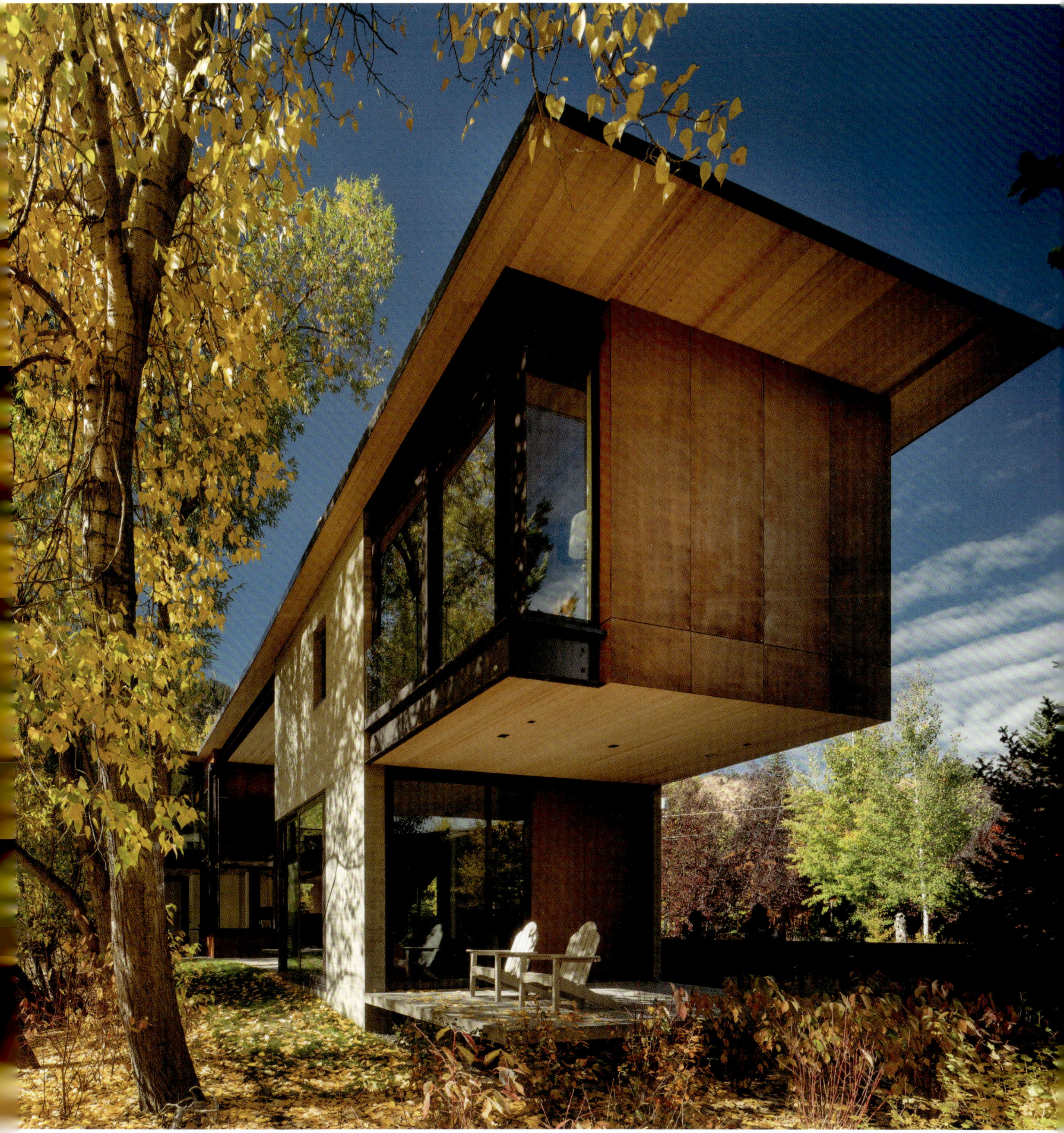

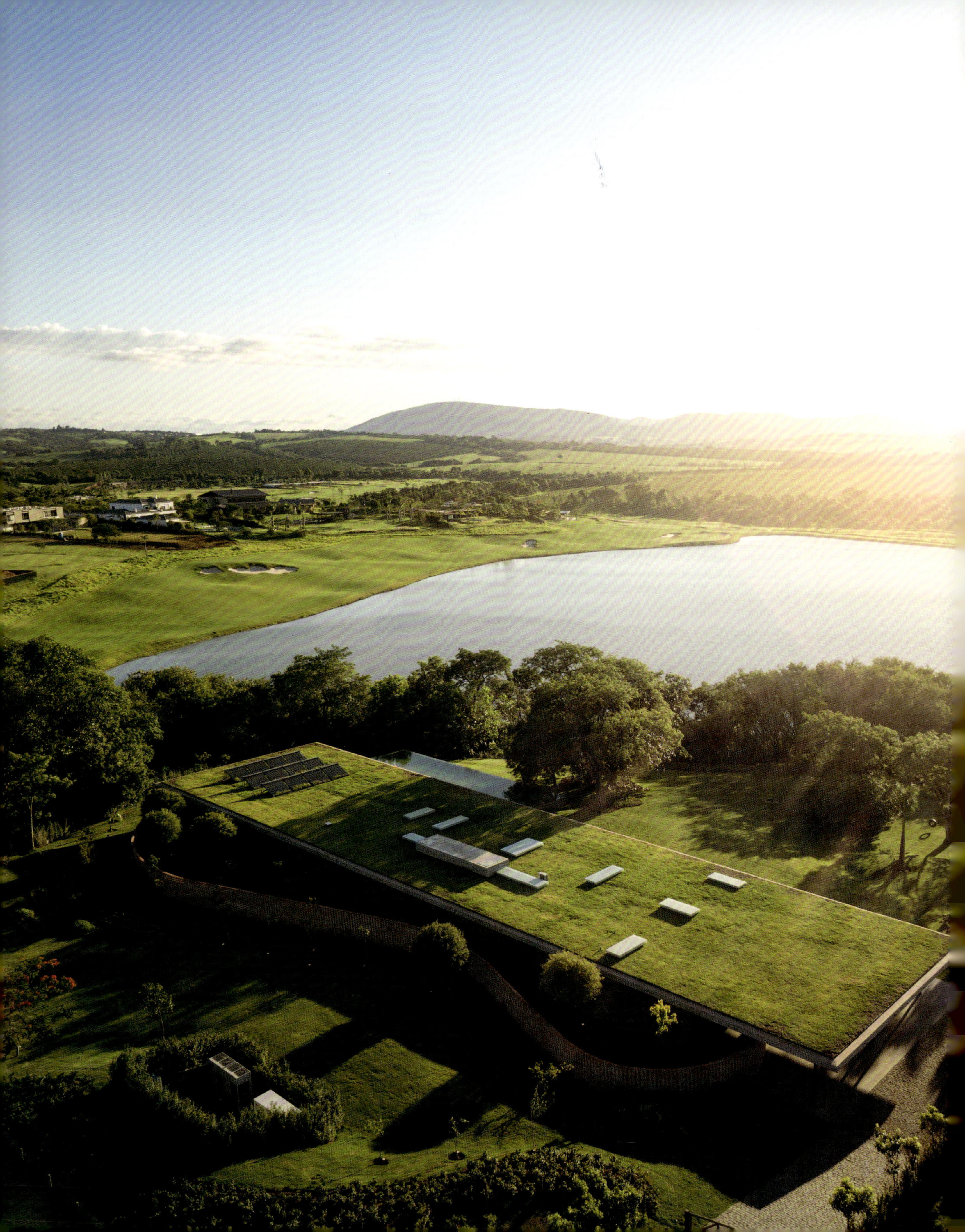

Porto Feliz, Brazil | 2018

CASA PLANA

Studio MK27

Photographs: Studio MD27 and FG+SG

"Almost every Brazilian architect considers concrete," says Lair Reis, architect and project manager at Studio MK27. "Putting aside the architectural history of Le Corbusier and Oscar Niemeyer, concrete is a fundamental material. There's the possibility of making light something that is very heavy." That makes it especially well suited to the firm's buildings, whose strongly horizontal proportions are inspired by founder Marcio Kogan's filmmaking background and interest in wide-screen cinematography. He often organizes his clients' programs as floating boxes, or a box within a box.

It was not just the program but also the remarkable site that inspired this treatment at Casa Plana, two hours by car from São Paulo. The house sits on a high point in the middle of the lot, which faces a lake and preserved area on the southwest. Asked for a low-lying house with open spaces connected to nature, the architects drew two flat concrete slabs, one for the floor and one for the roof. The roof extends dramatically past the perimeter walls, sheltering an open-air living and dining terrace to the south and parking on the north.

Utterly simple in plan, its austere rectilinearity is relieved by a free-standing red-brick wall that undulates dramatically along the east side, bending under the roof at the house's short ends to partially enclose the outdoor living spaces. This sinuous screen reinforces the sense that the roof is floating, and its light-filtering perforations add kinetic effects as the sun moves throughout the day.

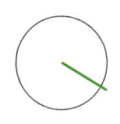

GROUND FLOOR

1 Swimming pool
2 Deck
3 Terrace
4 Outdoor kitchen
5 Living/dining room
6 Living room 2
7 Kitchen
8 Laundry
9 Mechanical room
10 Toilet
11 Bedroom
12 Main bedroom
13 Caretaker's bedroom
14 Caretaker's bath
15 Caretaker's living room
16 Gym
17 Bath
18 Playroom
19 TV room

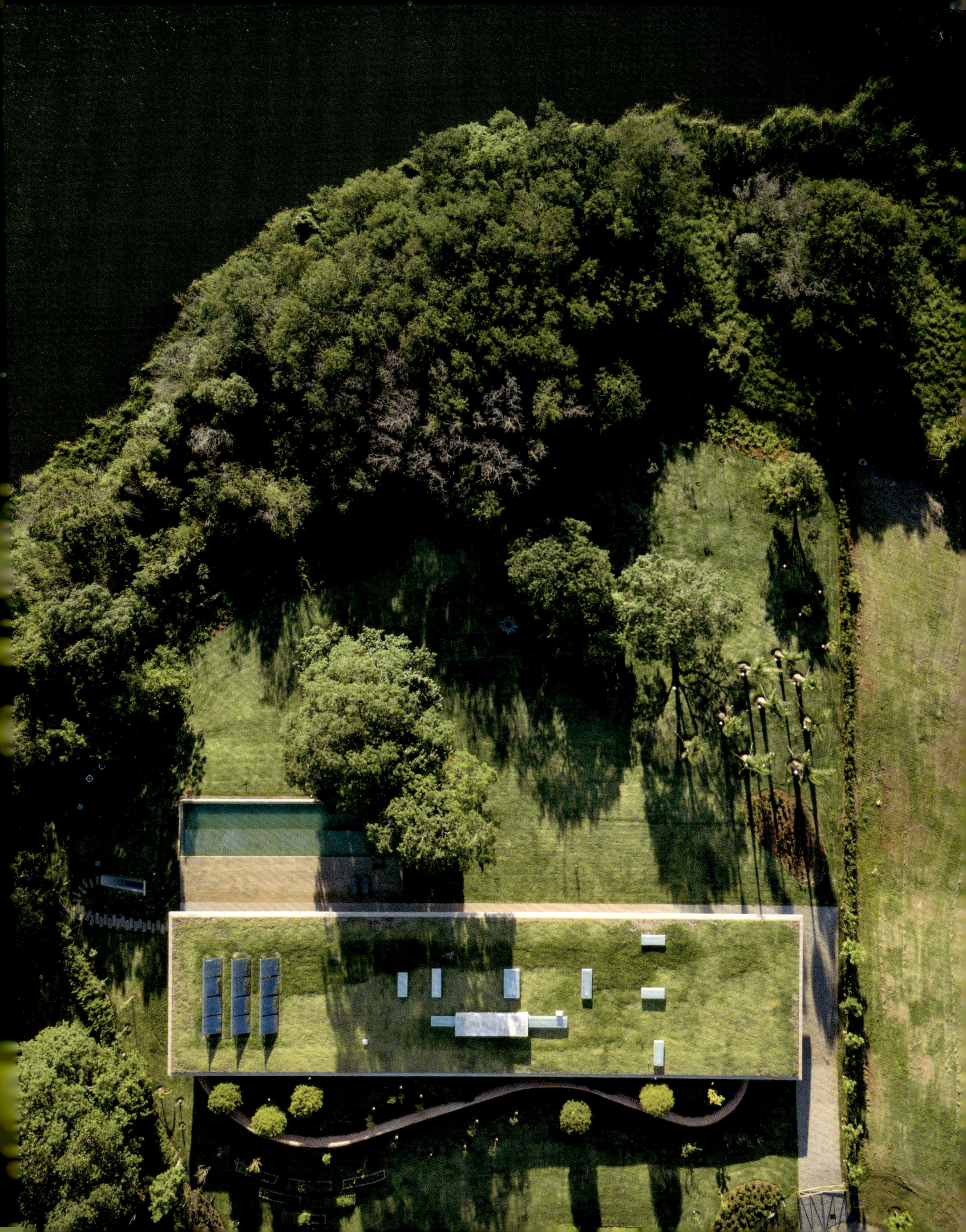

"It's almost like the house is a big shadow, just that slab, and over the slab we have this green roof that is responsible for insulation," Reis says. The caretakers access this cooling swath of lawn by ladder. "We wanted to make the house almost disappear into the environment since it was placed in the middle of the lot for privacy from the neighbors," he says. "When people choose a place for a weekend house, they want to feel they are alone."

Inside, the floor plan is divided lengthwise into two boxes separated by a central corridor, with glass on the outer edges. On the east the architects placed the staff quarters and a gym. Across the wood-sheathed hallway are a TV room and the family bedrooms with en suite skylit baths, which face the garden and lake. Entering from the parking area on the north, one is drawn down the long corridor—used as a photo gallery protected from ultraviolet light—and into the bright kitchen, living, and dining areas on the south. There, retractable floor-to-ceiling glass doors lead to the covered porch and a deck edging the pool.

"Concrete allows us to play with the volume; however, it's not easy to build with it," Reis says. "There is nothing to hide imperfections and mechanical systems. It is an investment in time, and expensive. But you can use the concrete to absorb and release heat, which helps to balance the costs. Now we're experimenting more with wood or a combination of wood and concrete, which can be interesting from a sustainable point of view. Here in Brazil most buildings are painted. If you protect concrete, you can forget it. But the process needs to be set up just right."

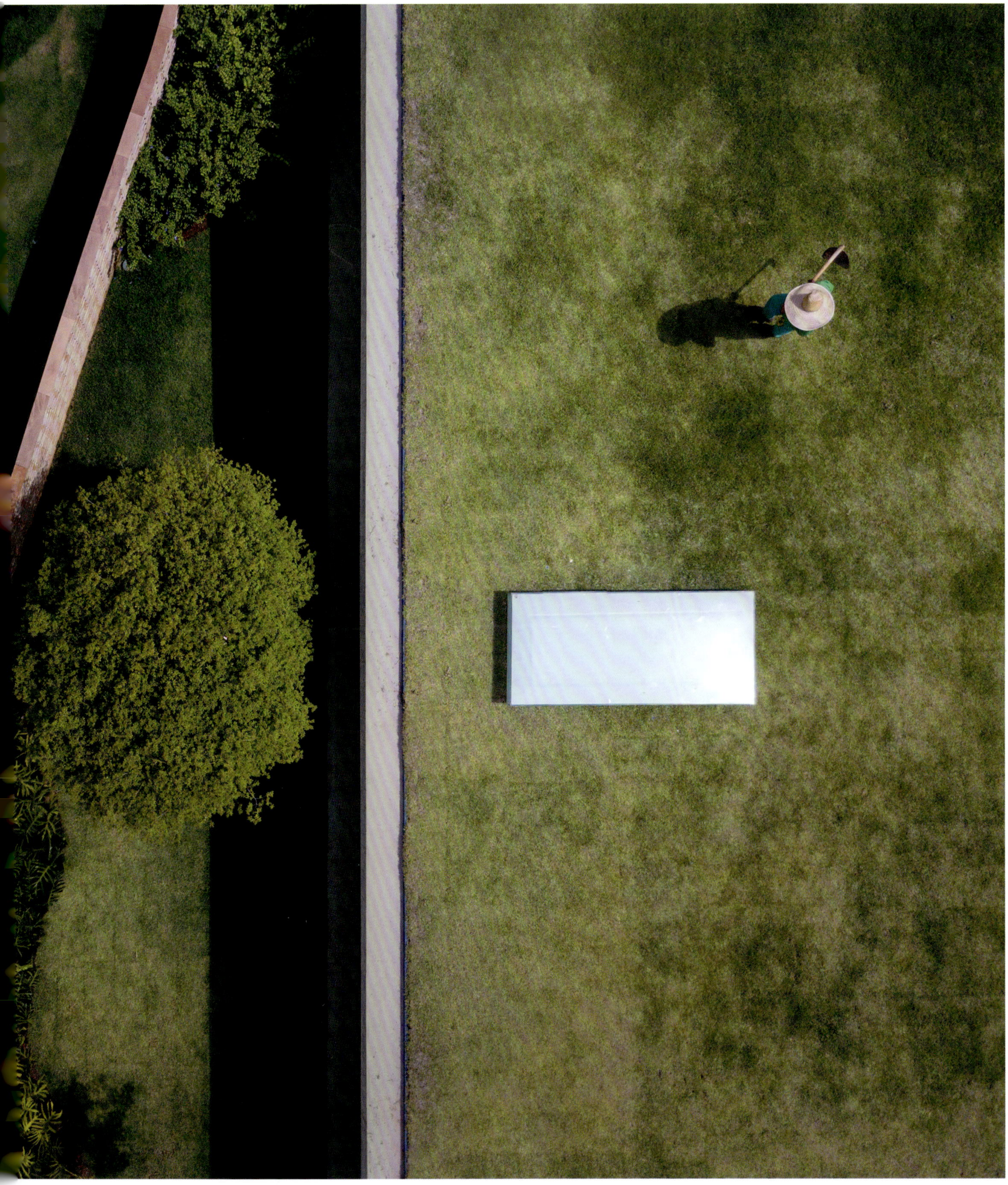

Concrete is a fundamental material. There's the possibility of making light something that is very heavy.
—Lair Reis

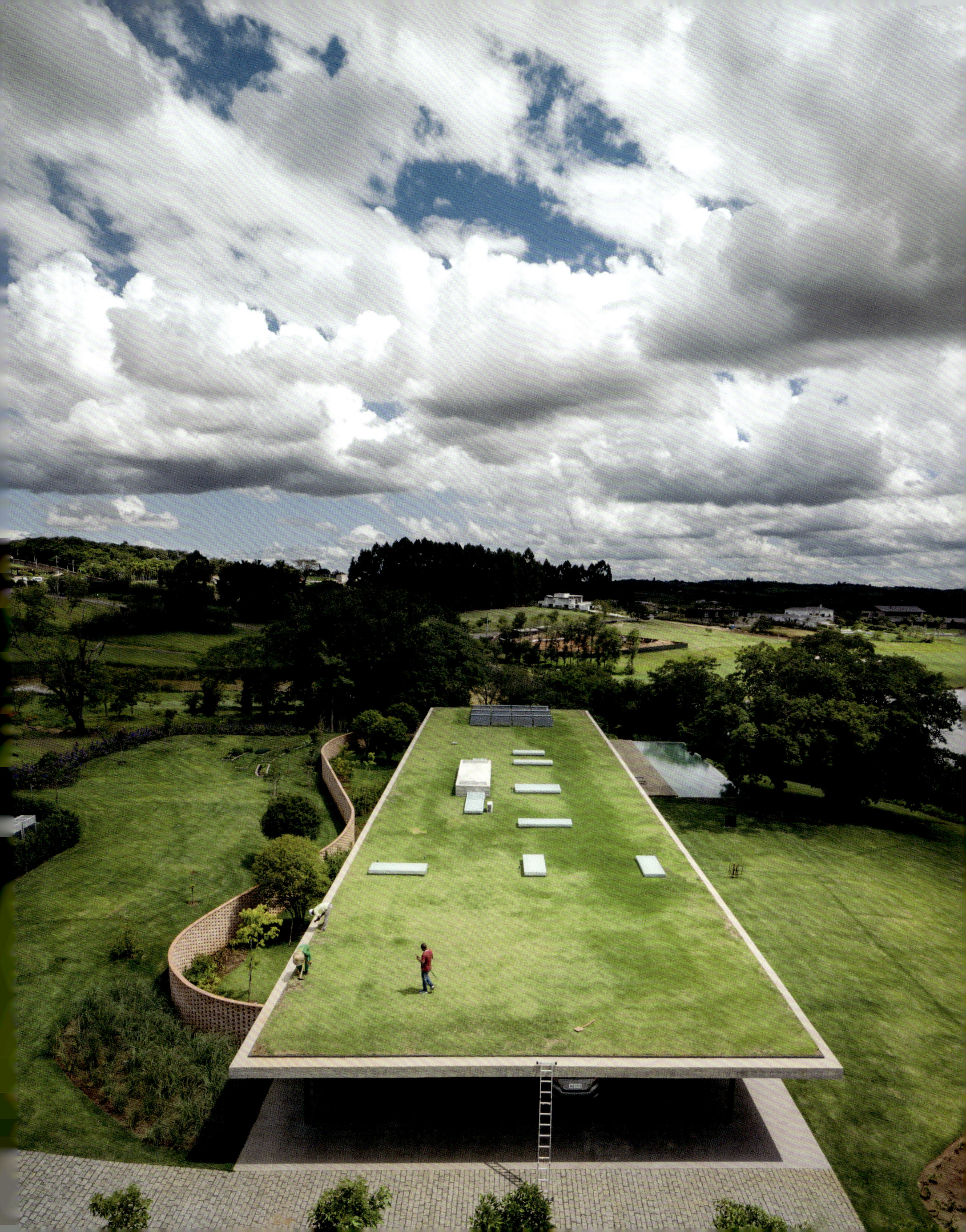

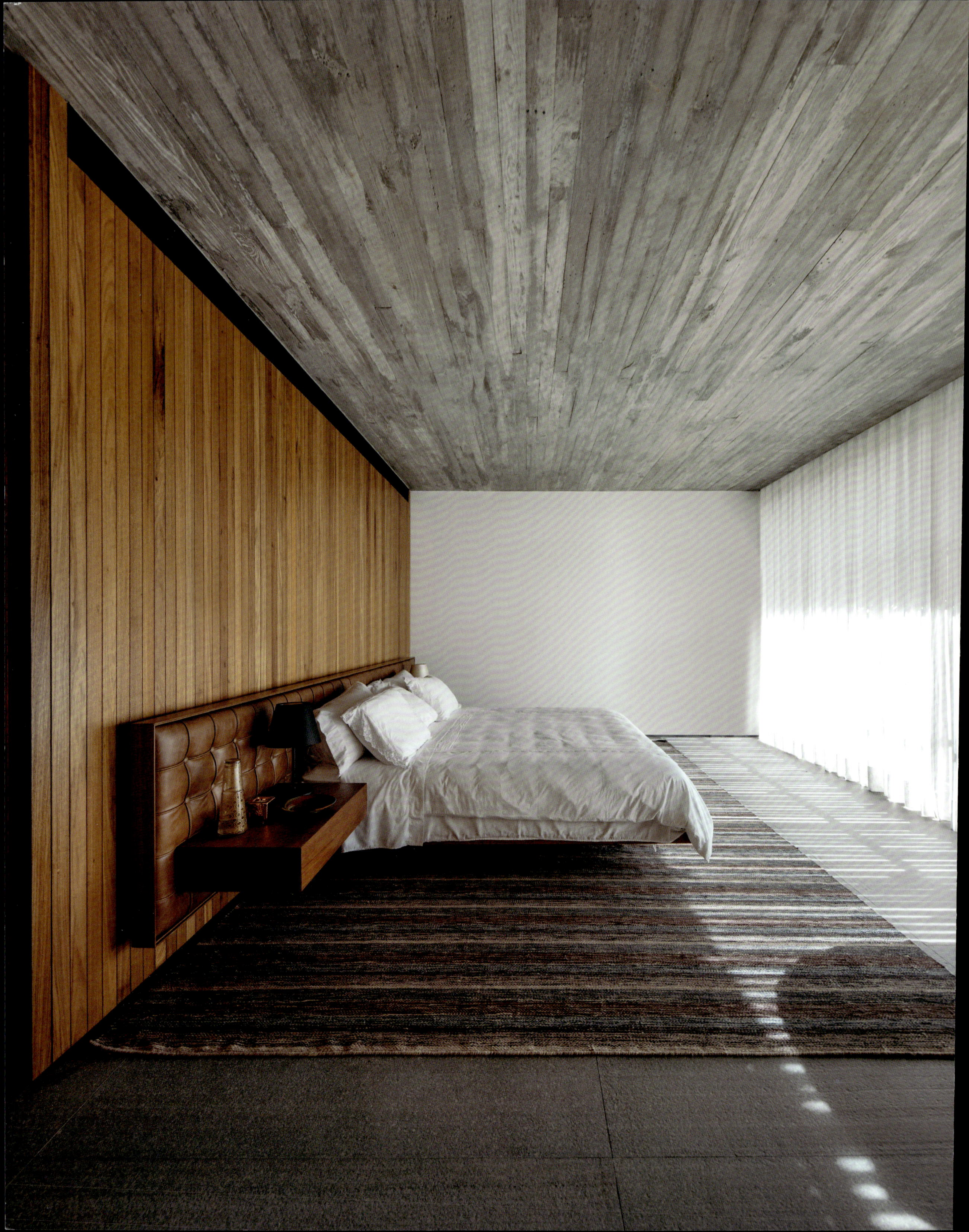

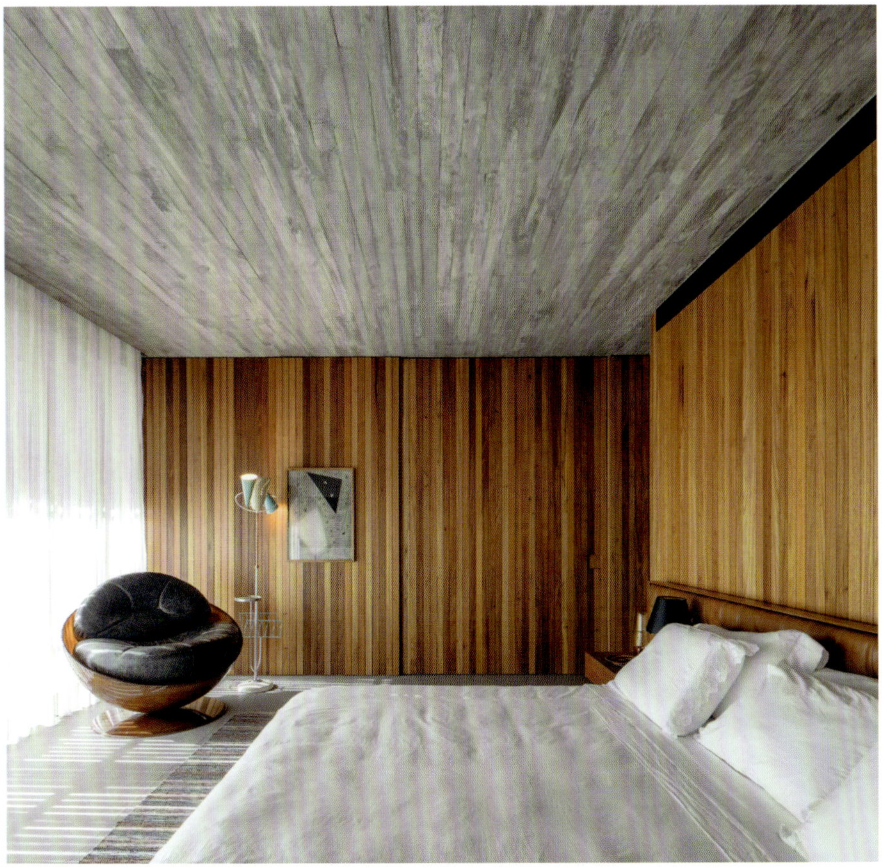

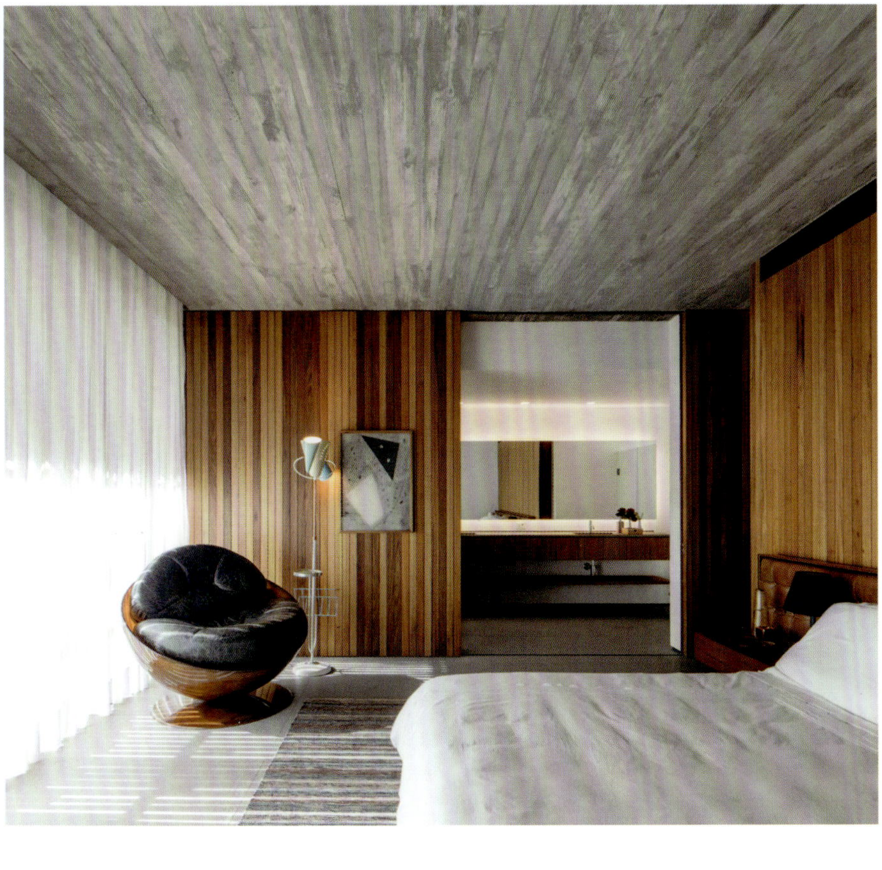

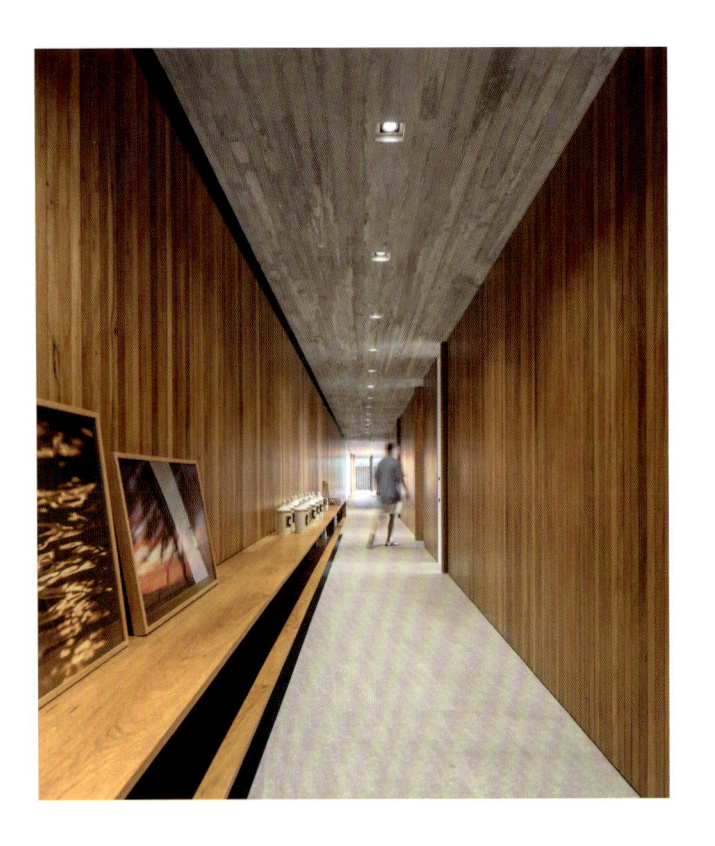

A long corridor protects the owners' photography collection from ultraviolet light. Walls are sheathed in Brazilian cumaru, and floors are Brazilian basalt.

Casa Plana

161

Casa Plana

To avoid the use of beams, concrete columns hidden in the interior walls support the roof, along with delicate steel columns in the open spaces.

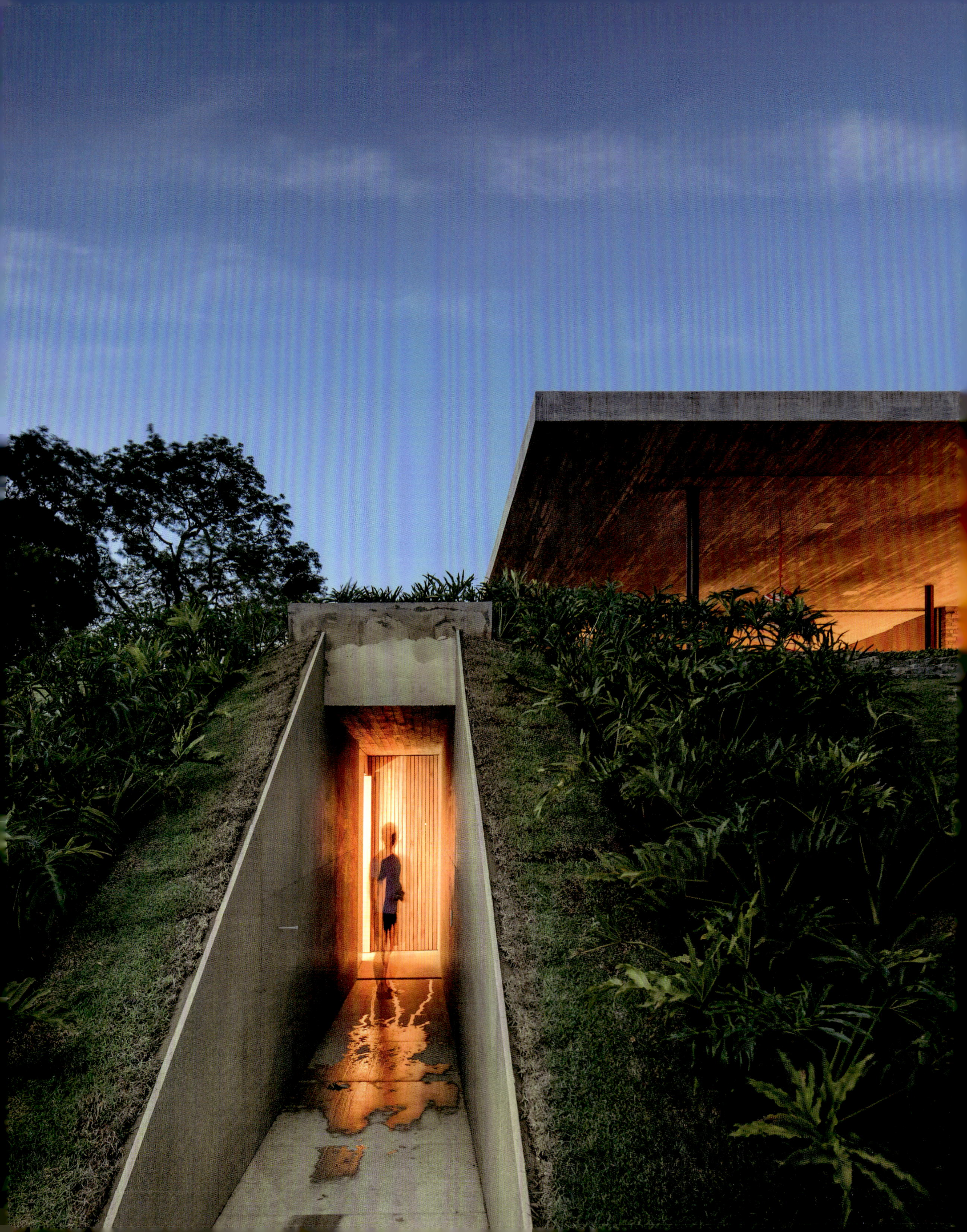

A tunnel cut into the landscape allows access to the mechanical area under the pool. Hidden water tanks collect rainwater for drinking, landscape use, and the swimming pool.

166 *Casa Plana*

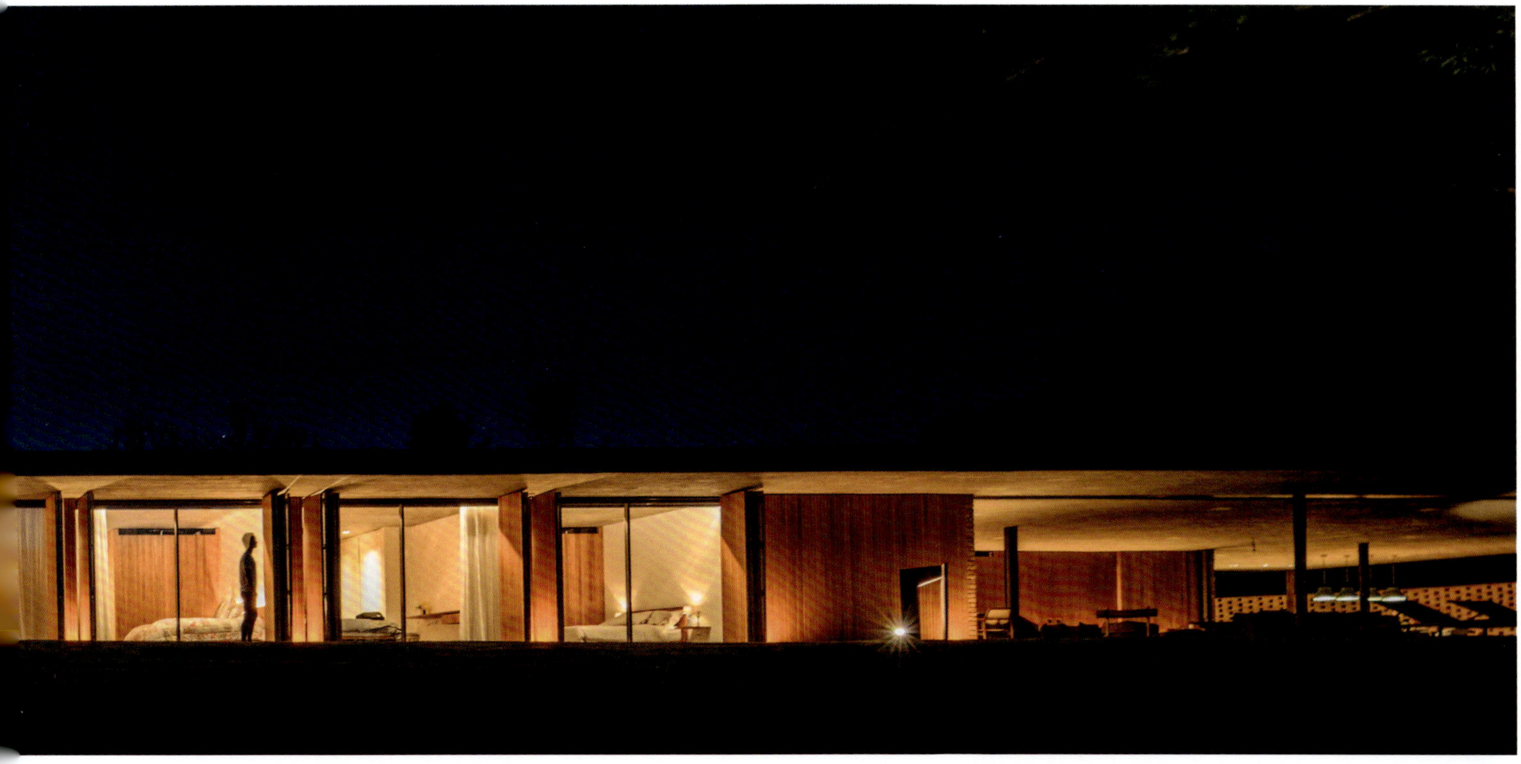

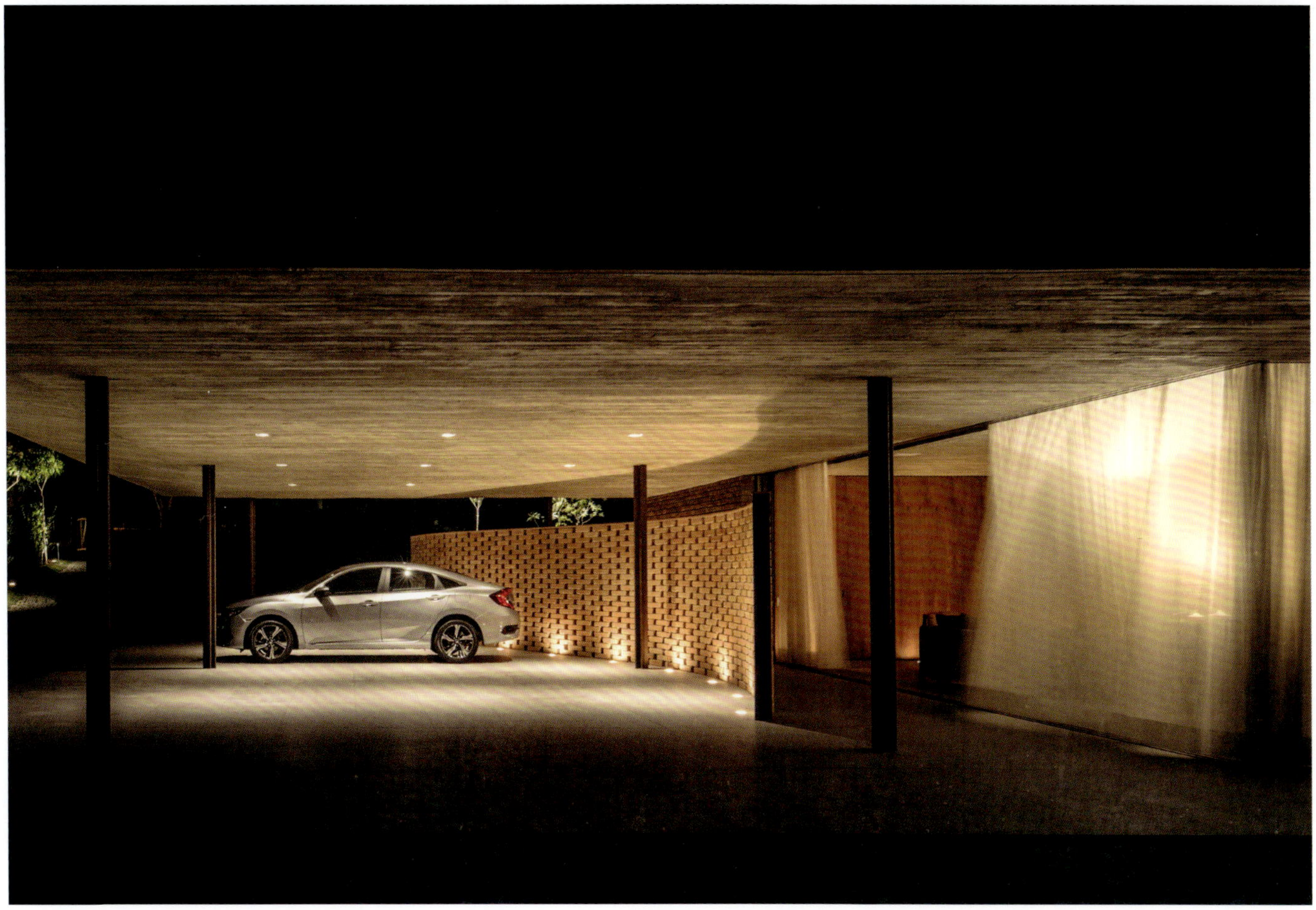

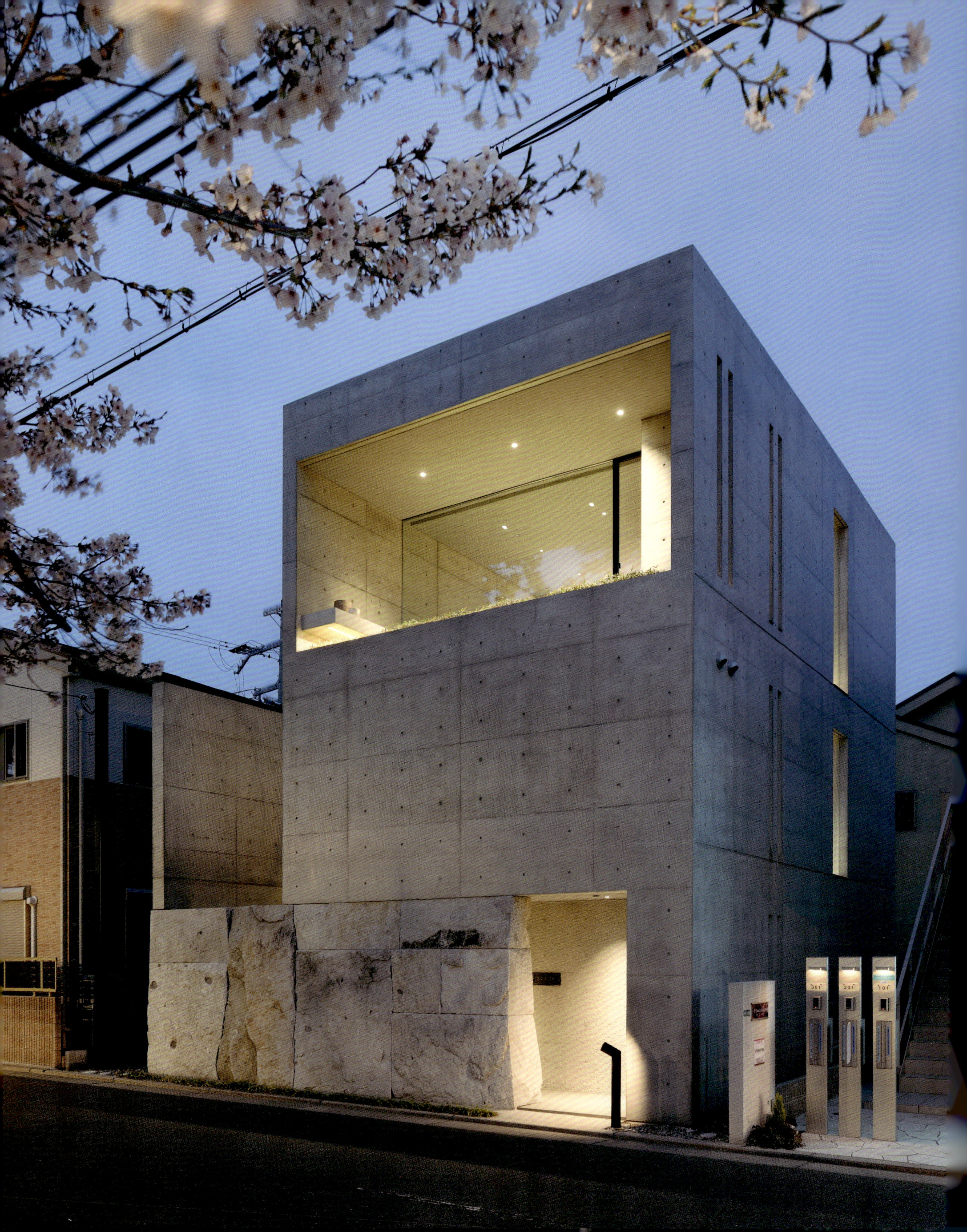

Hyogo, Japan | 2018

F RESIDENCE

Gosize

Photographs: Courtesy of Gosize

Not everyone will appreciate the brutalist minimalism of architect Go Fujita's own combined house and office. But the orthogonal tower exquisitely expresses his interest in subtle buildings that are inventively attuned to texture, light, and nature. It's located in a dense neighborhood in a part of Japan popular for its cherry blossoms, and Fujita took design cues from both the man-made and natural environment. Instinctively Japanese, its rough-hewn stone base hints at the interior vibe. "The stone is from Fukushima; it's a gray color that blends well with concrete," Fujita says. Extending off-center away from the house, it forms a wall that marks the entry at one end and encloses a private interior courtyard at the other.

Inside, the house embraces light and air with high ceilings and full walls that open to the outside. The double-height foyer, or *doma*, leads to a sliding glass wall containing the courtyard with a pool, rocks, fringy ferns, and a tree. "From the courtyard, you can see the sky that reflects the changing seasons, bringing a richness to the house," Fujita says. "It also makes the house seem relaxed and larger than it is." This level houses the office and conference room, plus a kitchenette and a small bath. With its chiseled chunks of stone flooring and light filtering through high cutaways in interior and exterior walls, a sense of the natural world permeates. Light from the vegetated courtyard throws elongated plant shadows into the room. "The interior is reduced so that light and shadow can be seen effectively," Fujita says.

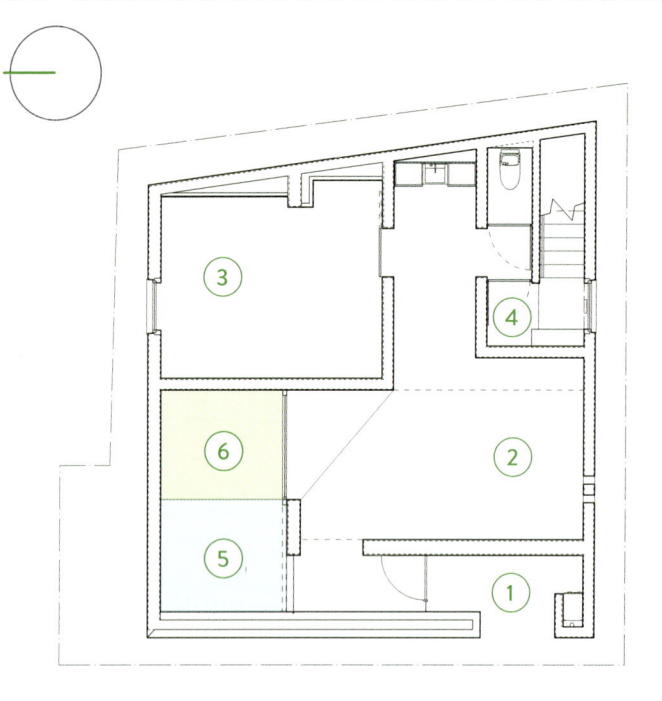

FIRST FLOOR

1 Entrance
2 Conference room
3 Office
4 Inner entrance
5 Pond
6 Courtyard with tree

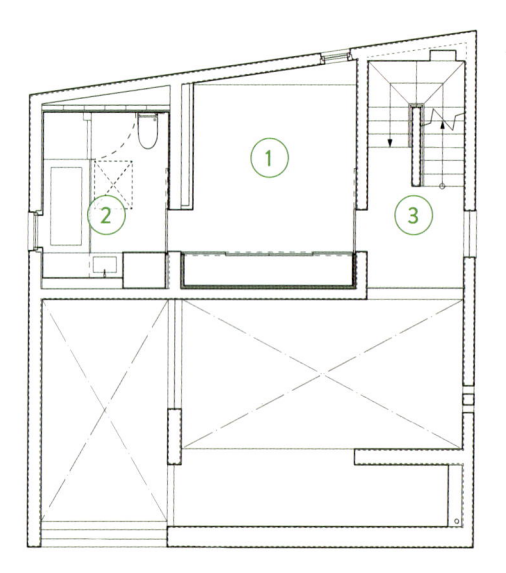

SECOND FLOOR

1 Bedroom
2 Bath
3 Open to tree and courtyard below

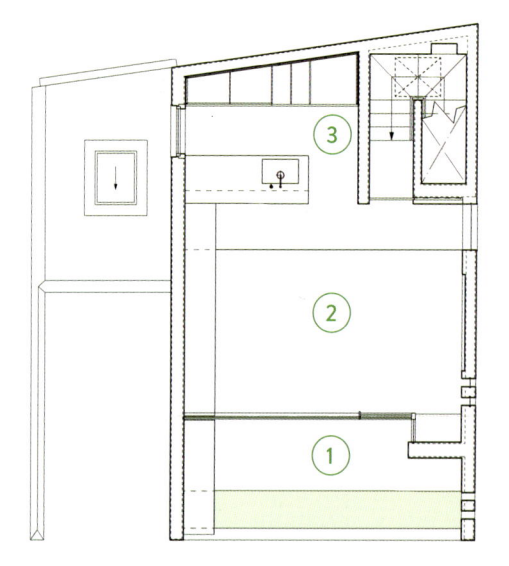

THIRD FLOOR

1 Terrace
2 Living
3 Kitchen

F Residence • Floor Plan

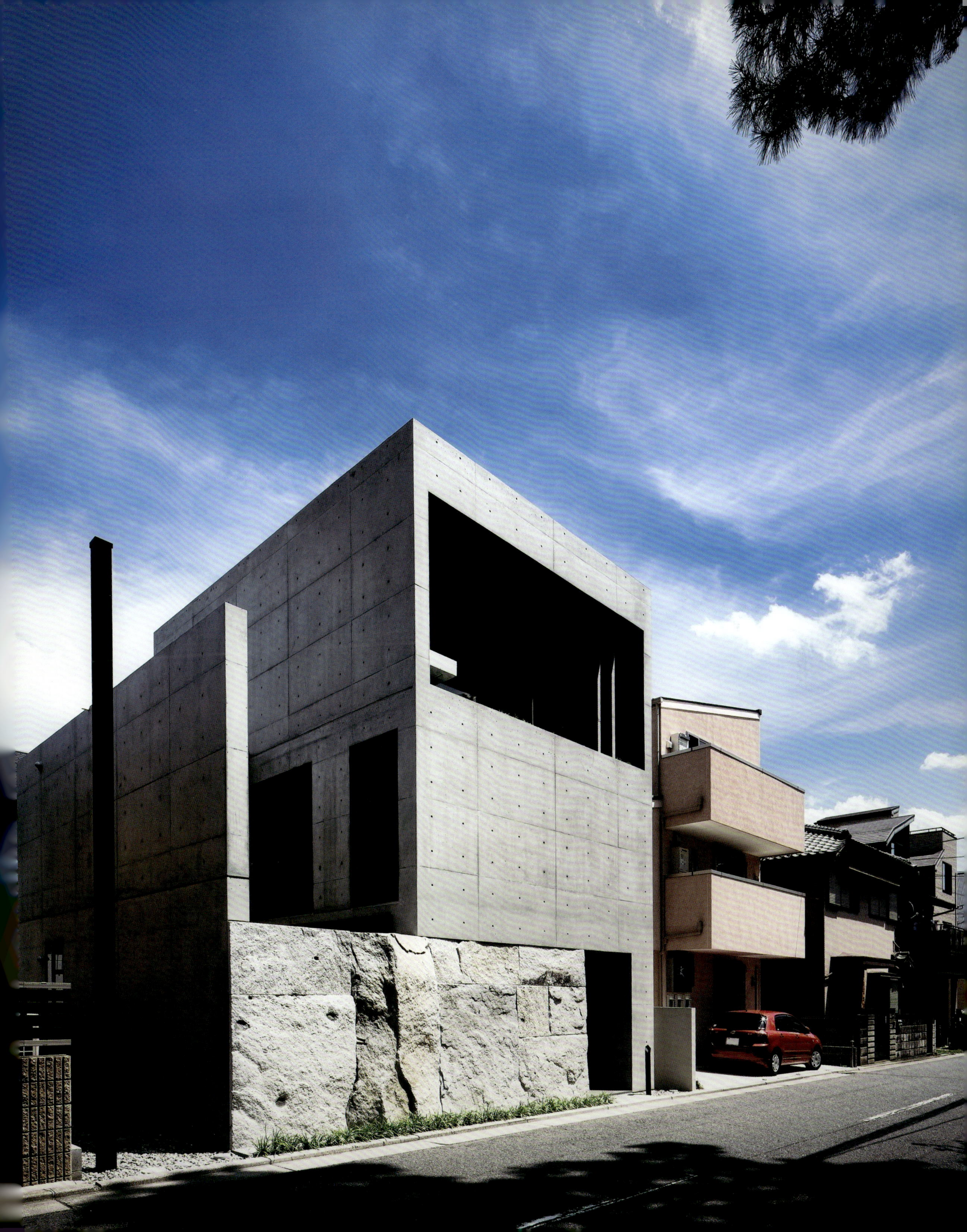

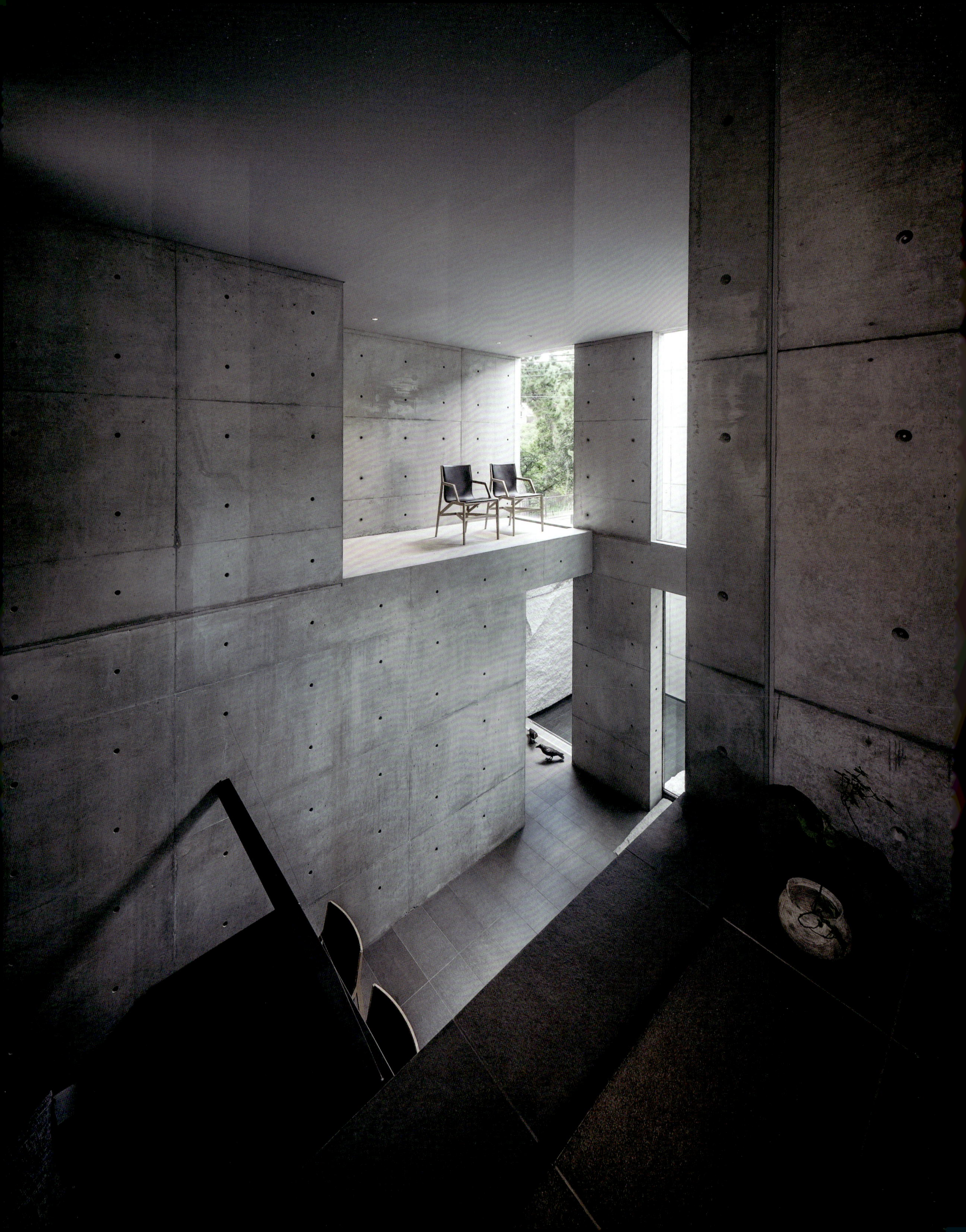

"I wanted to reflect a distinctive Japanese aesthetic of natural materials and beauty in simplicity," Fujita continues. "The design emphasizes plainness and blank spaces, with ambiguous boundaries between, inside and out, and a keen awareness of time."

As one moves up through the house, it becomes more open to the outside world. On the second level is a single bedroom and a bright, skylit bath that overlooks the double-height spaces below. The top floor contains the kitchen, dining, and living space, where dark, rippled oak flooring and oak cabinetry lend warmth and texture to the hard surfaces. A concrete bench spans one wall, piercing the sliding glass doors that open the entire front of the house to a covered terrace—a porch overlooking the street.

Relaxed and lively, and perhaps counterintuitively, this house has a charm that comes from its universality: stripped to its essence, it becomes a prototypical dwelling. "It is my hope that this residence and office will serve as a place to reconnect with the nature-based wisdom and spiritual culture our ancestors have passed down to us," Fujita says, "as well as to quietly reexamine my own life."

"From the courtyard, you can see the sky that reflects the changing seasons, bringing a richness to the house," Fujita says. "It also makes the house seem relaxed and larger than it is."

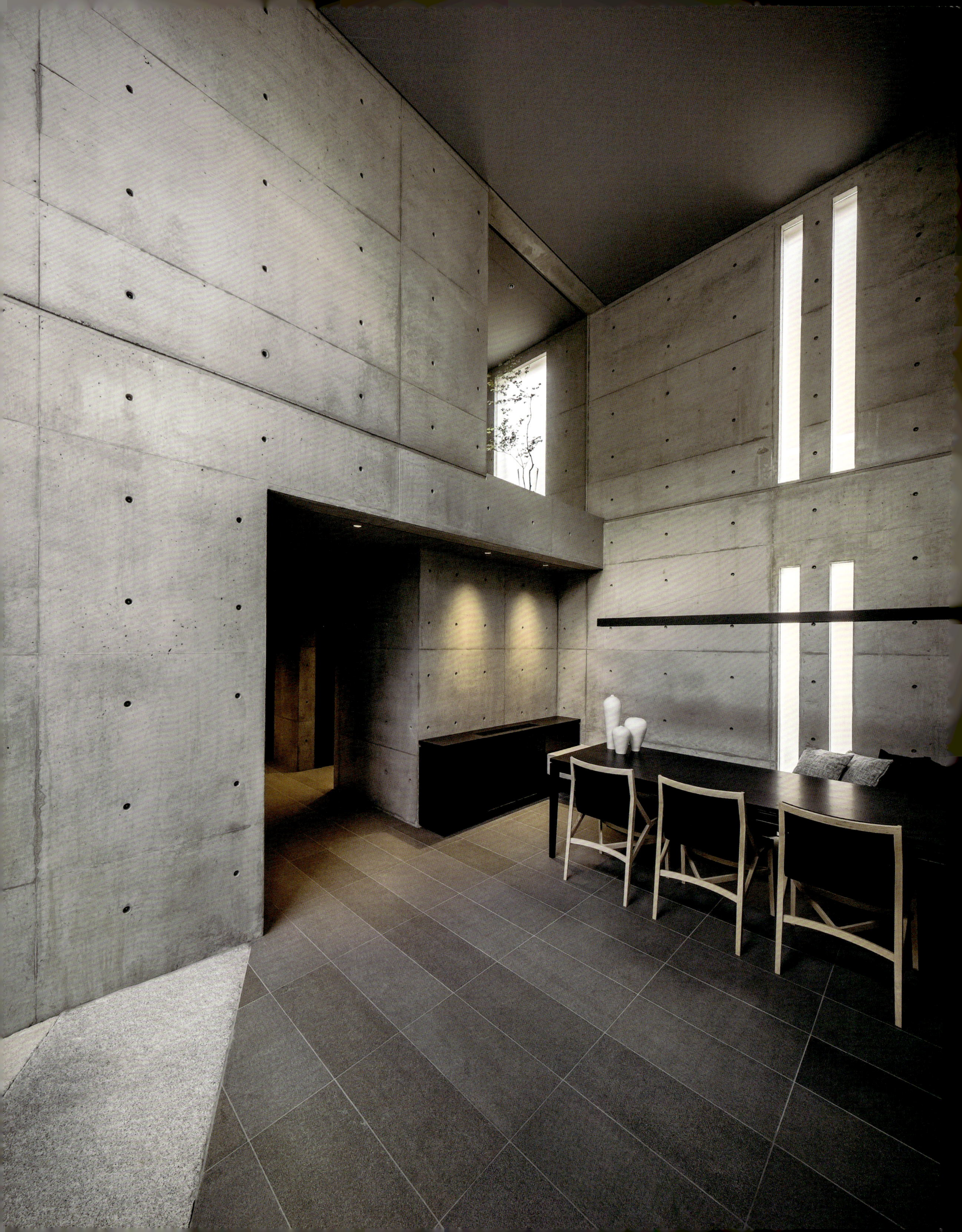

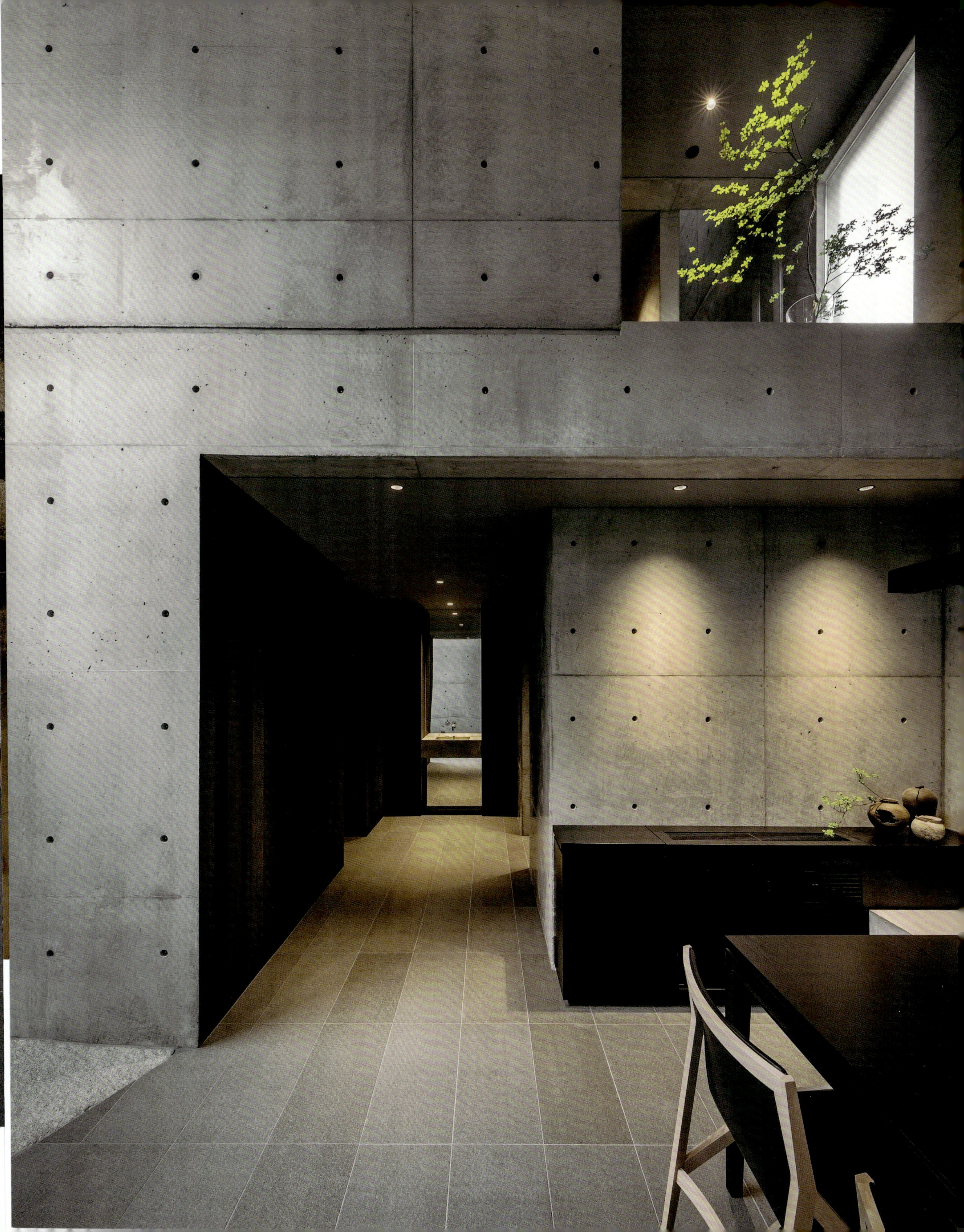

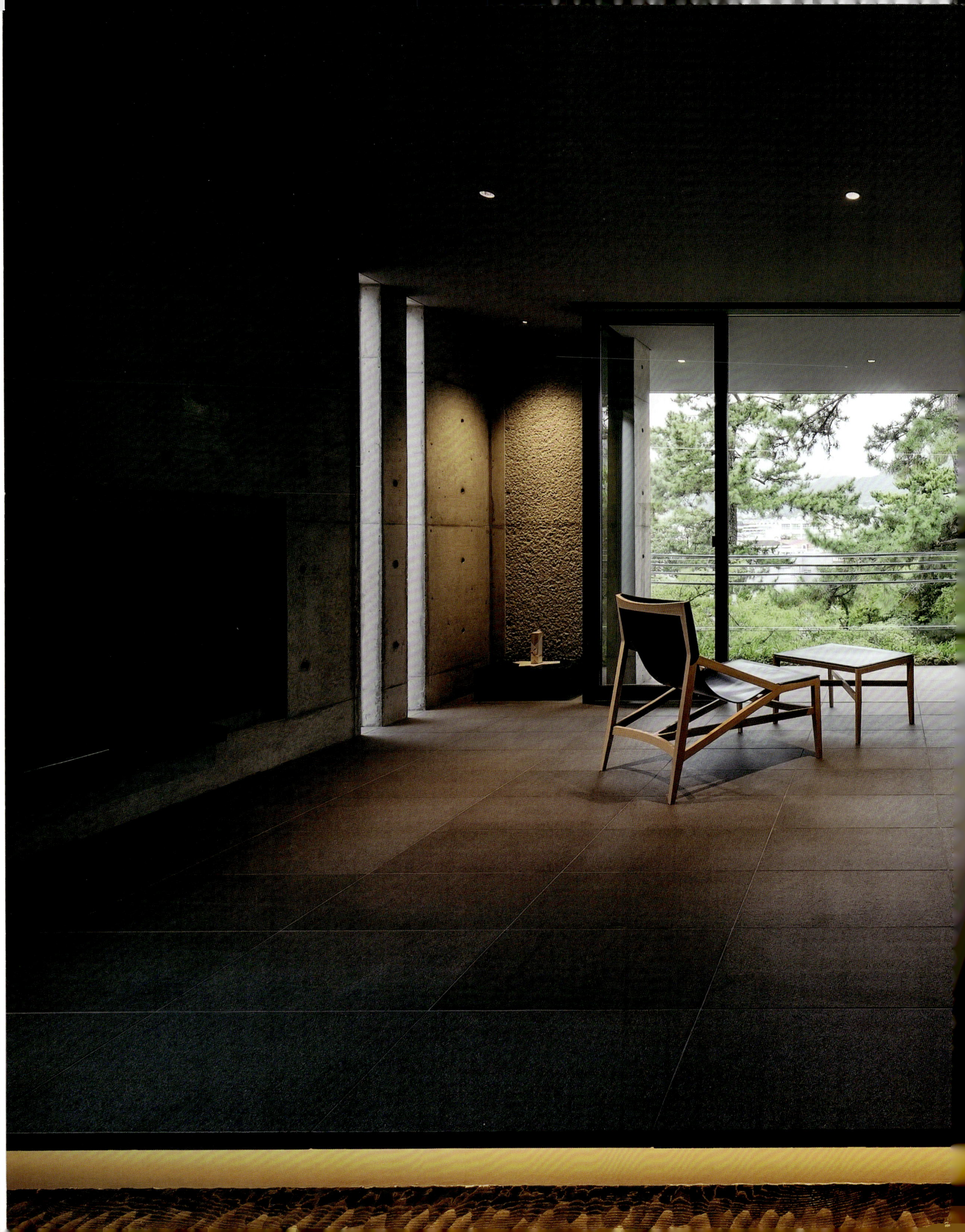

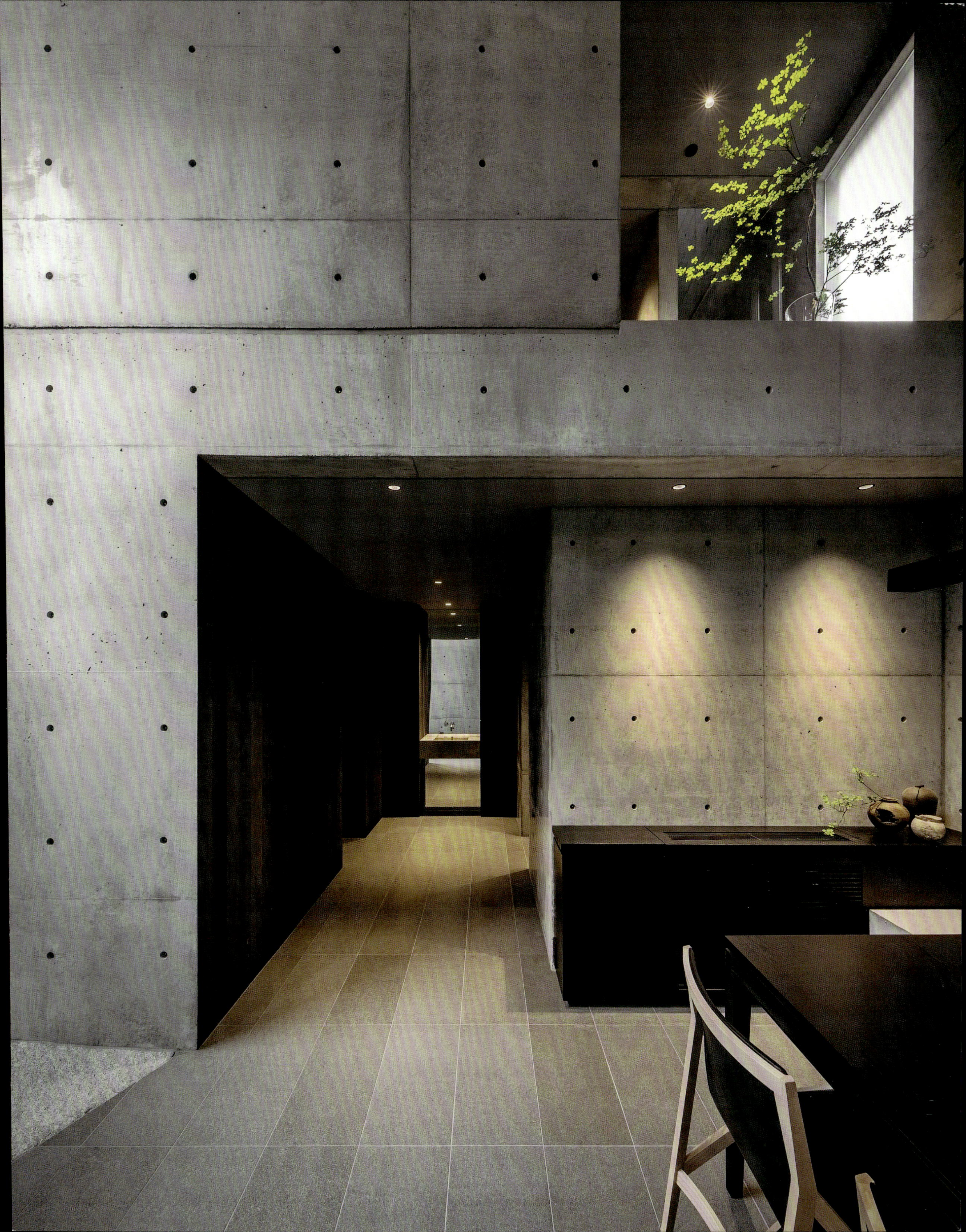

176   F Residence

The interior is reduced so that light and shadow can be seen effectively.... The design emphasizes plainness and blank spaces, with ambiguous boundaries between inside and out, and a keen awareness of time.
—Go Fujita

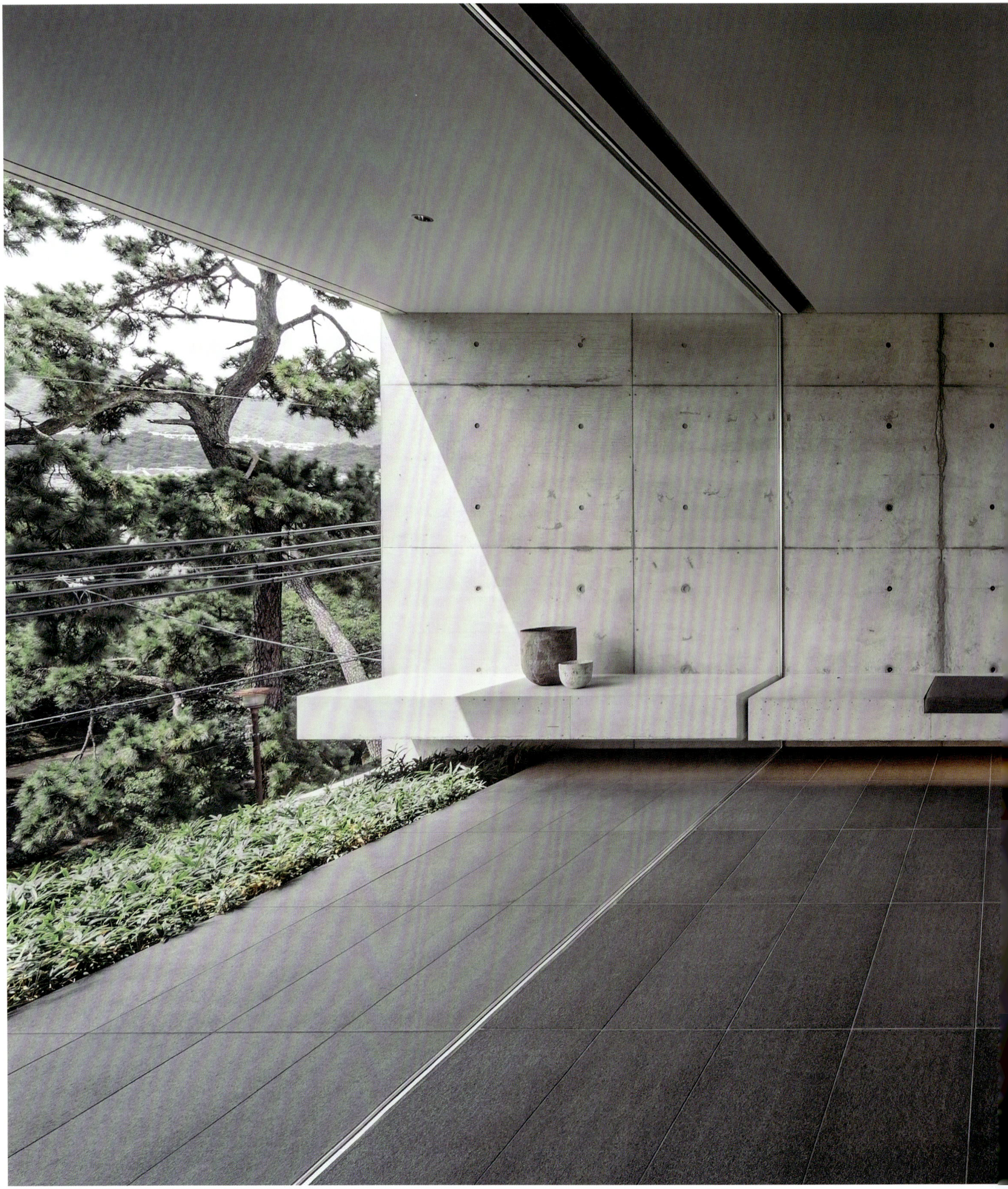

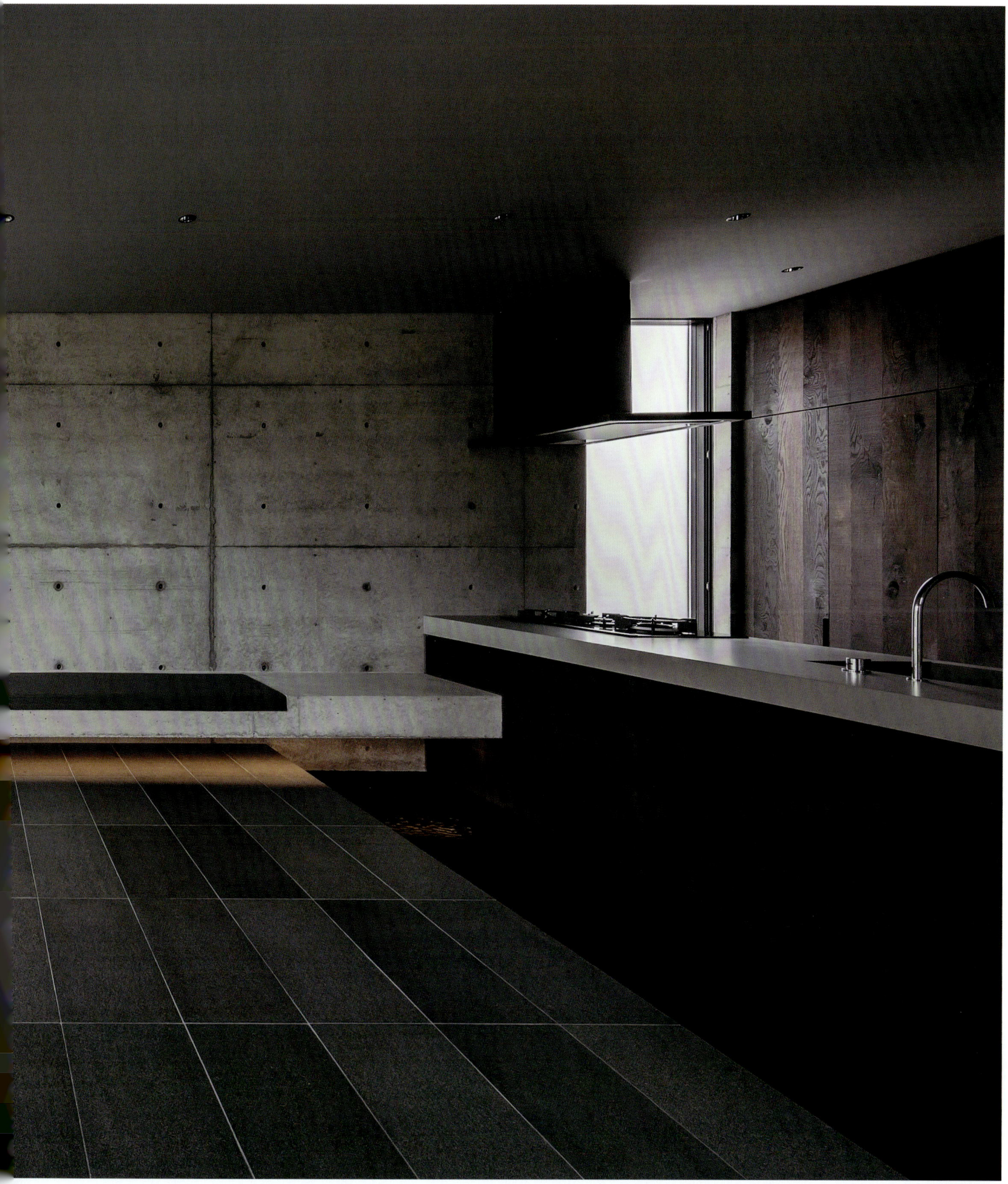

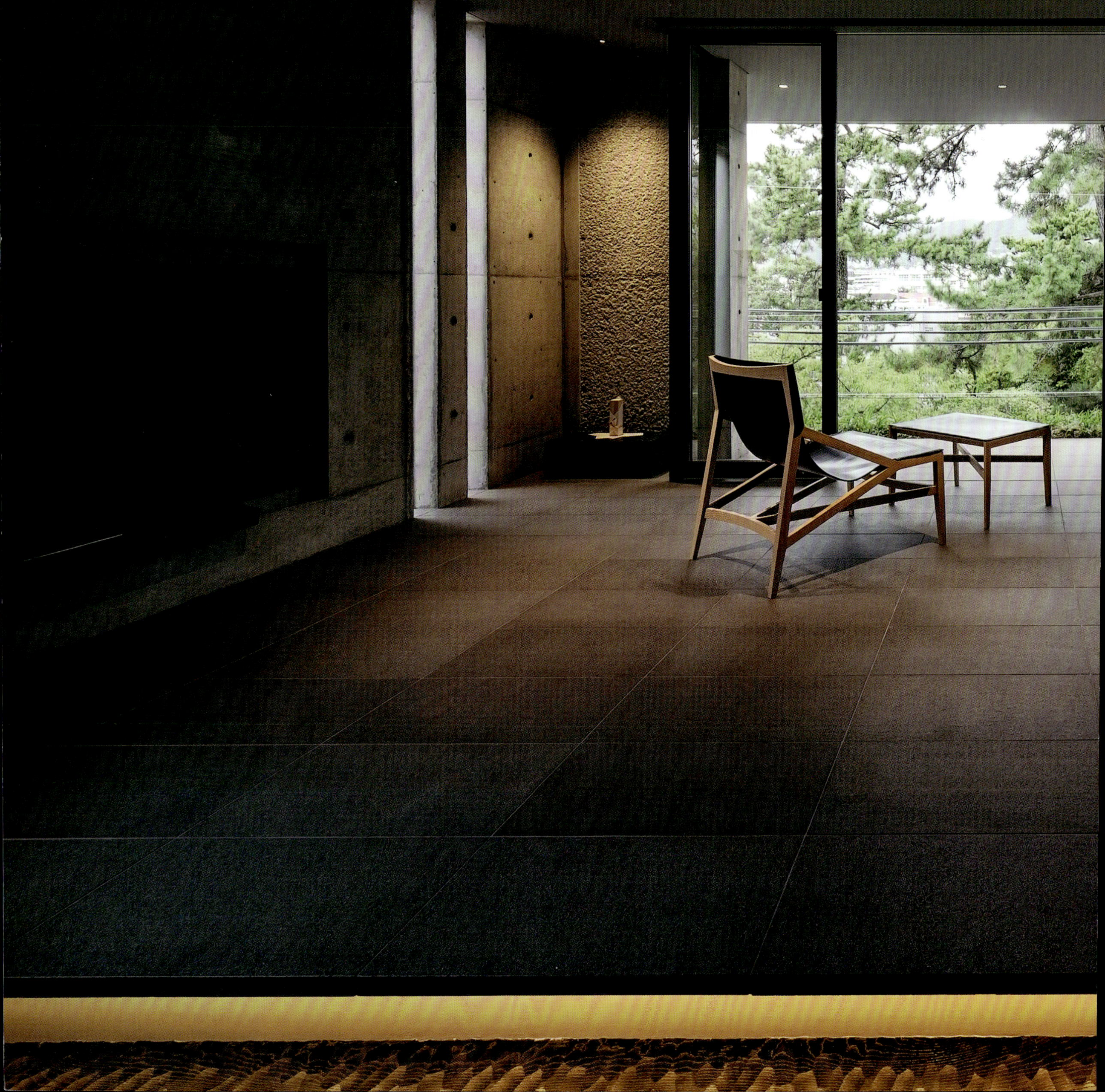

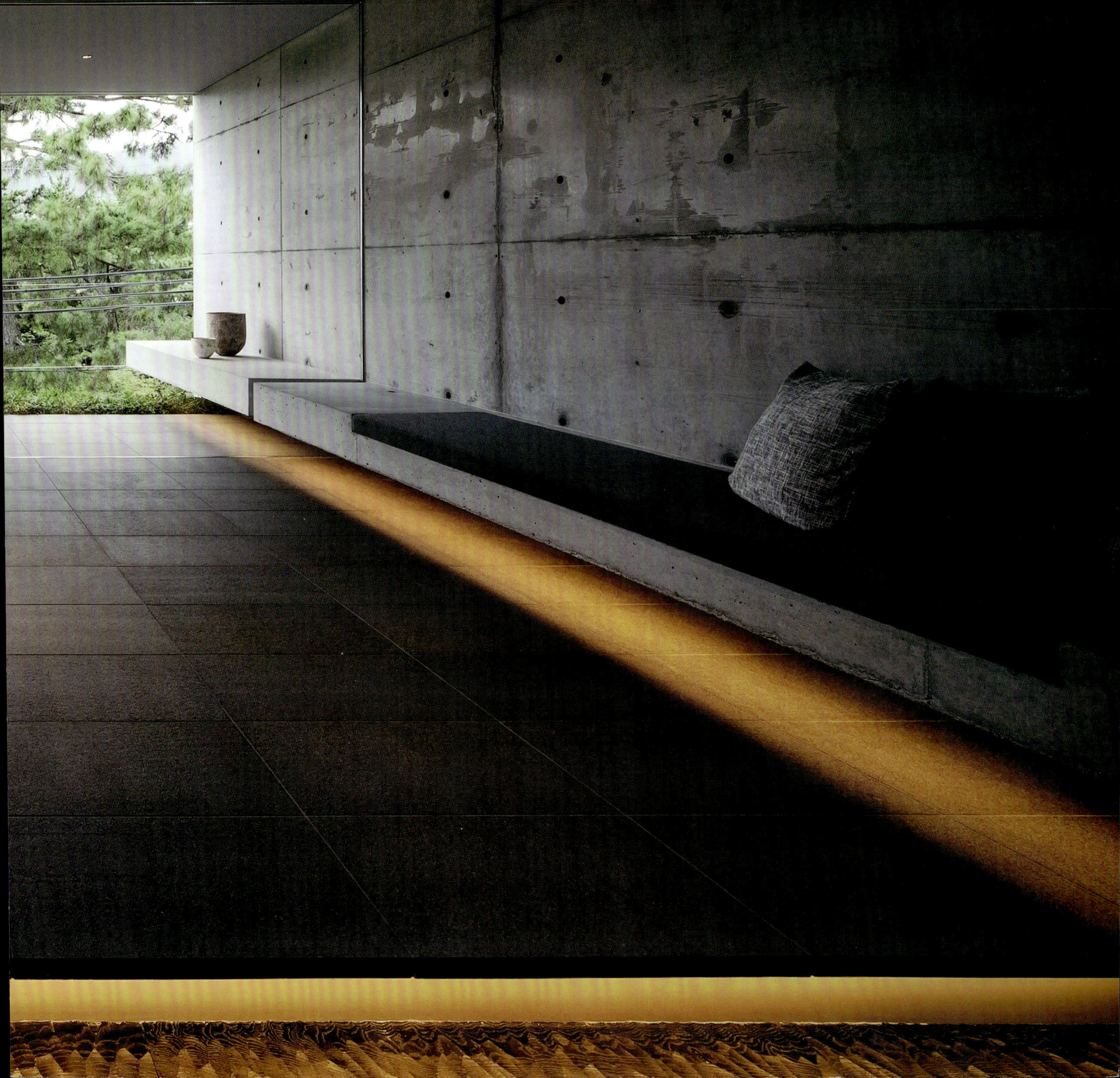

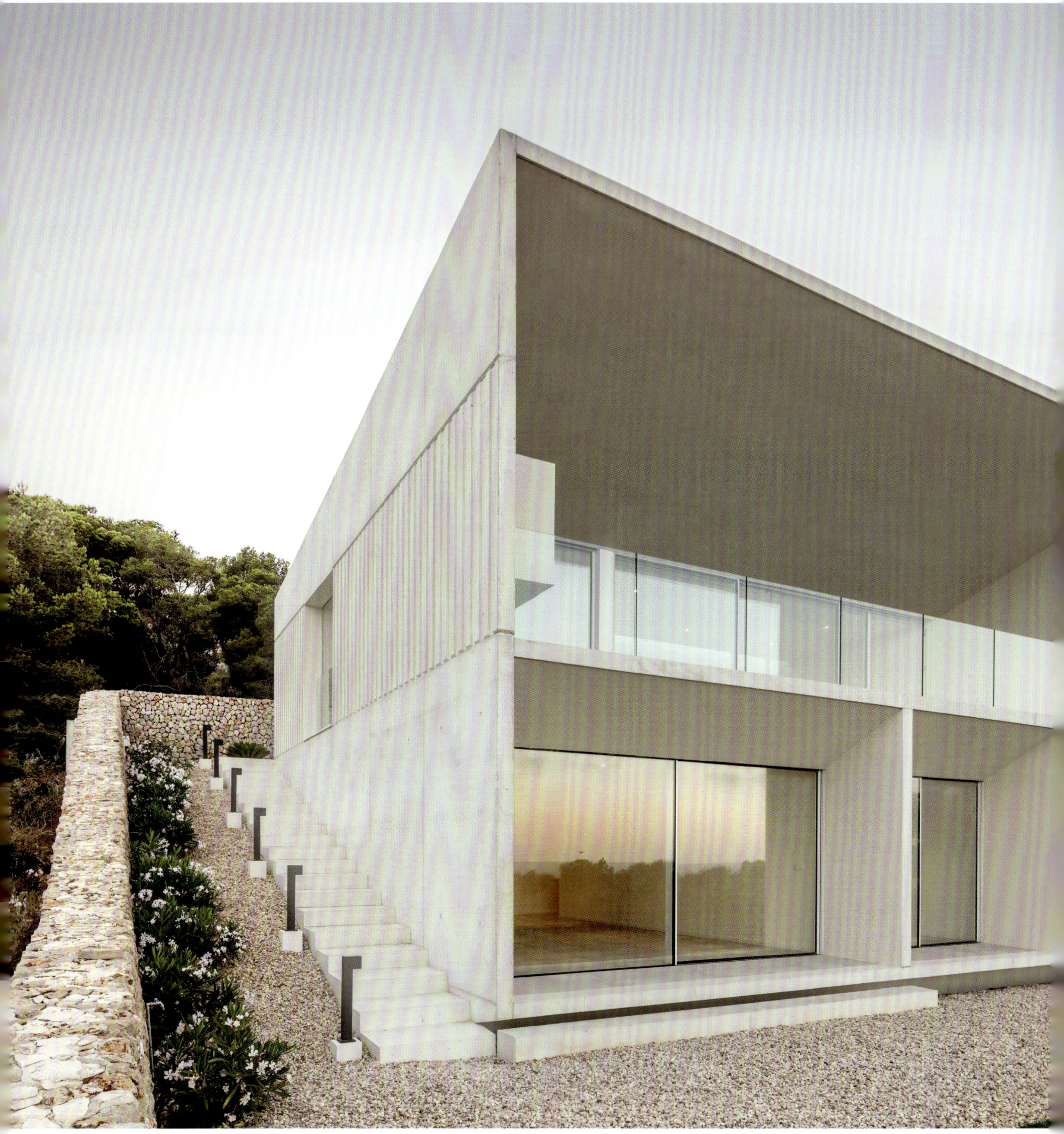

Minorca, Spain | 2018

FRAME HOUSE

Nomo Studio

Photographs: Courtesy of Nomo Studio

For architects designing a summer house on the sea, the goal is always to find ways to encourage people to be outside. On the northern coast of Minorca, though, that agenda is already in place—most of life happens outdoors. In that regard, Frame House serves Spain's Mediterranean climate well. It opens entirely toward the sea view, beckoning the owners onto a wide terrace extension of the living spaces. By contrast, the sides and back are closed, creating a sense of prospect and refuge, and a strong framing effect.

The couple asked Nomo Studio for a house that they and their three children, plus frequent guests, could enjoy together and apart. Designed as a simple, two-story concrete box, its insertions, deletions, and detailing respond directly to the light and site conditions. With close neighbors on either side of the steeply sloping lot, the off-white concrete facade reads as a monolith from the front. A horizontal band of vertically striped relief goes around the front and sides, organizing the windows and doors. "We felt that concrete without any decorative element would be a bit too hard," says architect Alicia Casals. "On the lower floor, containing the bedrooms, the pattern becomes a vertical column that hides the windows, so you don't see into the house from the street."

The stone wall becomes part of the landscape, and the off-white facade blends in with the ocher and terra-cotta soil around the house. The poured concrete is 8% gray to soften and hide the stones in the concrete mix.

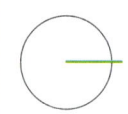

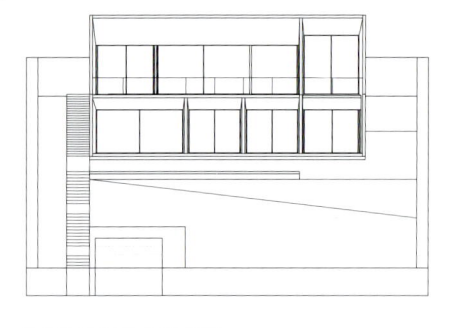

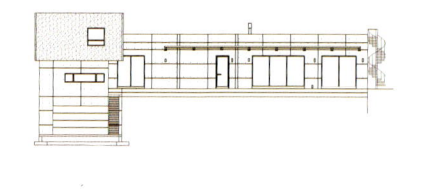

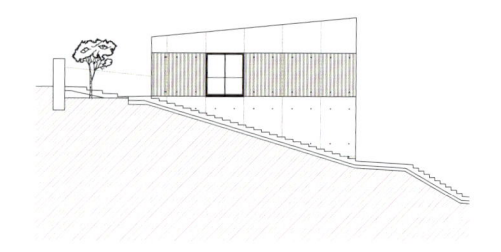

EAST ELEVATION

WEST ELEVATION

SOUTH ELEVATION

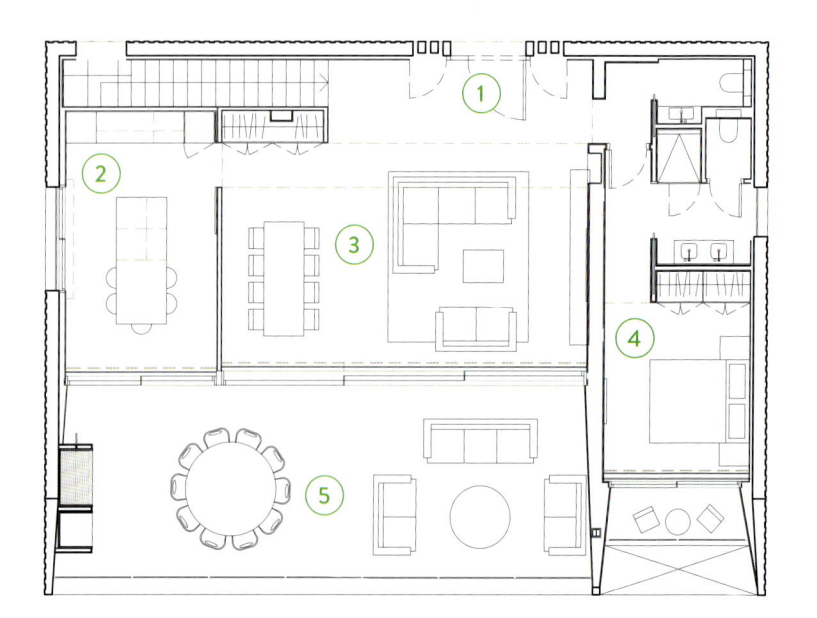

FIRST FLOOR

1 Entry
2 Kitchen
3 Dining/living
4 Main bedroom suite
5 Terrace

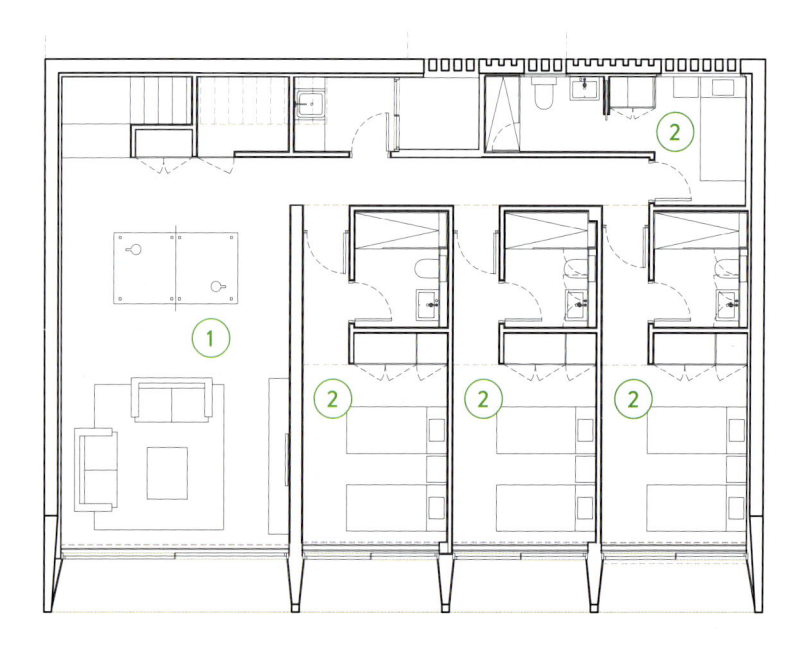

GROUND FLOOR

1 Lounge
2 Ensuite bedrooms

184   *Frame House • Floor Plan*

Veiled yet inviting, the approach is through a wooden gate in a tall wall made of island stonework, then over a bridge to the wooden front door. Inside, a large skylight at the entrance floods the living and dining room with light. To take best advantage of the view, the traditional program was flipped: living spaces are on the top floor, while three en suite bedrooms and a guest living room are below. An exception is the main bedroom on the top floor, which opens to a private patio. The idea was to treat the house as a single-level loft that would be easy to open and close for short weekend stays when only the couple is there, Casals says, and a lower-level extension for their children and guests.

Inside, a quiet color palette—gray flooring and white plaster walls—takes a deferential position to the view. Heightening this effect, the roof slopes up toward the sea view on the east, creating extra-high ceilings on the 463-square-foot terrace, where the owners spend most of their time. Sliding glass walls in the kitchen and dining/living room open seamlessly to their outdoor-furnished counterparts and a picturesque view of Addaia Harbor.

The entire house is constructed of poured-in-place white concrete with 8 percent gray and a precast, hollow-core slab roof. This structural roof plate system allowed for a 36-foot span that extends over the terrace, eliminating the need for view-blocking columns. And the removal of one roof module left a void for a large, frameless skylight that brings light to the windowless back.

The thick-skinned building material is a better match for the humid, salt-soaked air than wood or steel. "Concrete is one of the few structural materials you can leave exposed here," says Casals, "and it has this plastic characteristic; it's not as restrictive as beams." On the closed side of the house, for example, the walls are 10½ inches thick, tapering to 6-inch-thick walls and roof on the view side. "You get this very thin view from the front, in contrast with the rest of the house," she says.

186   *Frame House*

We felt that concrete without any decorative element would be a bit too hard. On the lower floor, containing the bedrooms, the pattern becomes a vertical column that hides the windows, so you don't see into the house from the street.
—Alicia Casals

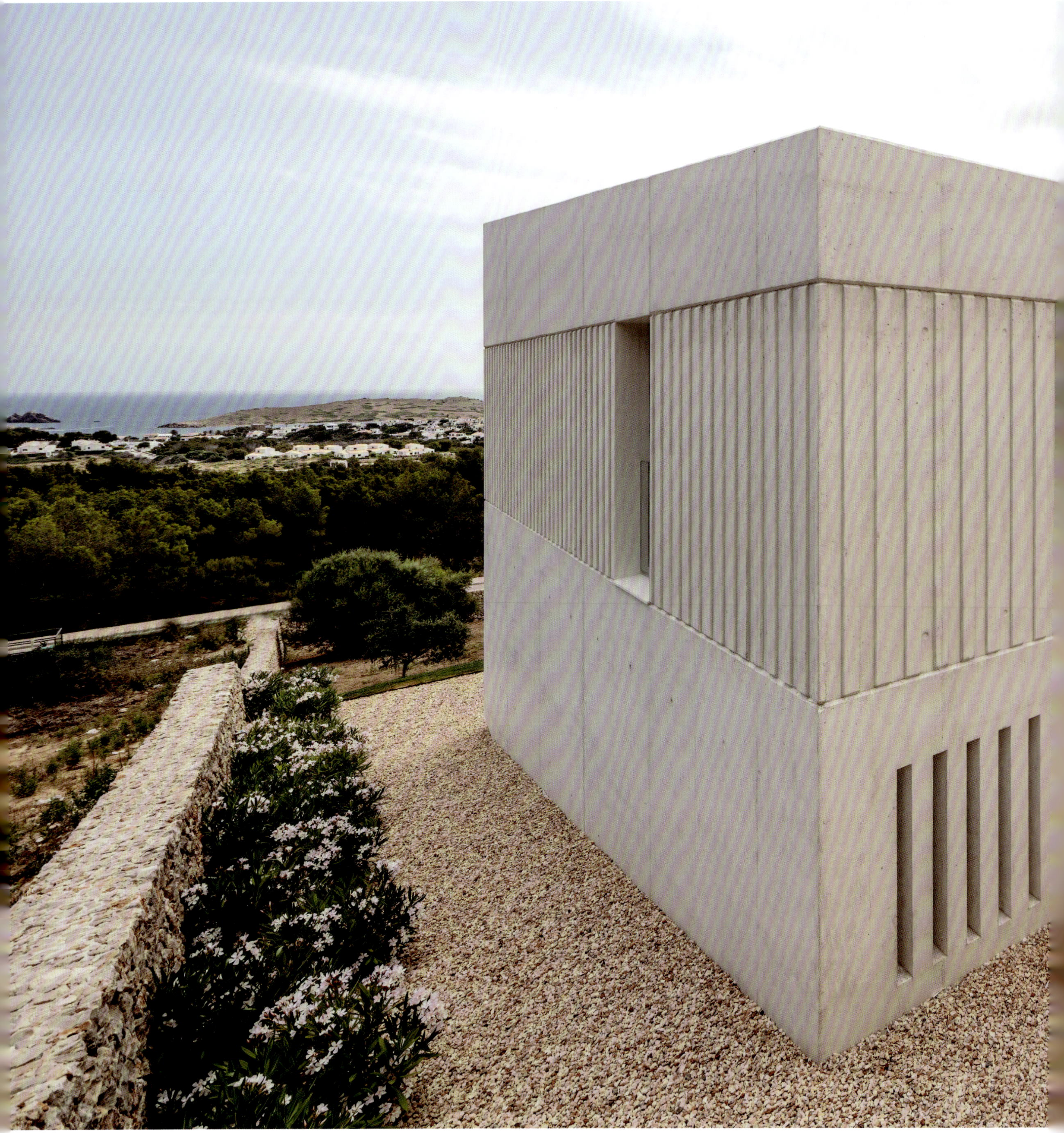

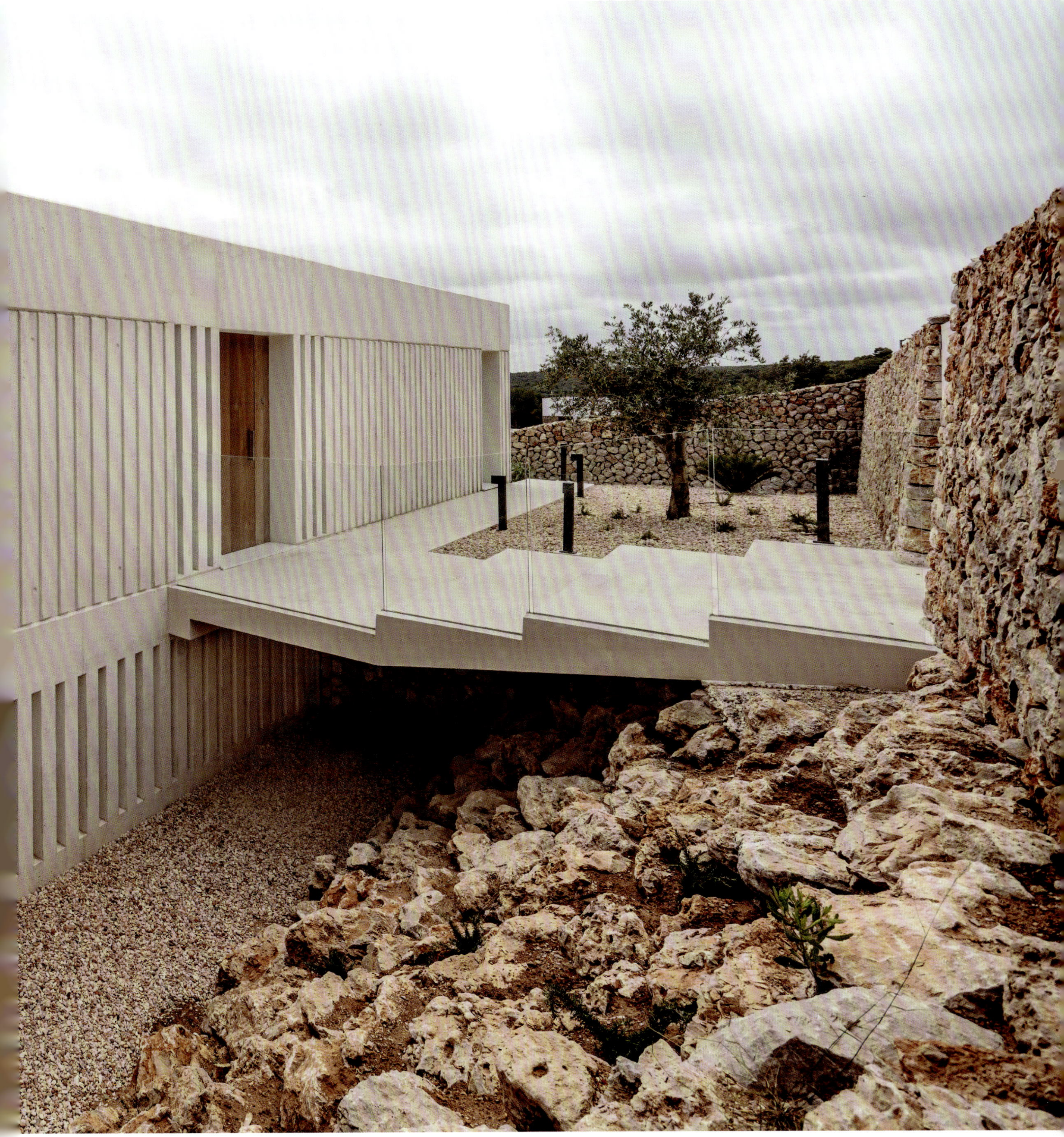

Frame House

Walls are 10½ inches thick on the street side, tapering in plan to achieve a thin profile on the view side of the house.

192 Frame House

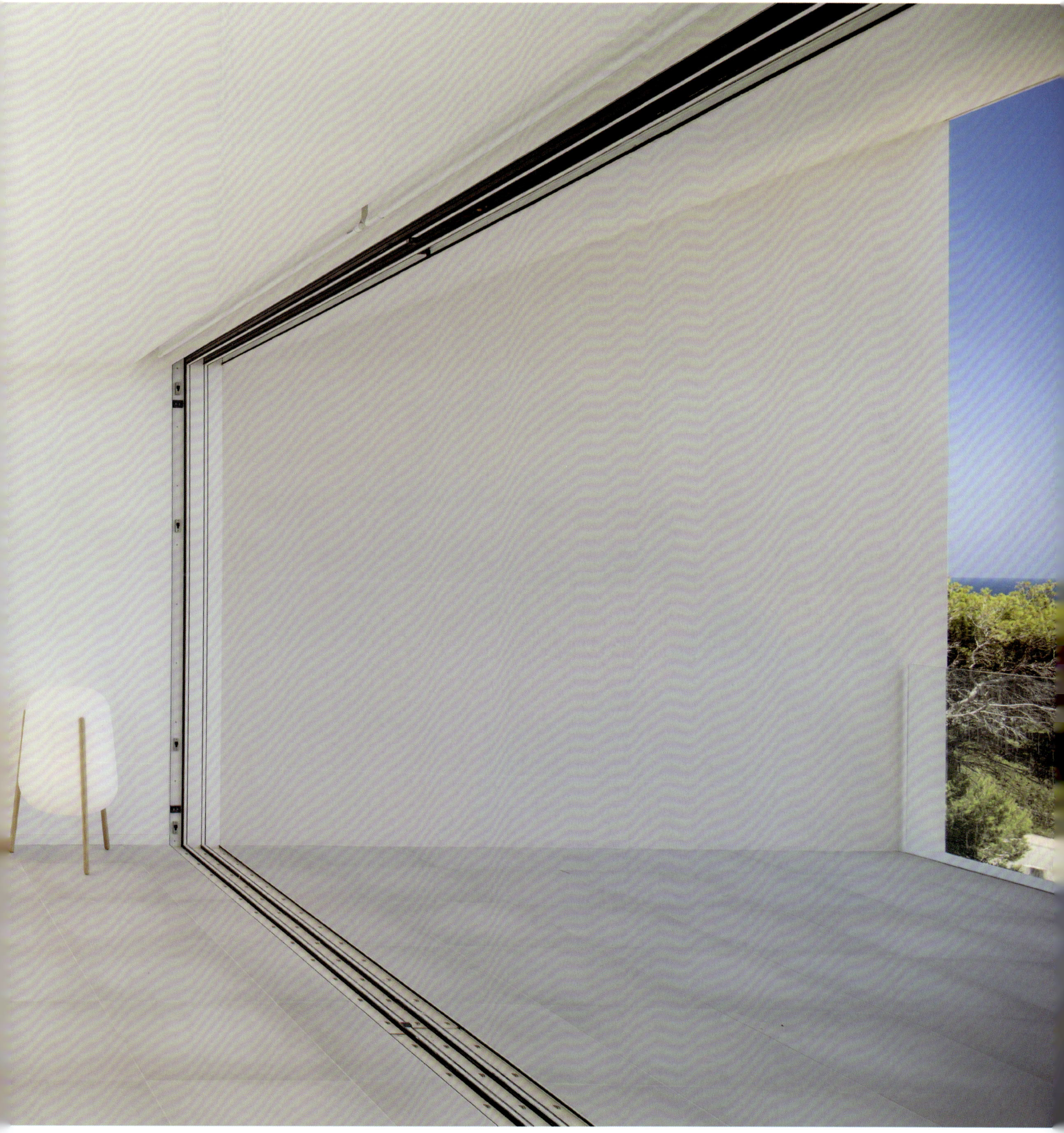

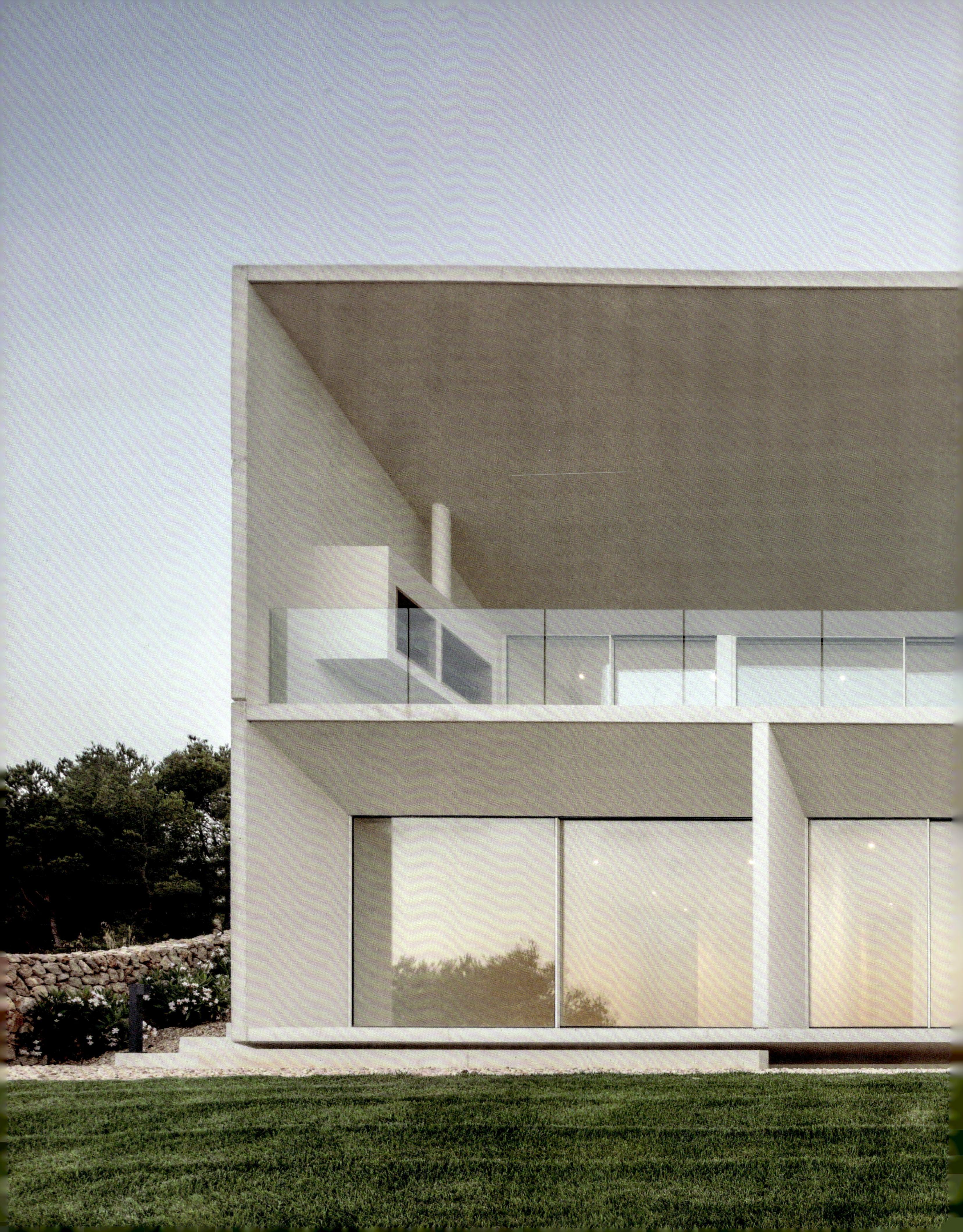

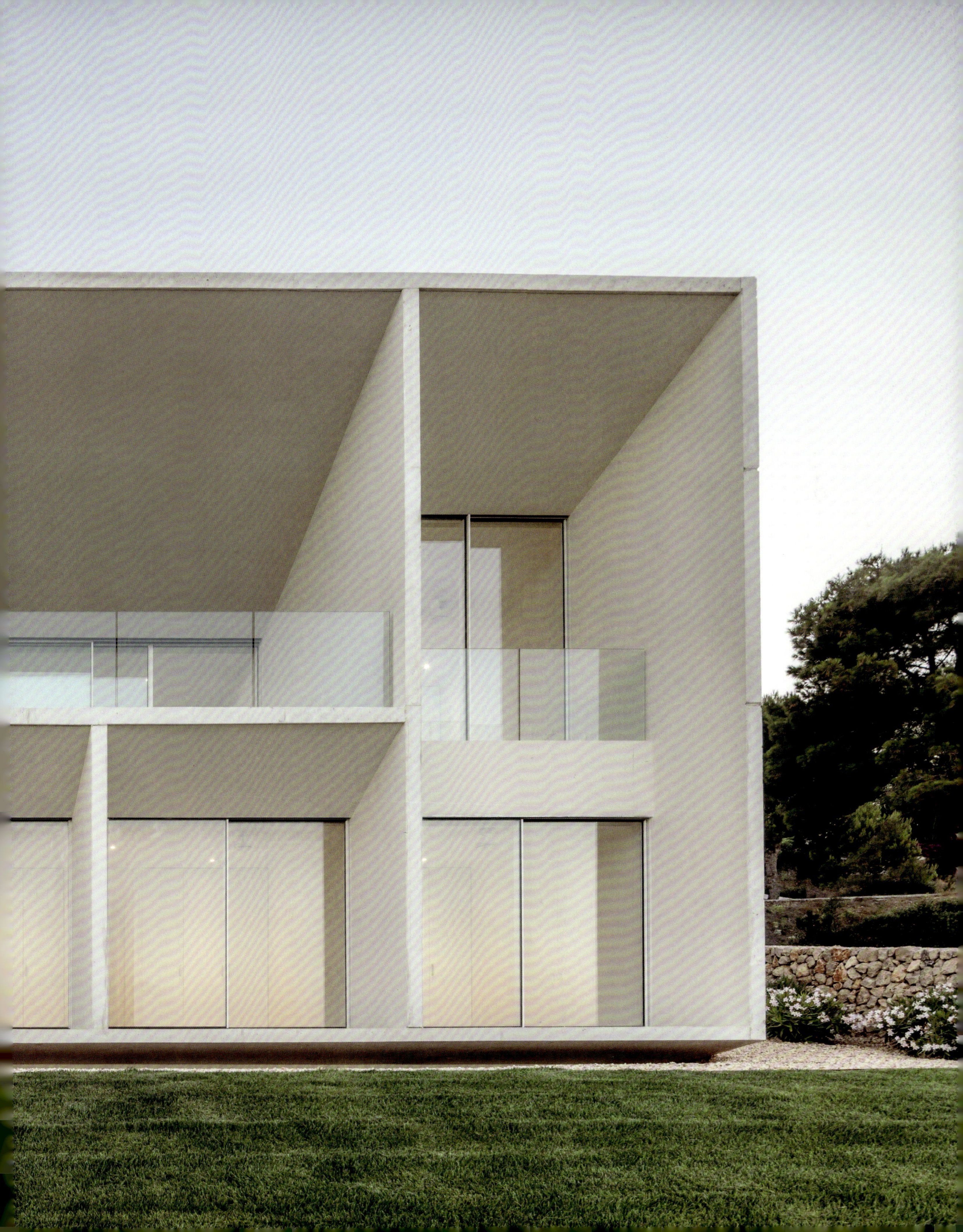

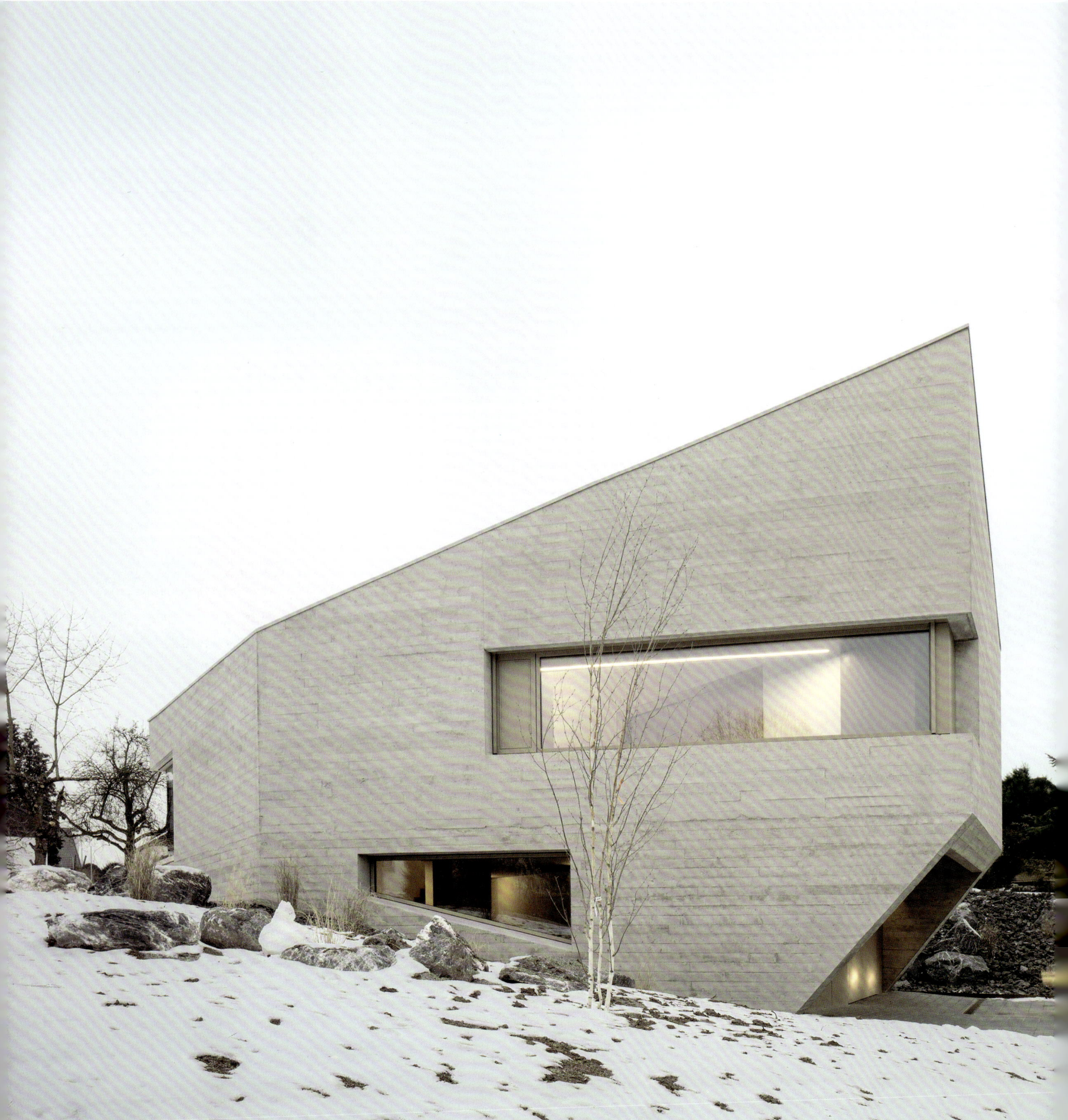

Pliezhausen, Germany | 2016

E20 HOUSE

Steimle Architeckten

Photographs: Brigida González

This house, by Steimle Architeckten, sits in Pliezhausen, a quiet village some 19 miles south of Stuttgart, where the firm is based. Designed as a primary residence for a couple with two children, it strikes a distinctive note, to say the least, in a neighborhood of conventional 1970s and 1980s houses. Originally the owners wanted to build a simple, modernist cube with a flat roof on the vacant lot, but the municipal powers rejected that idea. This vaguely parallelogram-like building is the result of the workaround, reinterpreting cubist geometries in a way that satisfied local code.

Designed on a hexagonal footprint, its faceted planes create dynamic interior and exterior effects while controlling views into and out of the house. The monolithic concrete structure maintains a conventional street face with a front-facing garage and long side walls running parallel to the surrounding houses. However, the tapered end walls and asymmetrical pitched roof form oblique facades that open the building to the outdoors and distant views. A gently sloping terrain reinforces the home's sculptural presence.

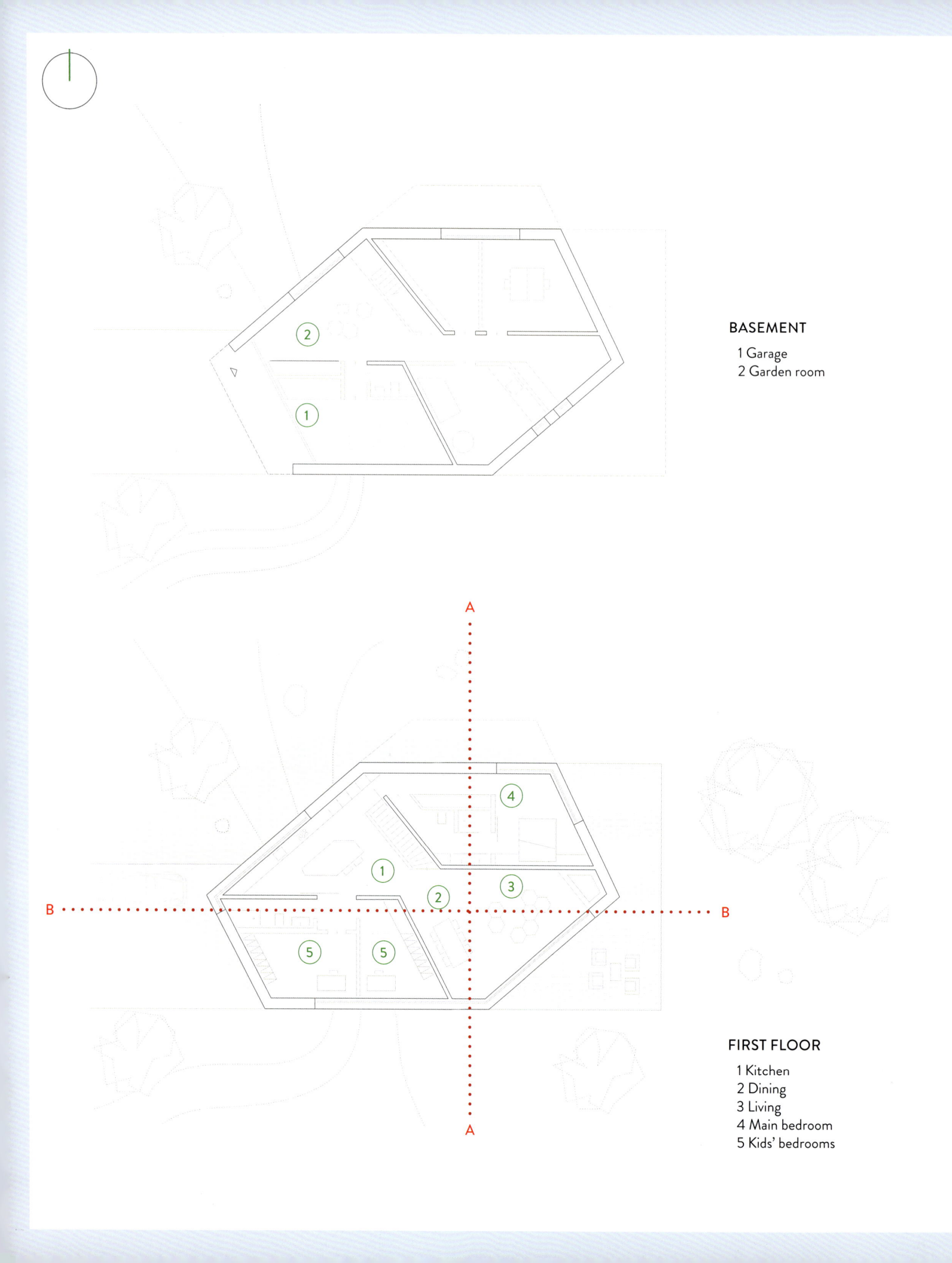

BASEMENT

1 Garage
2 Garden room

FIRST FLOOR

1 Kitchen
2 Dining
3 Living
4 Main bedroom
5 Kids' bedrooms

SECTION A-A

SECTION B-B

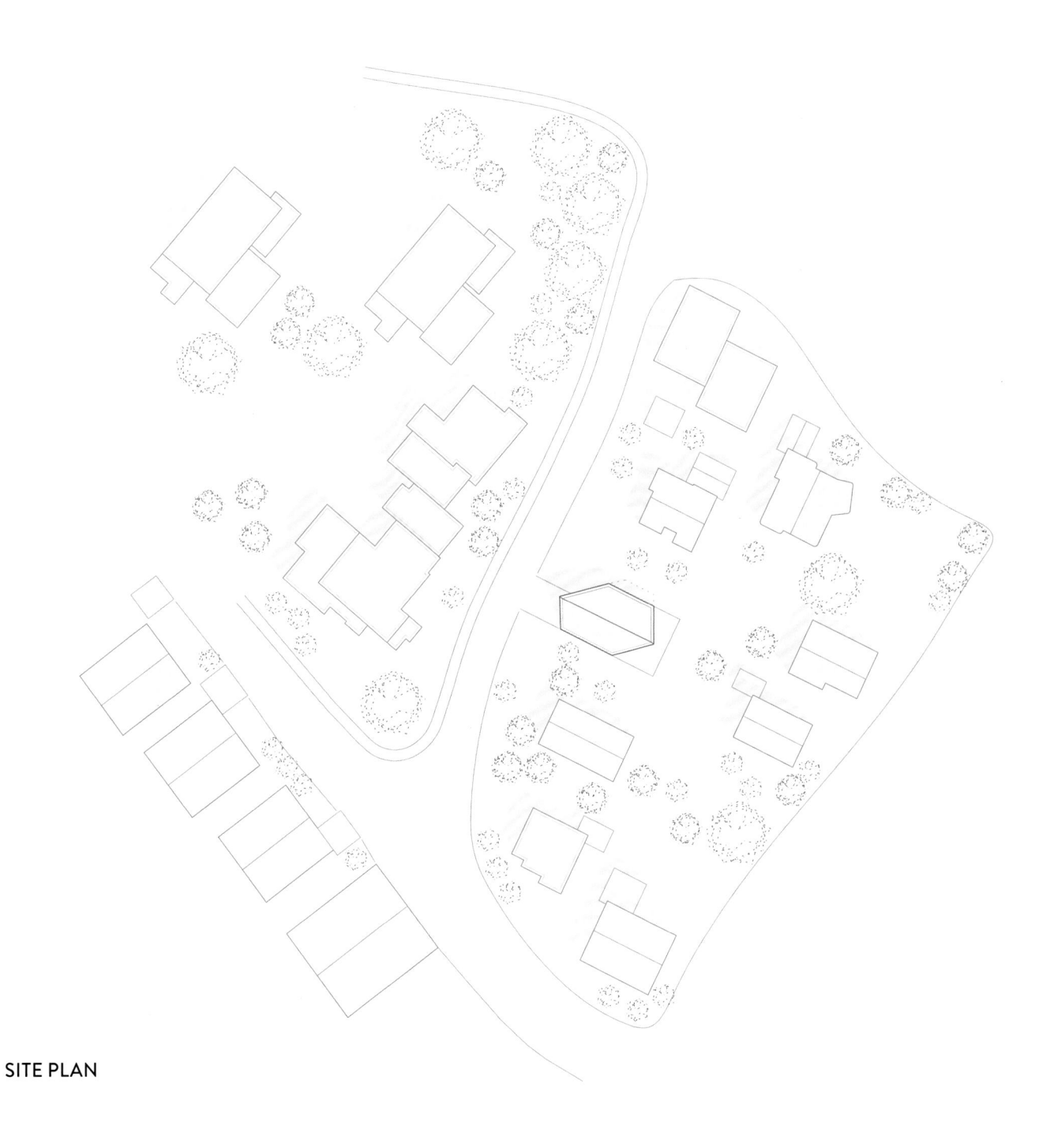

SITE PLAN

E20 House • Floor Plan   199

E20 House

Those angles create a series of kinetic interior spaces that play with compression and expansion as one moves from room to room. "The intention for the diagonally cut sides of the house was to provide a view of the wide expanse of landscape and thus fade out the neighboring buildings," says architect Thomas Steimle. "There is a constantly shifting dialogue between enclosure and openness."

The entrance, through a deep cut in the concrete, leads to a garden room and then up a flight of stairs to the main level, where trapezoidal walls reach upward under sloping ceiling planes. The floor plan squeezes and expands too. At the top of the stairs is a minimalist kitchen on the right and a dining/living room straight ahead. It narrows to a fireplace at one end, while the long wall opens entirely to a terrace overlooking the undulating landscape. The main bedroom and two kids' rooms lie like opposing parallelograms on either side of the living space, dividing the open kitchen and living zones.

Minimal yet muscular, the massive concrete shell defines the house inside and out. Steimle describes it as "a sensuous, atmospherically dense place of dwelling." The gray tile roof and beige-colored, anodized aluminum windows blend with the concrete facade. Window indentations reveal the 20-inch thickness of the insulated walls, which were poured in place on a rough-sawn wood form. On the interior, the concrete is troweled smooth, a serene complement to the minimalist palette of pale oak floors and casework and white plaster walls. The effect of the light on these surfaces is magical, and so is the lofted study area in the kids' bedrooms, reached via zigzag stair treads that pique a child's imagination.

Gentle angles and seamless surfaces give this unusual house an enigmatic allure, with spaces that envelope yet raise one's awareness of the outdoors. Steimle's unremitting approach to spatial control and clean details gives the house a subtle combination of German identity and joy of life.

202 E20 House

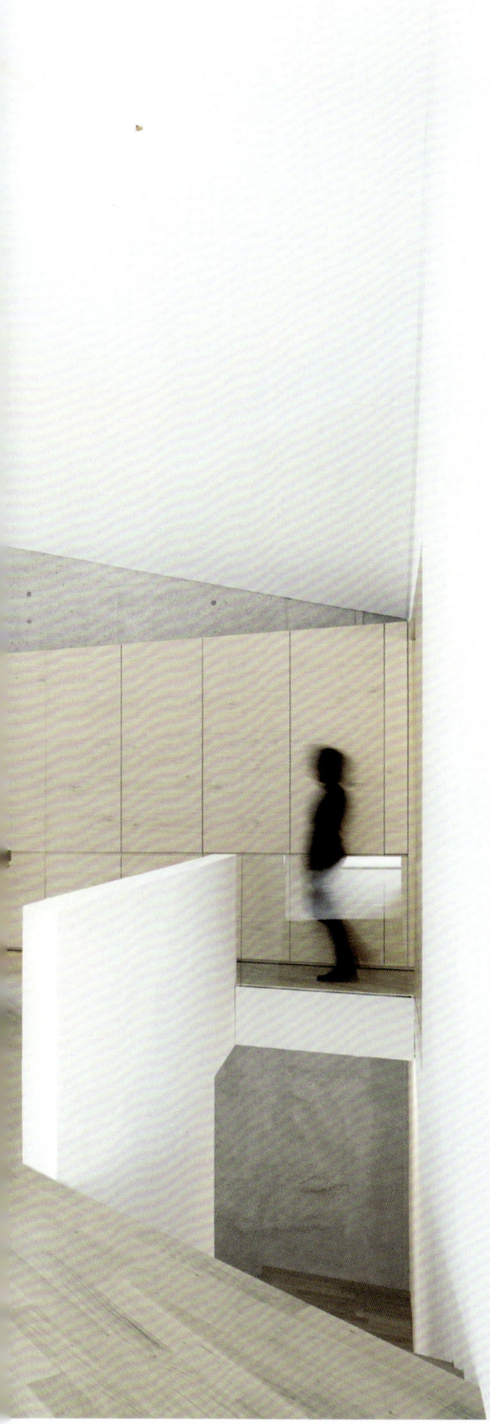

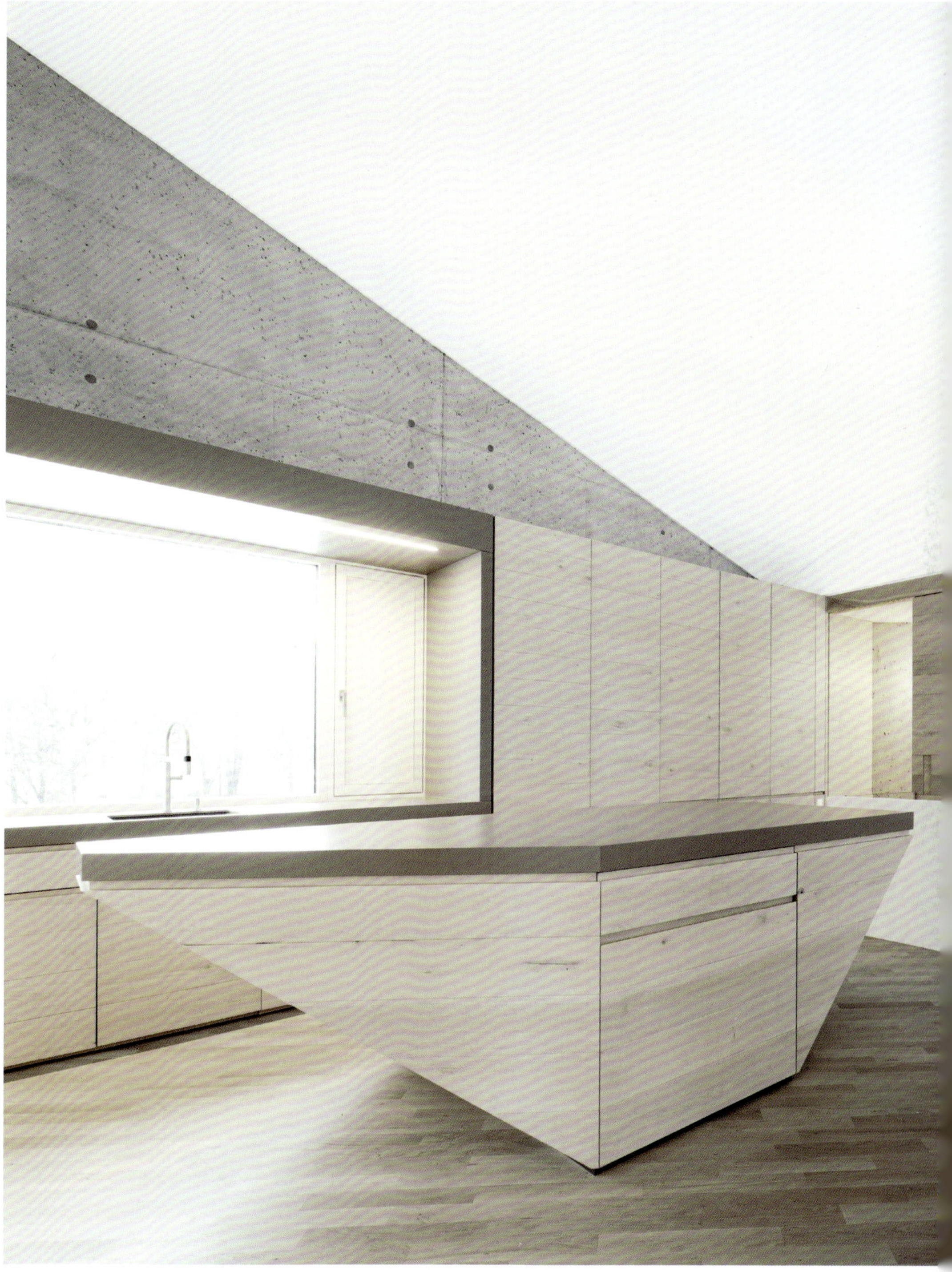

E20 House

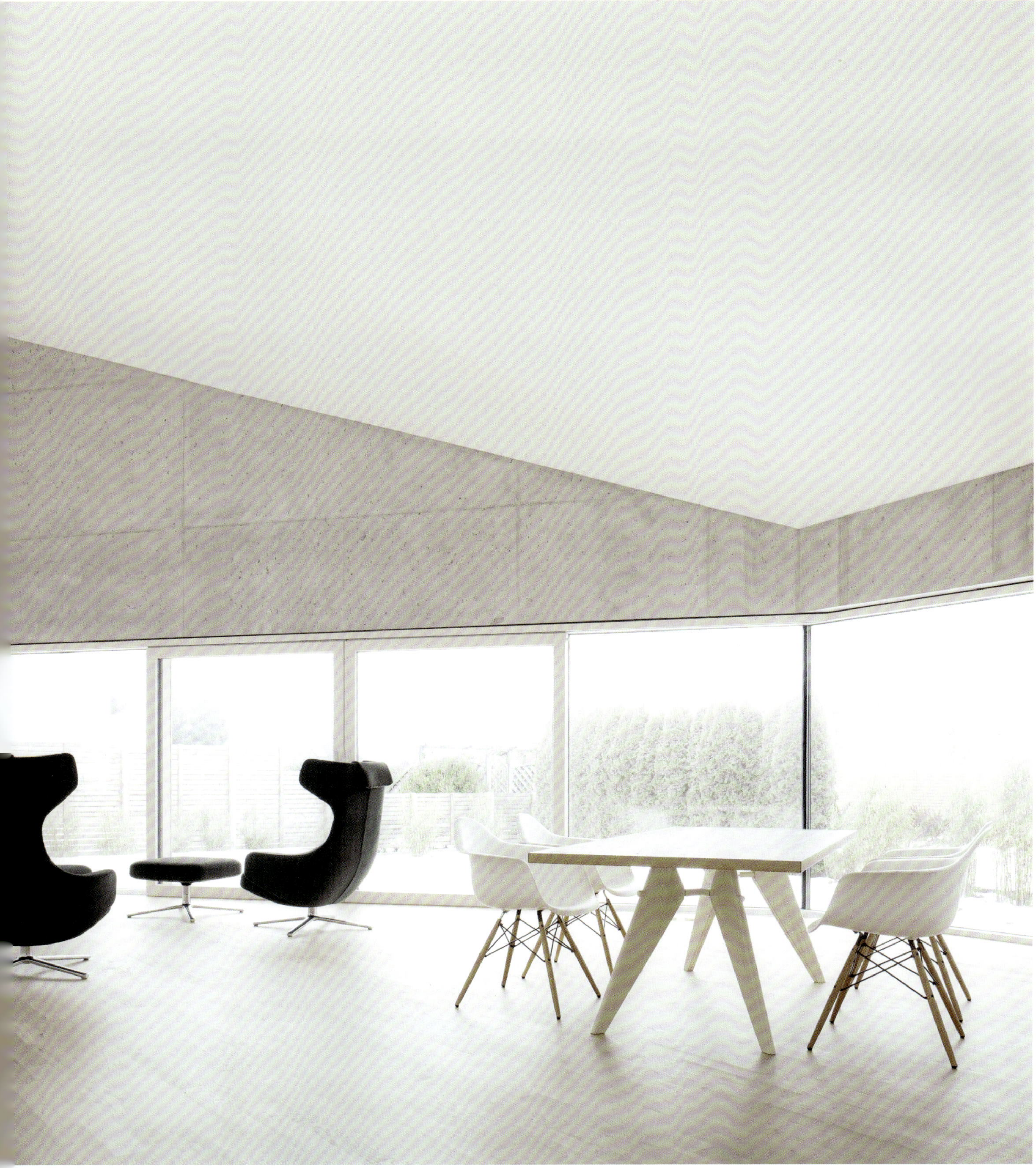

E20 House

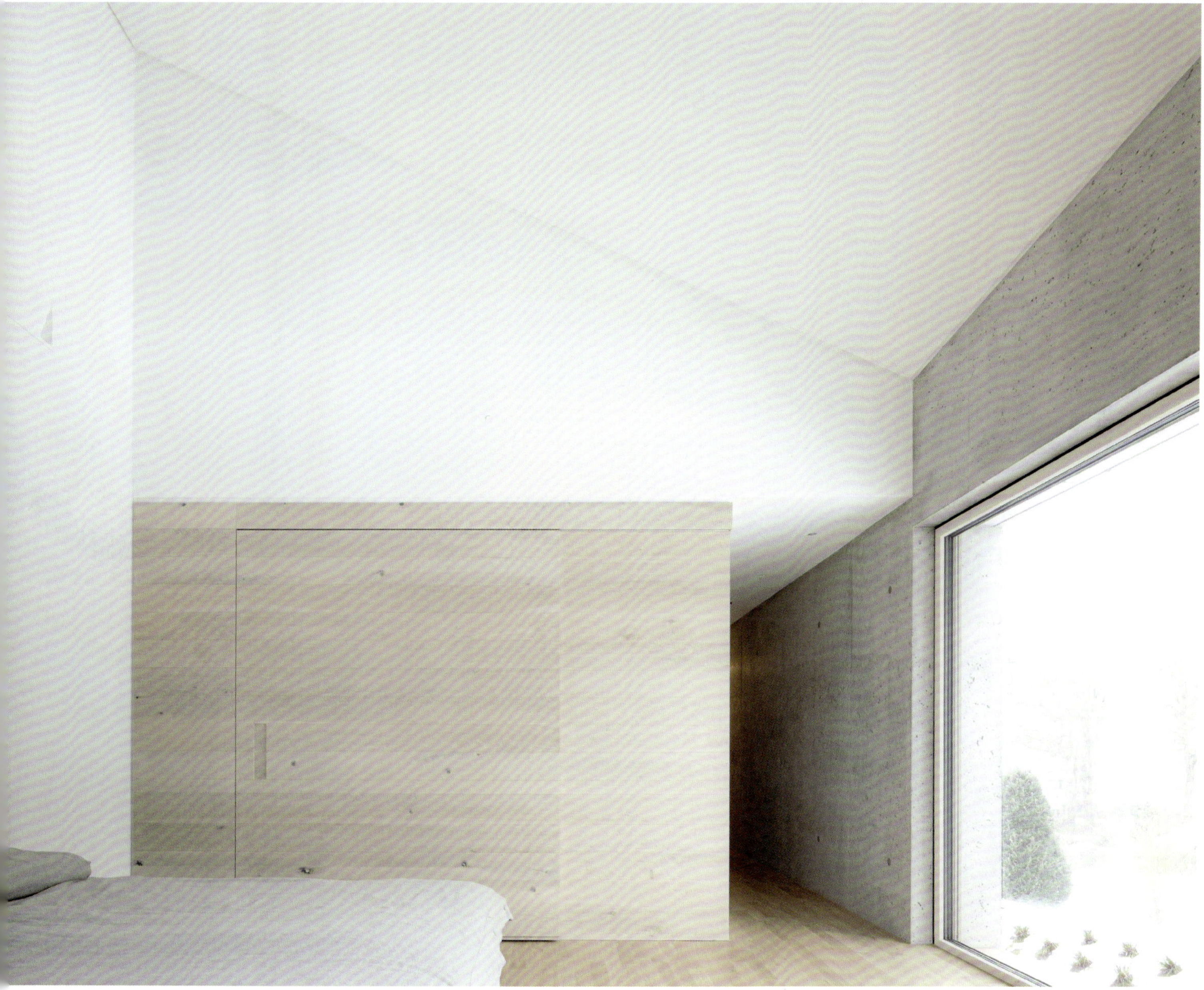

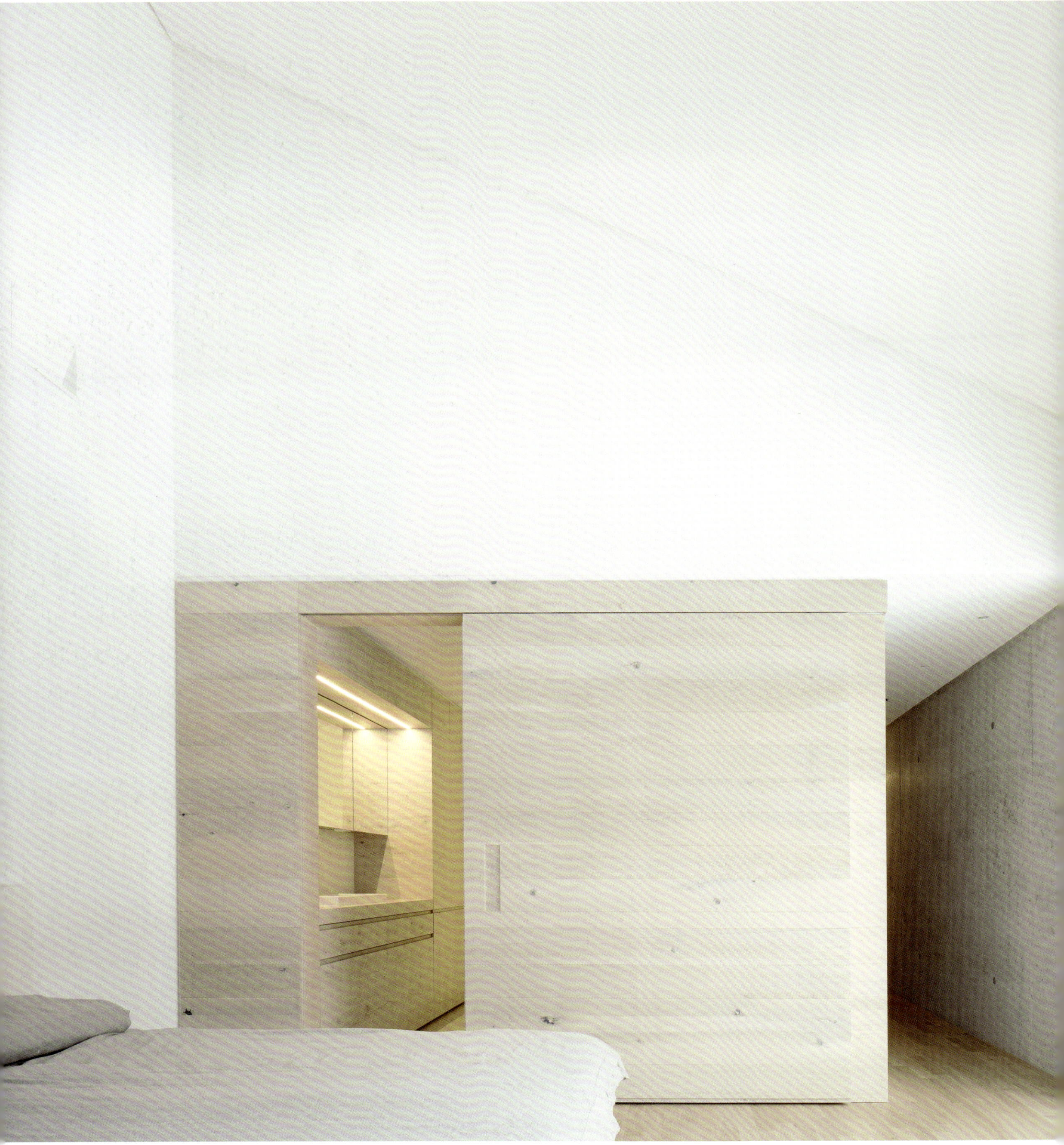

The intention for the diagonally cut sides of the house was to provide a view of the wide expanse of landscape and thus fade out the neighboring buildings. There is a constantly shifting dialogue between enclosure and openness.
—Thomas Steimle

In two bedrooms, zigzag stairs to a lofted study area delight the children of the house.

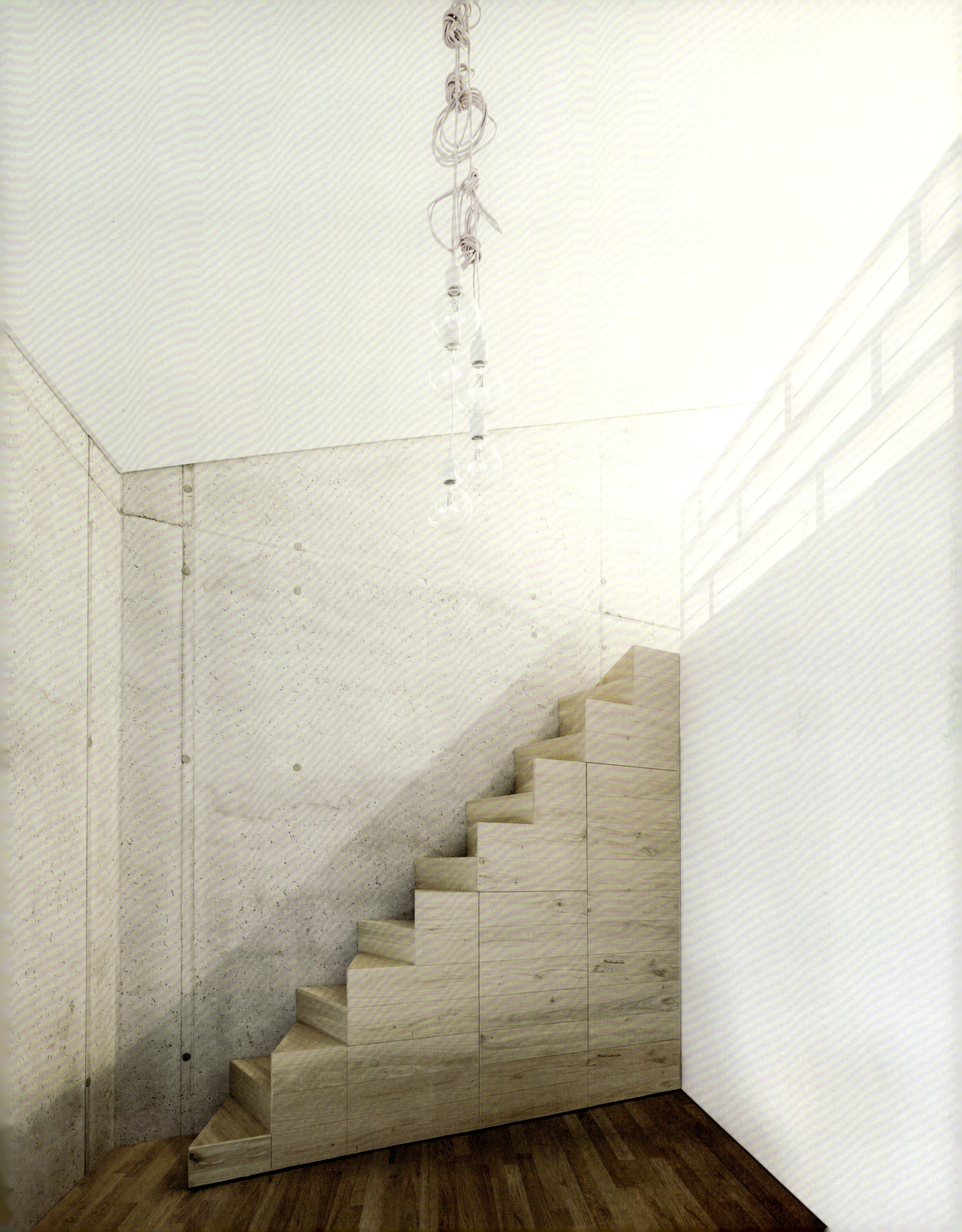

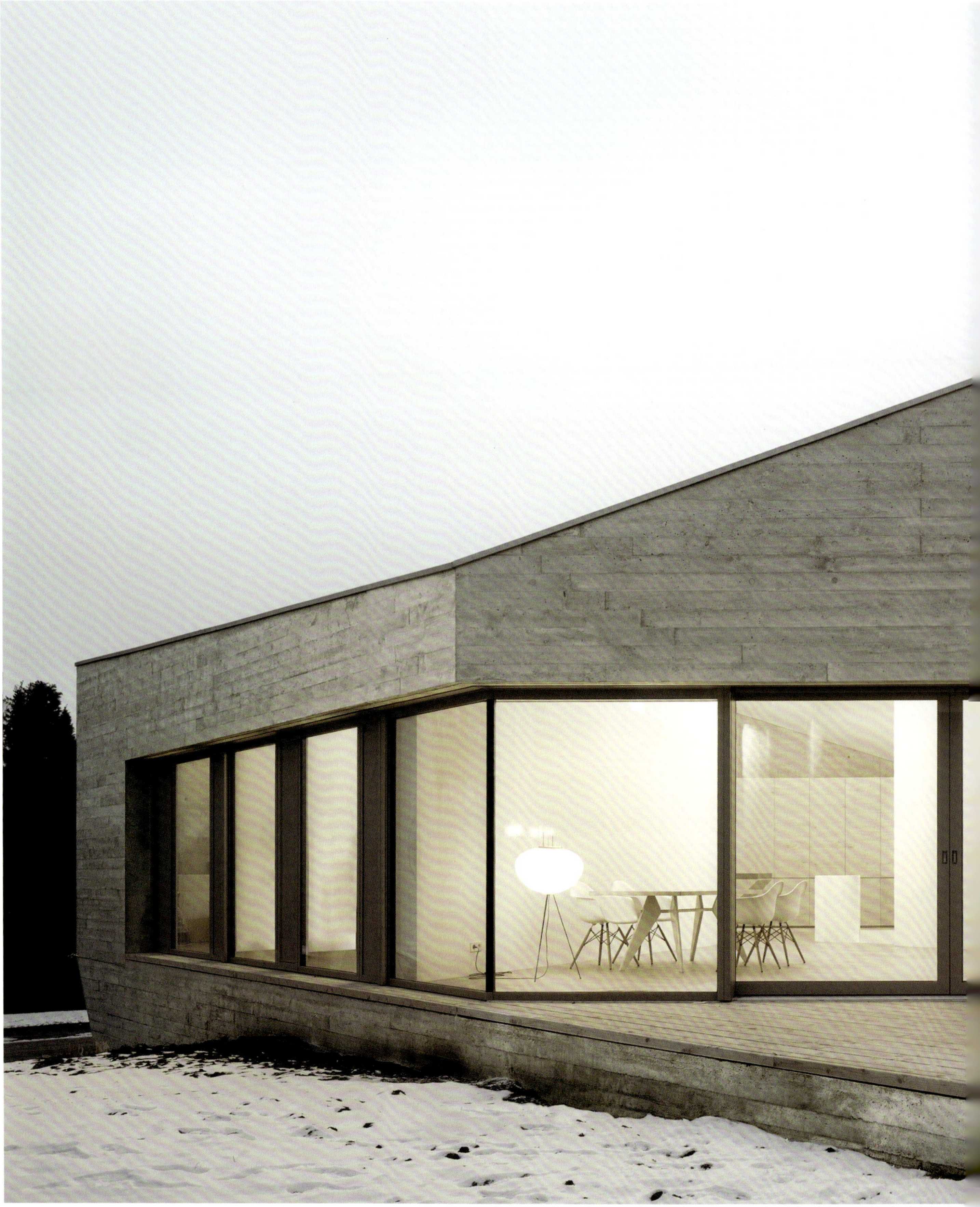

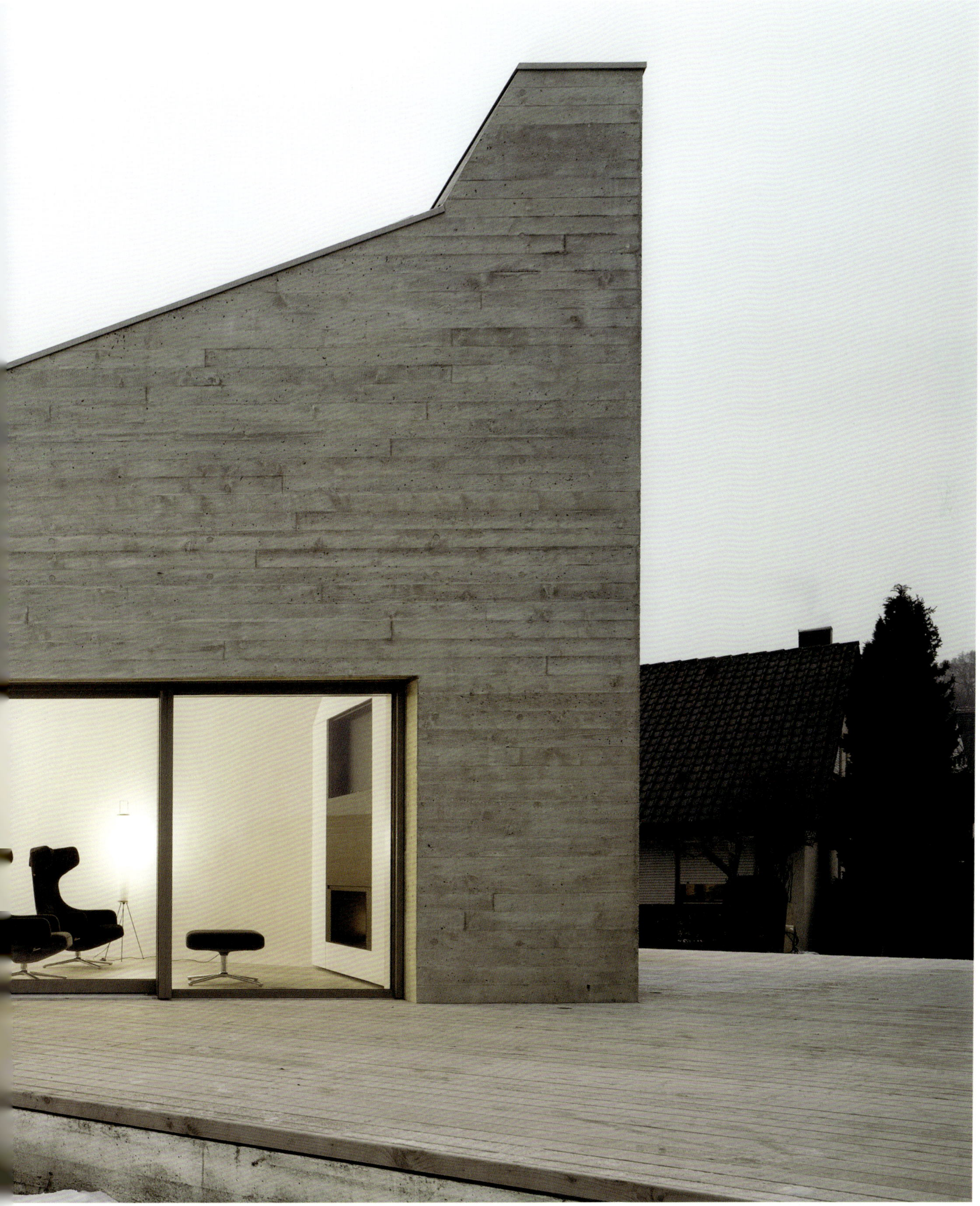

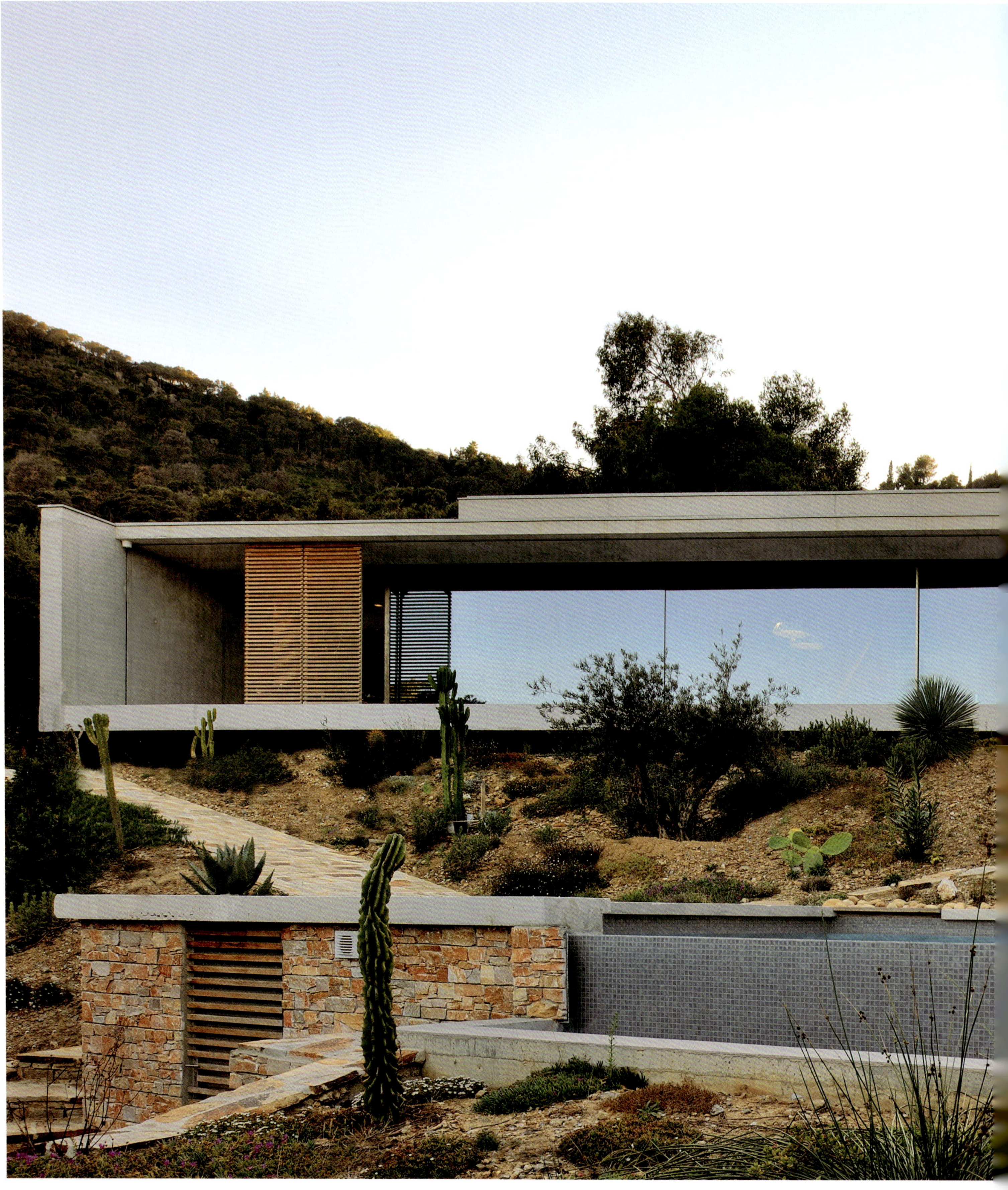

South of France | 2017

LA MIRA RA

Minassian Architects

Photographs: Studio Erick Saillet

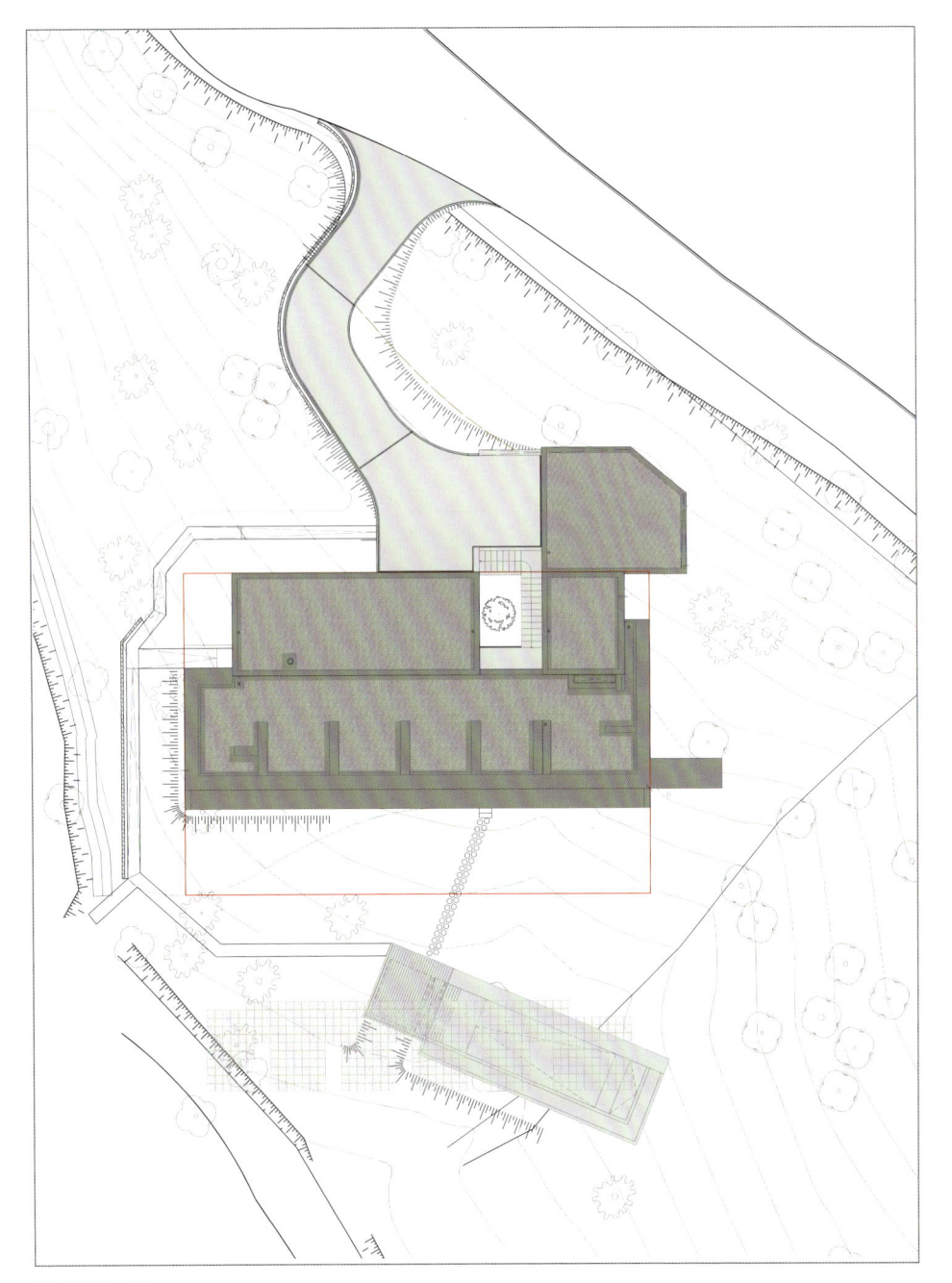

SITE PLAN

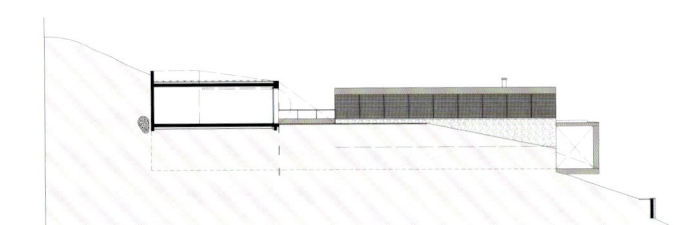

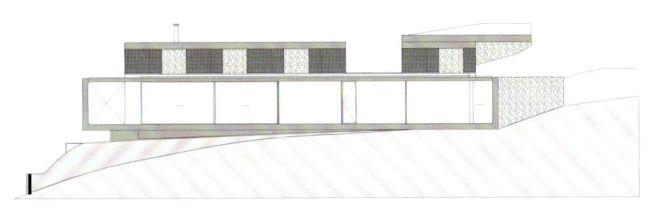

WEST ELEVATION

EAST ELEVATION

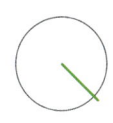

FIRST FLOOR

1 Guest bedroom
2 Bath
3 Bedroom
4 Patio
5 Office
6 Mechanical room

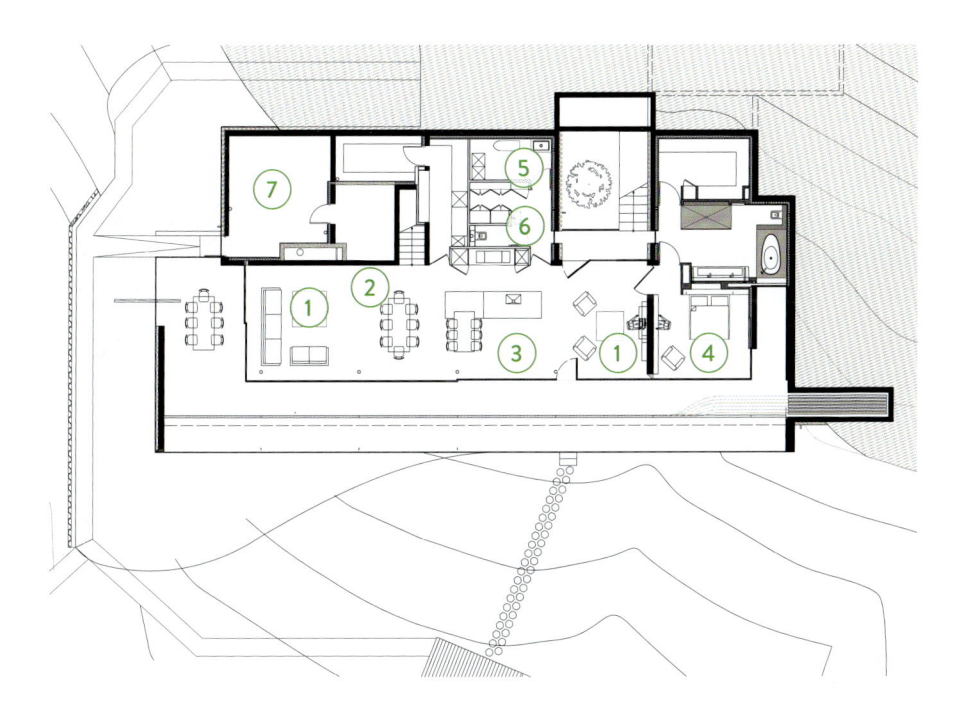

LOWER FLOOR

1 Living room
2 Dining room
3 Kitchen
4 Main bedroom suite
5 Utility room
6 Powder room
7 Basement with wine cellar

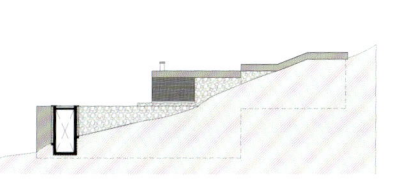

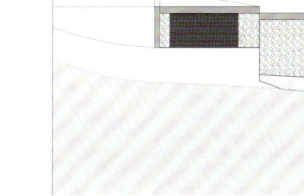

NORTH ELEVATION

SOUTH ELEVATION

La Mira Ra • Floor Plan

La Mira Ra

Architecture is nothing if not adaptable, and at La Mira Ra the designers used a variety of devices to fit it harmoniously into its sloping site and the private older community. The homes surrounding it had all been designed by one architect in the early 1960s, and any new houses were required to have flat roofs and use local stone like the originals.

On the community's last empty lot, facing the sea, "the aim was to make ours different and similar," says architect Pierre Minassian. It is a formidably long, horizontal house and so well integrated into the environment that whether viewed from above or below, it barely registers. Designed for a family of five, with the owners intent on retiring there, the structure consists of two concrete bars wrapped in stone on three sides. The upper-bedroom volume protrudes only a half story above ground so as not to block the neighbors' views. The lower volume, housing the public rooms and main bedroom, is pulled forward beneath it, extending the living spaces toward the view. A planted roof on each level merges with the scrubby hillside.

The requirement to use stone made sense given the rocky Mediterranean terrain. Flecked with gold, it reflects the color of the soil and the sunsets. An admirer of concrete's peaceful quality, Minassian decided to combine the two. "Concrete is a really interesting material and a good answer to that kind of site," says Minassian. "We developed a patented process with the builder we work with to allow a very thin and pure structure, almost like the house is a sculpture." Walls were poured on-site using double layers of concrete with insulation inside. "This allowed us to make a whole house with the outside and inside complete, whereas with wood or steel you have to add a number of layers," he says. "The inner shell of raw concrete creates a calm atmosphere, and the smooth skin reflects light coming into the house at sunset."

Viewed from the downhill side, the thin boxes open fully to the water view through floor-to-ceiling glass walls. Strictly speaking, curtain walls were not allowed, but the full-height teak louvers address that restriction while providing solar protection and reducing the scale of the glassy facade. They are fixed on the street-facing bedroom wing, and fold and slide out of the way on the northeast view side, dissolving the boundary between house and terrace.

Outside, a walkway leads to the pool facing the sea, ending in a desert garden filled with native flowers. "La Mira Ra house is the fruit of a long reflection about the marriage of the wild nature of the Mediterranean and the minimalist purity of contemporary architecture," Minassian says.

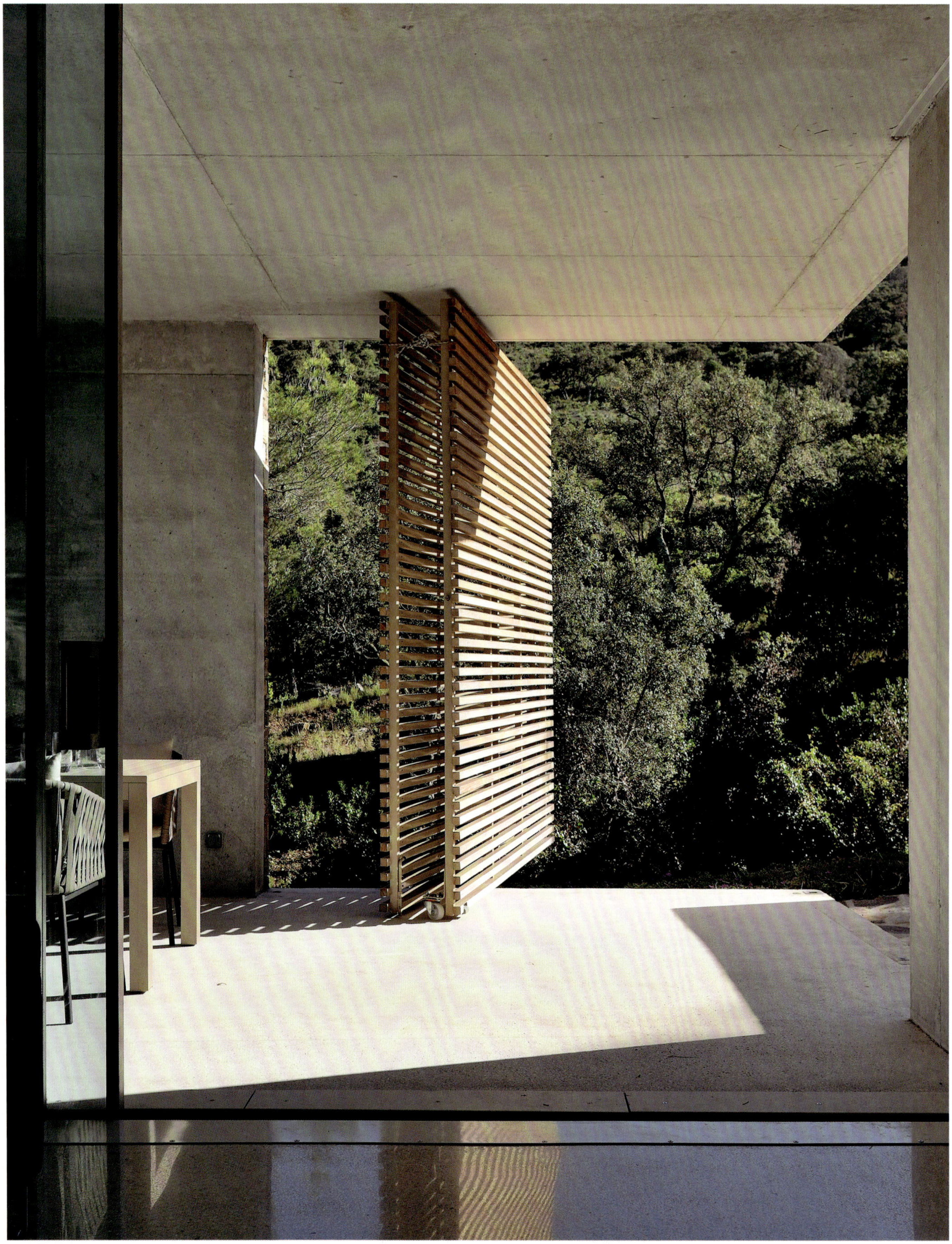

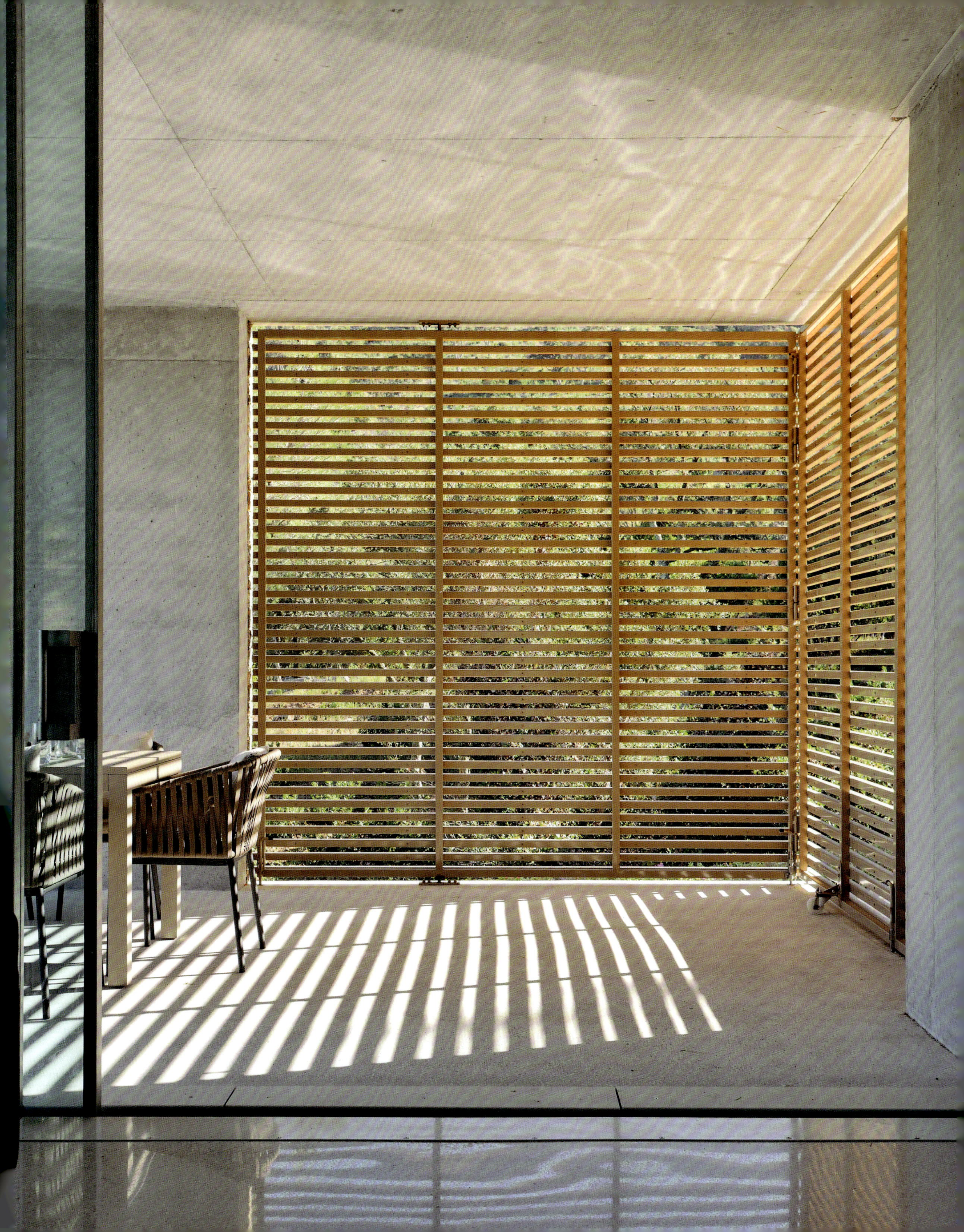

La Mira Ra

With our builder we developed a patented process to achieve a very thin and pure structure consisting of double layers of concrete with insulation inside. This allowed us to make the house almost like a sculpture, with the inside and outside complete.
—Pierre Minassian

La Mira Ra

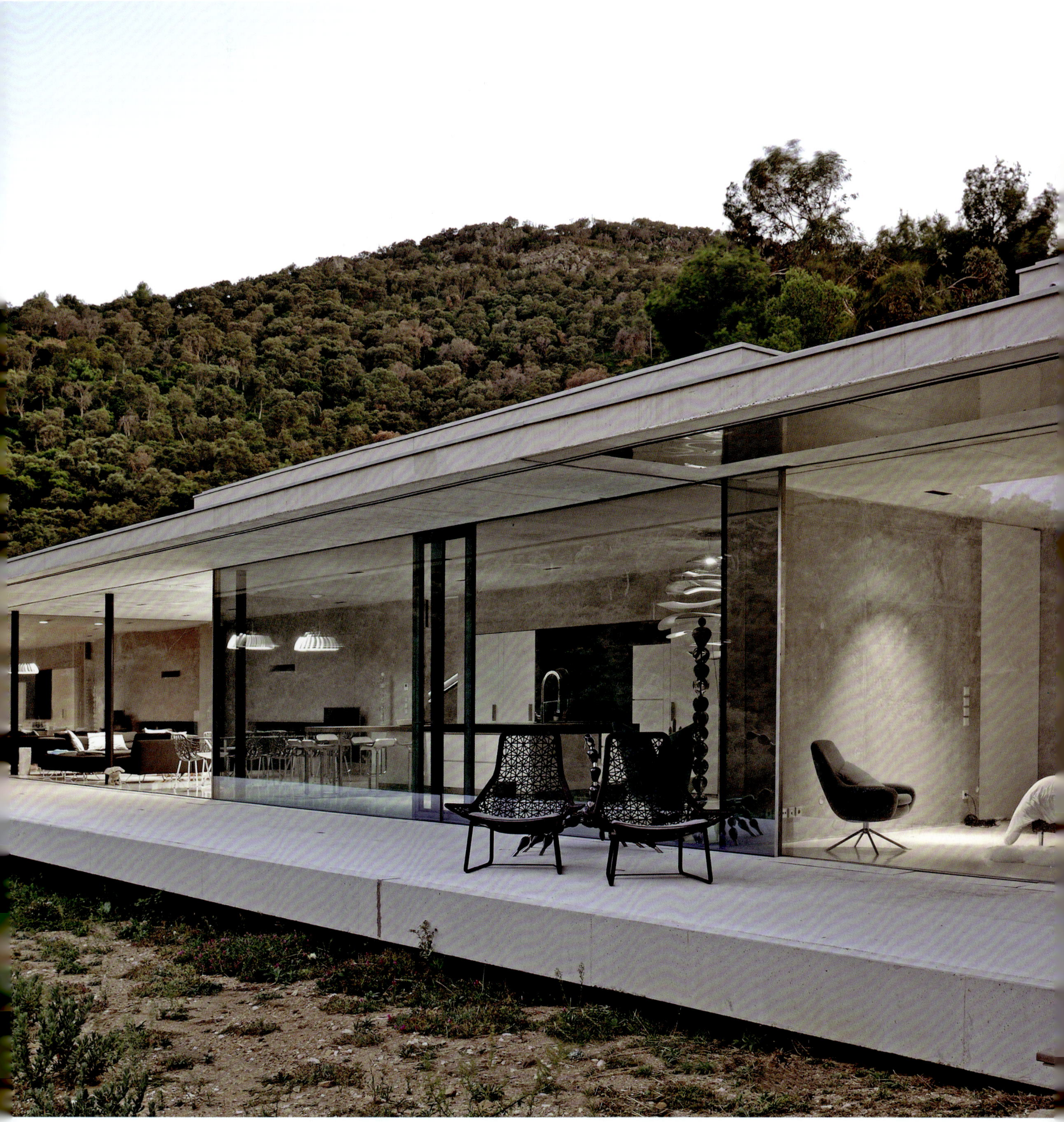

La Mira Ra

Full-height teak louvers provide solar protection and reduce the scale of the glassy facade. They are fixed on the street-facing bedroom wing (*opposite, bottom right*), and fold and slide out of the way on the northeast view side.

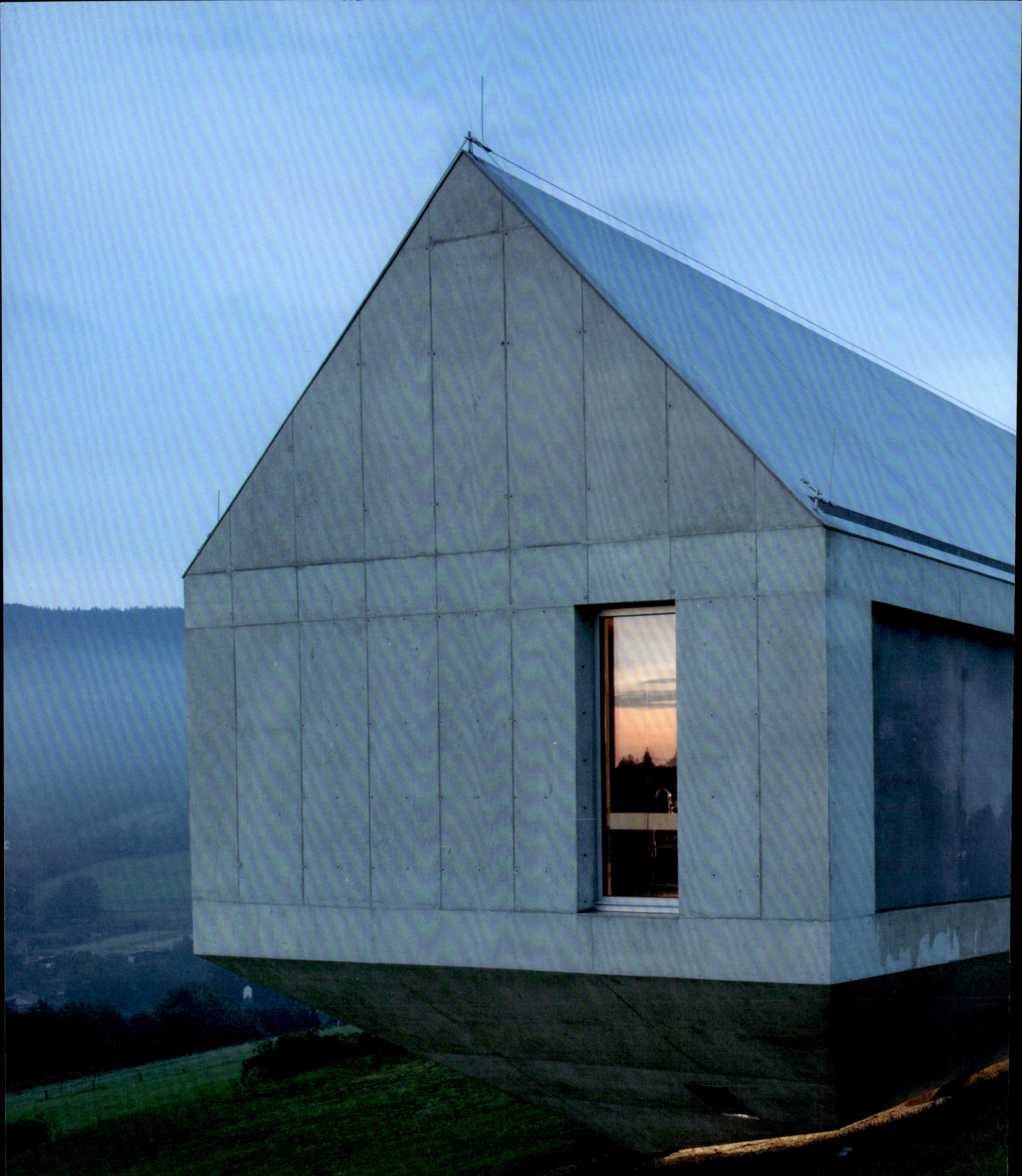

Kraków, Poland | 2015

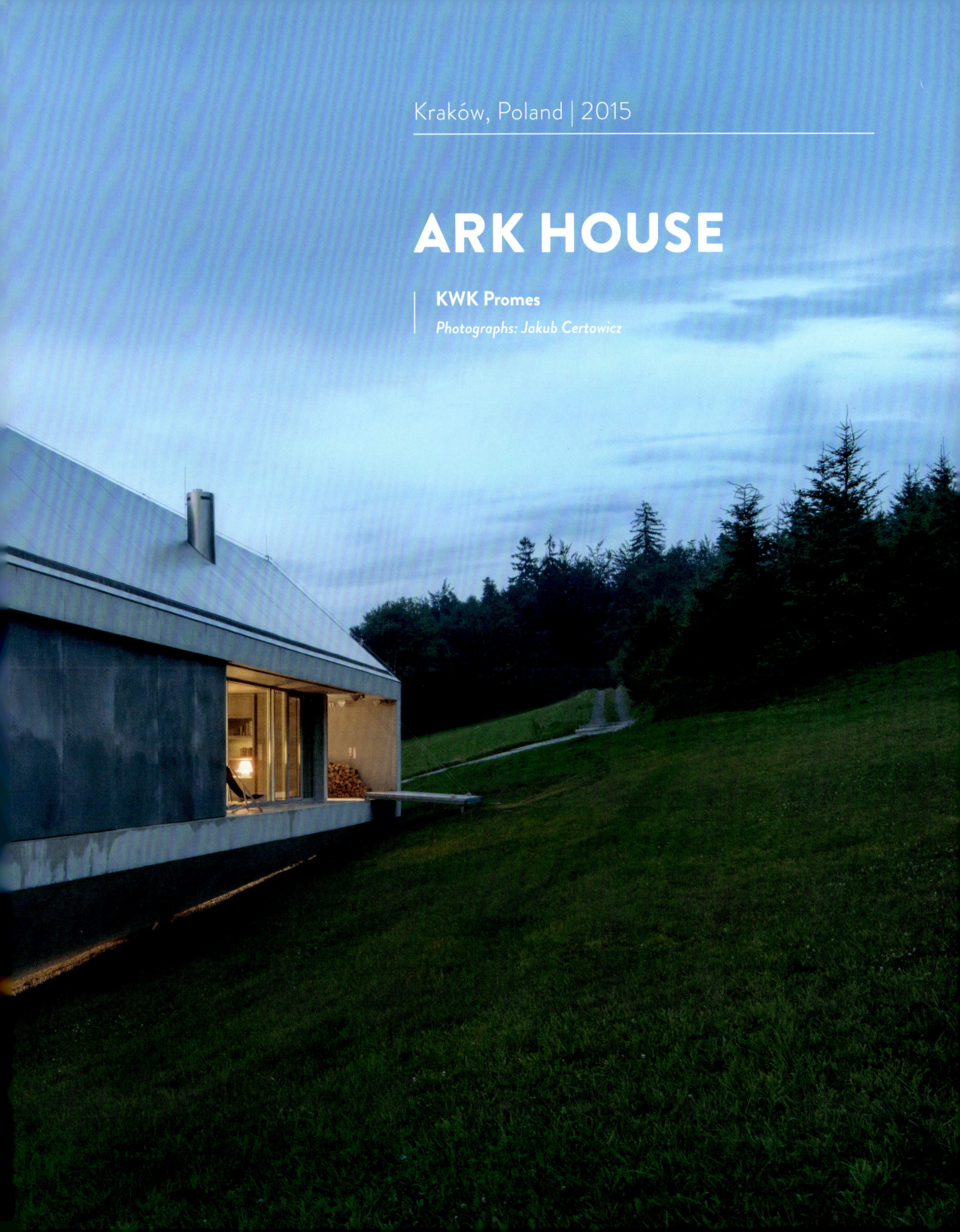

ARK HOUSE

KWK Promes
Photographs: Jakub Certowicz

FLOOR PLAN

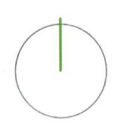

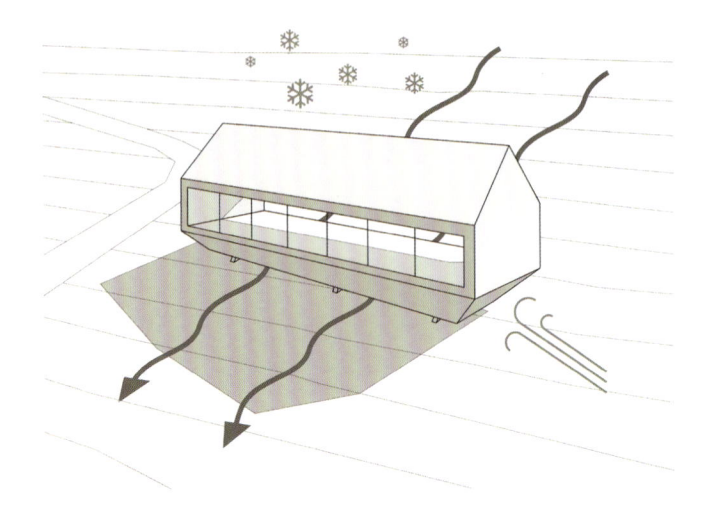

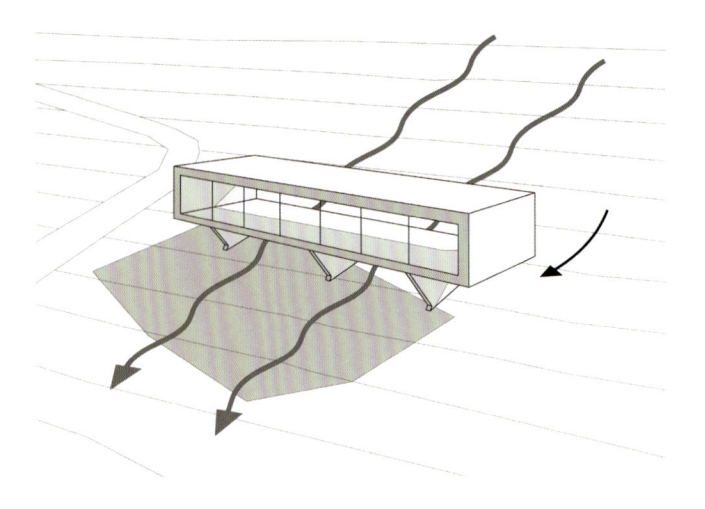

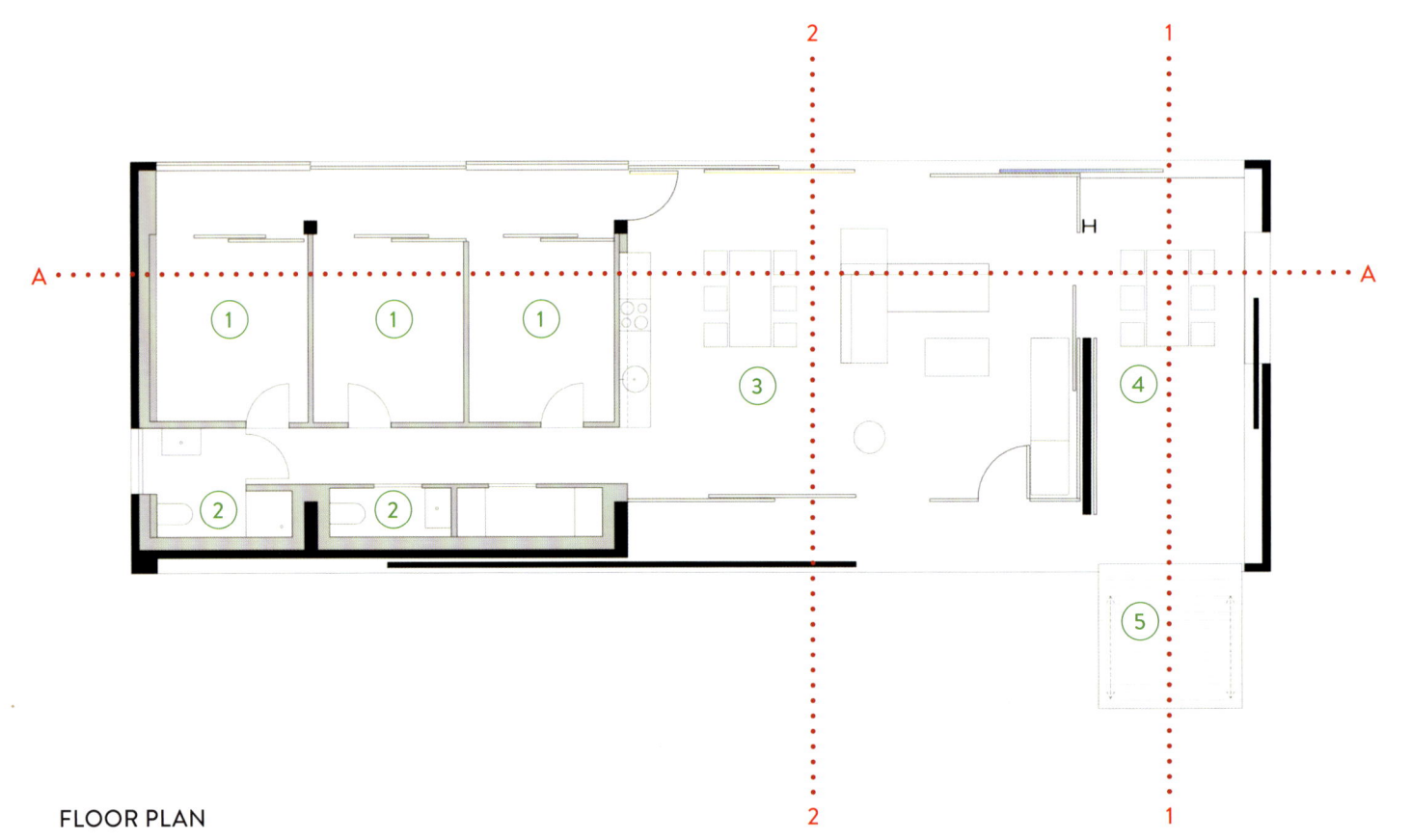

1 Bedrooms
2 Baths
3 Kitchen/dining/living
4 Dining terrace
5 Entry drawbridge

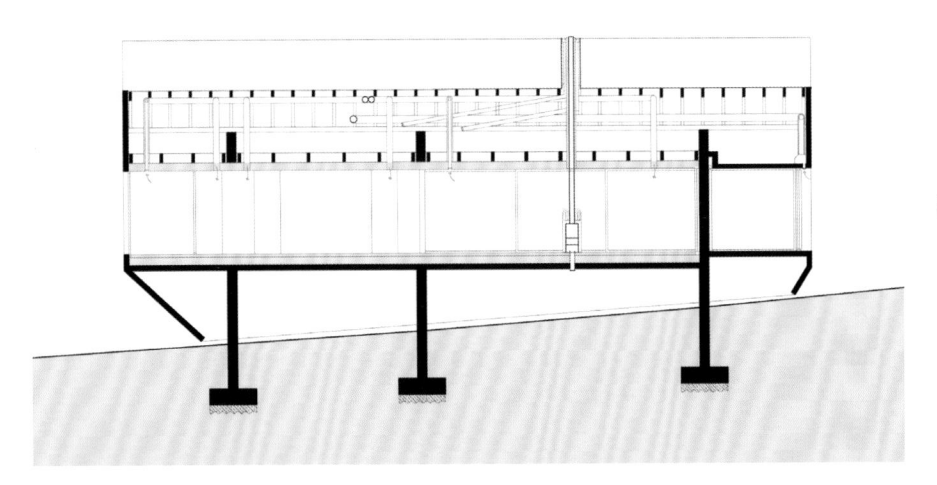

SECTION A-A

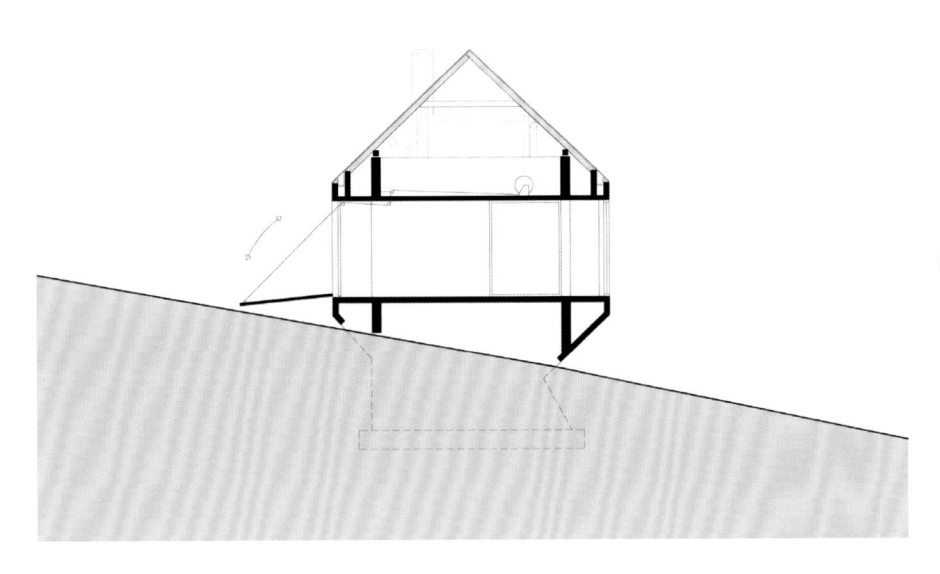

SECTION 1-1

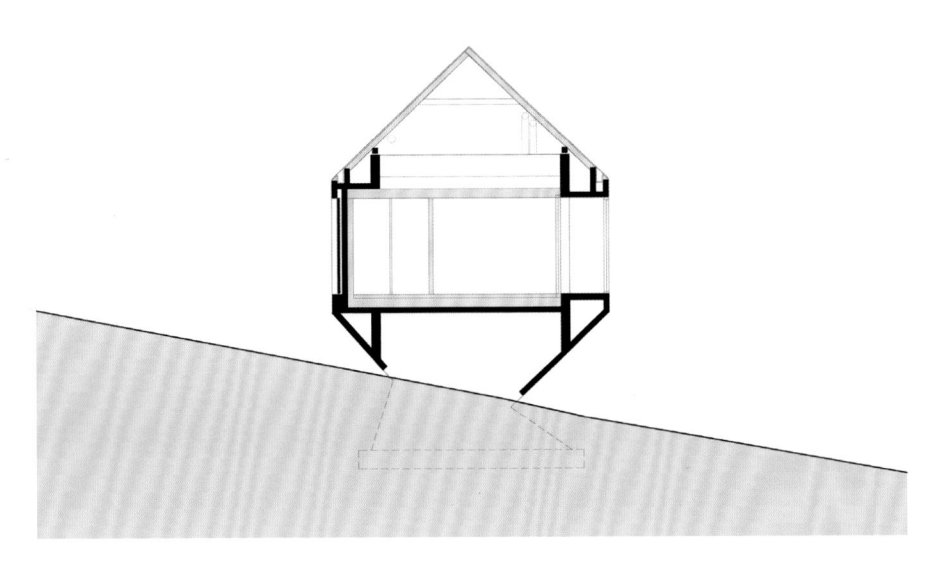

SECTION 2-2

Ark House • Floor Plan

Robert Konieczny's own family house makes the most of its bucolic setting, small plot, and footprint. His innovative Ark House was designed as a frame for viewing the landscape, but it is so much more than that. Part barn, part bridge, part giant eave, it handily addresses a list of environmental and security issues.

From early on, the design concept was for a bar-shaped house that would keep a low profile against the sloping pastureland. Board-formed concrete was a natural choice for expressing the simple, self-contained shape and would not need successive layers of finish. As the design evolved, however, the gabled structure—reminiscent of local barns—morphed into something that looks, depending on the angle, like a prototypical boat in drydock.

Several conditions drove the ultimate design. Because first-floor windows raise security concerns, Konieczny slightly twisted the ground floor away from the slope so that only one corner is in direct contact with the ground—effectively putting the bedrooms out of reach. This move also allowed water to flow unimpeded through the 0.4-acre plot. Essentially resting on horizontal concrete piers like a bridge, the bottom of the house was enclosed with canted walls that give the structure rigidity and provide storage, accessed from a second drawbridge that is released down.

About the unusual form, the architect says, "We created a house with two roofs that protect it from water. The top one is watertight, while the lower one has to be in a sense hollow to allow water to flow

235

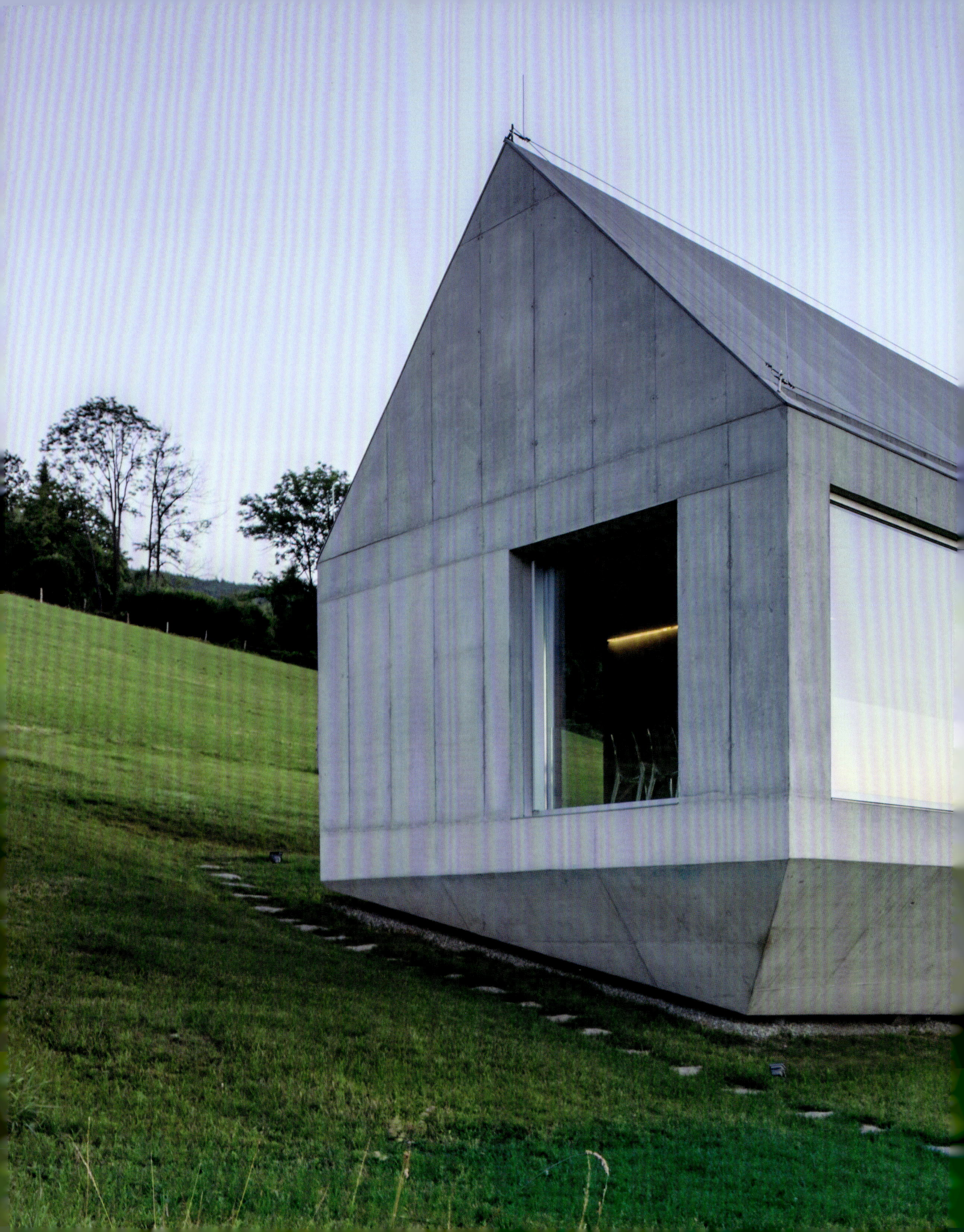

The plot around the house looks as if there were no borders, but it's just an illusion. Actually, it's quite small—1,694.0 m² (0.4 acres). At some point, I realized that the house should be a part of the nature surrounding us. That's why I gave up the idea of a garden and fence. It also influenced the way of designing the entrance to the house. Abandoning the fence resulted in moving it to the outline of the building, which let the nature reach the house. What's more, I achieved a natural symbiosis with the animals, who graze around it, mowing our lawn at the same time. When there is rain or wind, they treat the space beneath the house as a shelter. The Ark was given real and sublime meaning.
—Robert Konieczny

238 Ark House

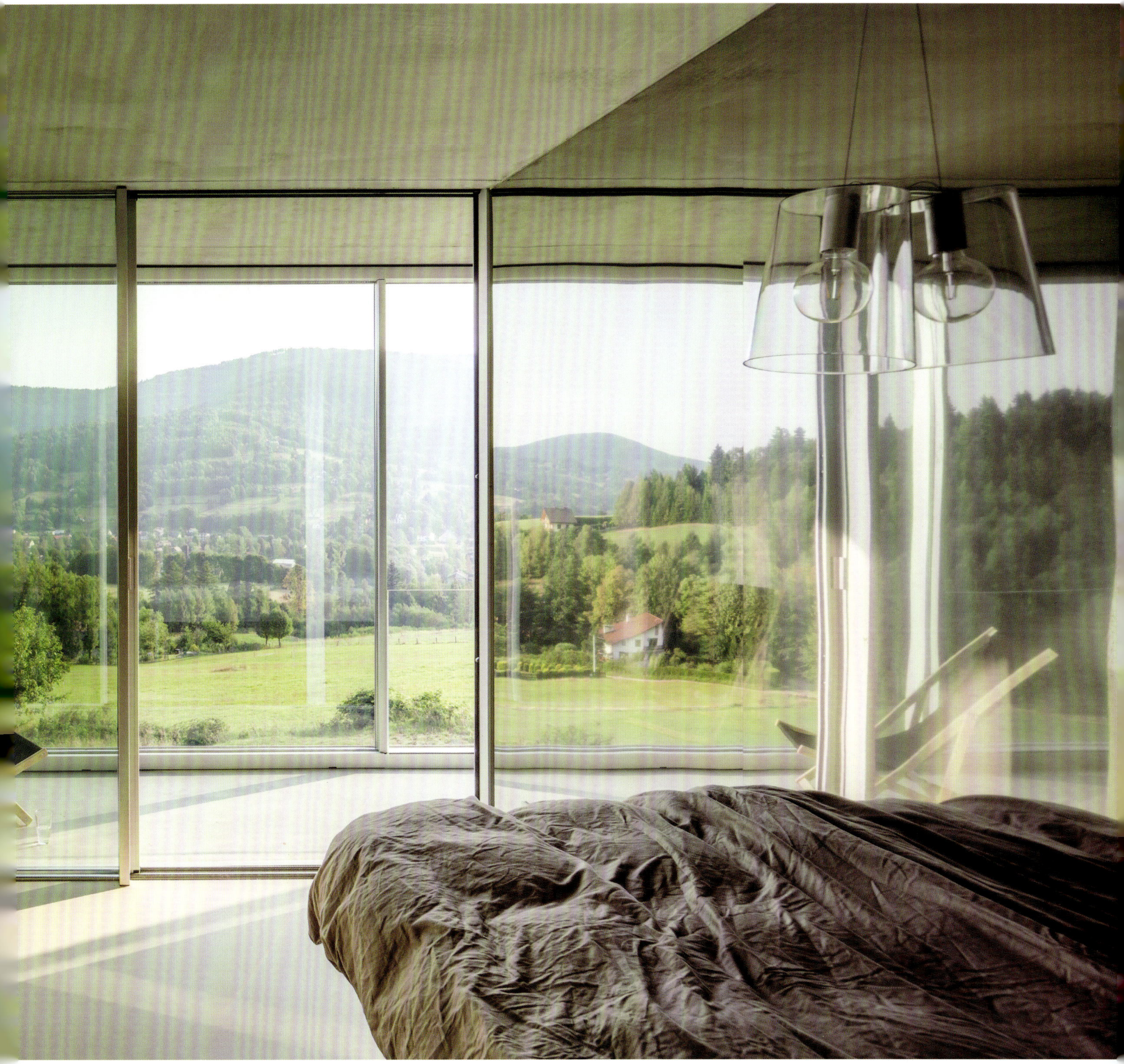

240 Ark House

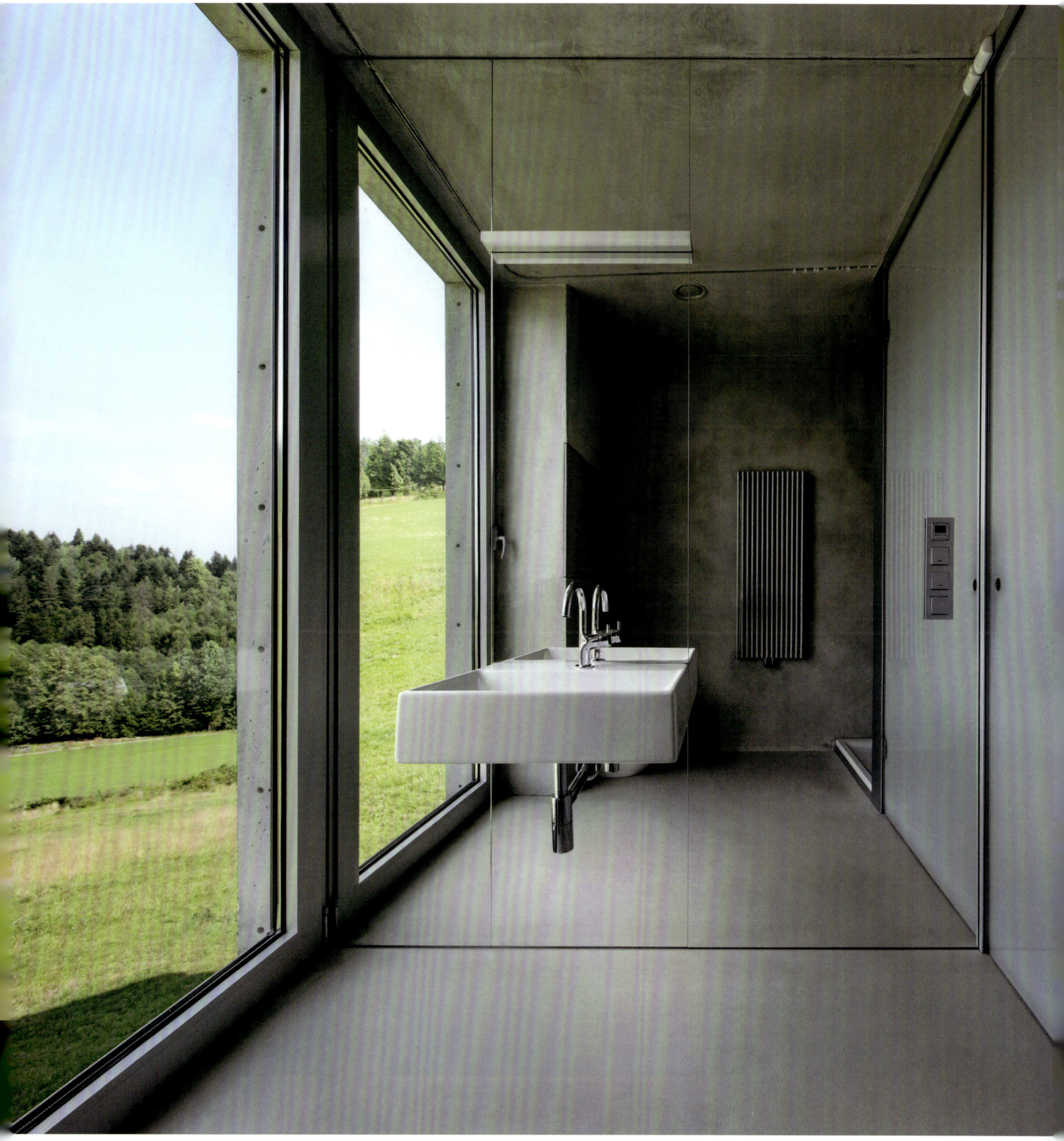

242 Ark House

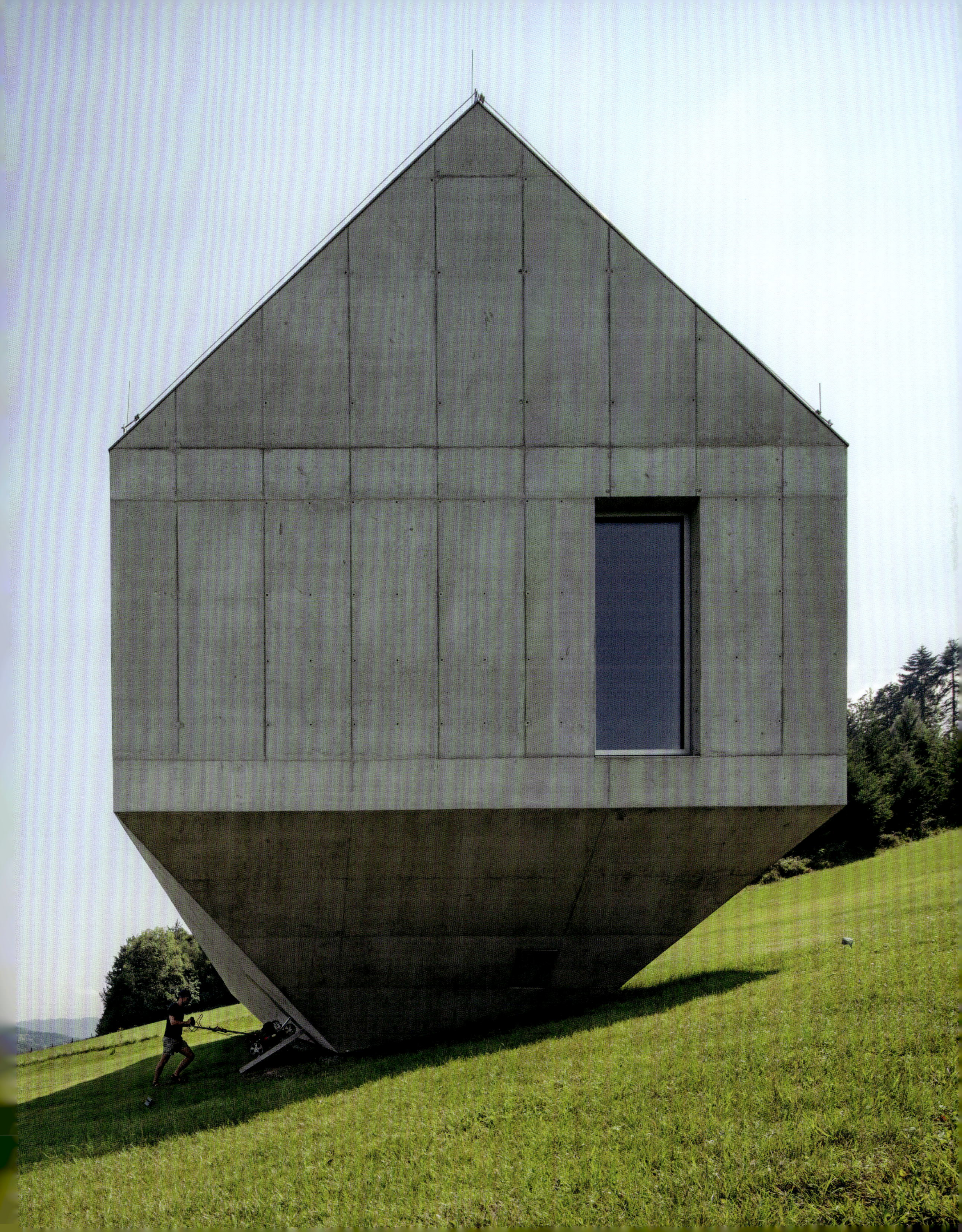

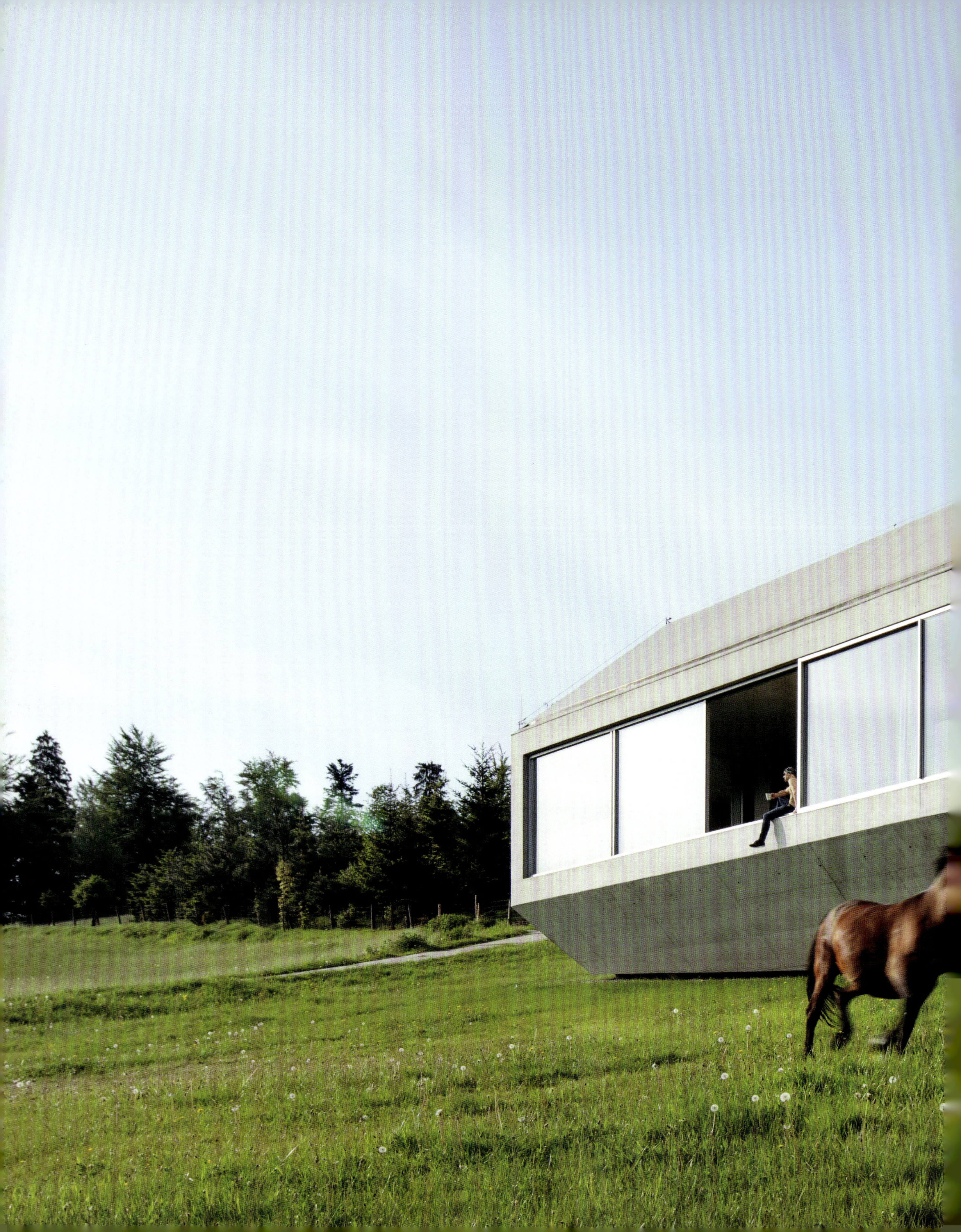

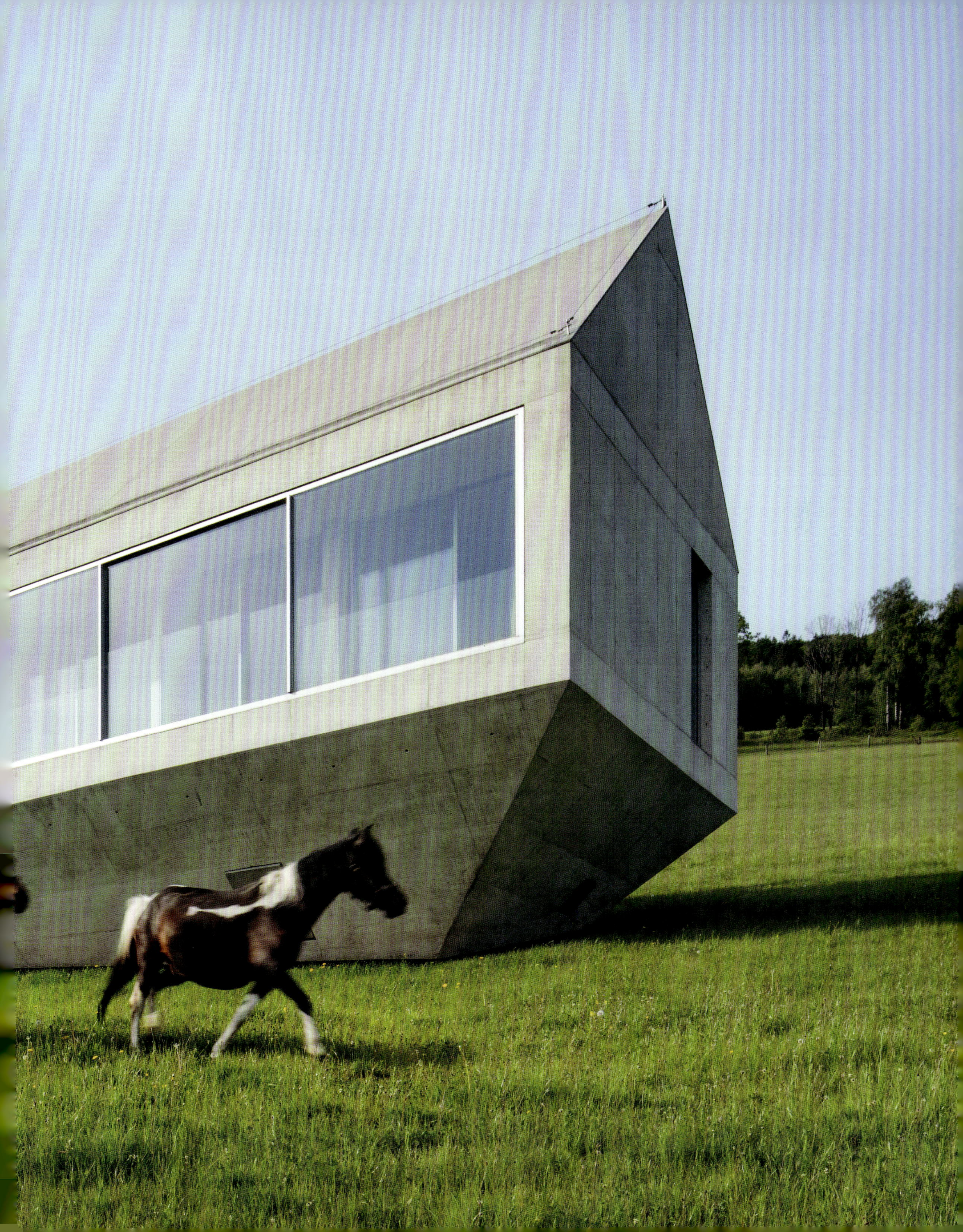

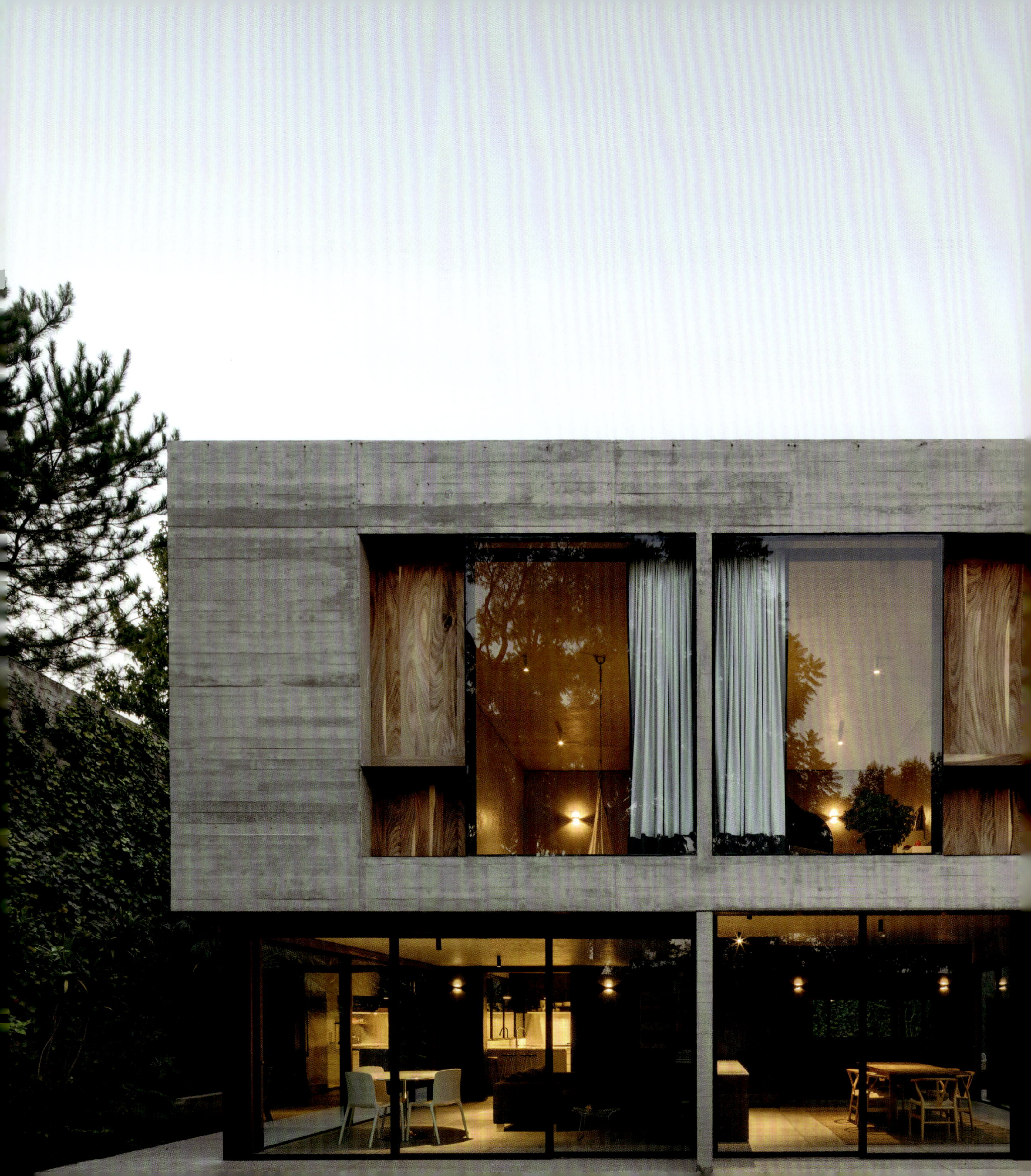

Mexico City, Mexico | 2018

CASA SIERRA FRIA

PPAA Arquitectos

Photographs: Rafael Gamo

For architect Pablo Pérez Palacios, concrete's most desirable quality isn't how it looks but what it can accomplish. His team at PPAA Arquitectos used it to stack three volumes on this tight urban lot in Mexico City's Lomas de Chapultepec neighborhood, where setbacks are 10 feet on each side. "We say that we do architecture about intentions rather than forms," he says. Here the puzzle was "how to make the floor plan as open as possible and use the setbacks."

Ultimately, the architects devised a design that turns the open-plan idea on its head. The 3,767-square-foot house has a cross-shaped internal structure with a skylit stairwell at the center. This gesture enabled a glassy first floor whose concrete beams effortlessly lift the second-story concrete box into the air. The public rooms open out rather than in to each other. Each discrete space has two outdoor exposures, an open corner, and access to the walled property that turns the setbacks into private gardens. "Everyone wants a corner office," says Palacios.

Visitors enter through a door in the tall, dark wall along the front property line. To the right of the entry walkway, the living room spills out to the garden, where a large rock is a "memory piece" saved from excavation. Ahead is the main entrance at the heart of the plan. There, a stair hall divides the kitchen on one side from a service core on the other and leads to a lounge and dining room occupying the rear corners of the house.

SECOND FLOOR

1 Study
2 Main bedroom suite
3 Kids' bedrooms

FIRST FLOOR

1 Entry
2 Living room
3 Kitchen
4 Lounge
5 Dining room
6 Gravel courtyard
7 Garden

ROOF TERRACE

Totaling 3,767 square feet, the three stacked volumes decrease in size as you move up. The second story is a more solid block containing the couple's bedroom and a study at the front and two children's bedrooms at the rear. Perched on top, gazing over the city, is a rooftop pavilion under a concrete canopy. The concrete envelops a glazed volume that scoops light into the floors below. "The stairway becomes an opening to the sky," says Palacios.

In section, the design explores the meaning of weight and weightlessness. "The open ground floor literally carries a rock on top," the architect says. "It's the idea of lifting a huge rock from the ground. The circulation became the way we brought light into the house from the sky; there is literally a hole in the rock you're carrying."

This sense is reinforced in the darkly plastered crosswalls that support the concrete block—and nod to the front garden wall. "It's a way to make the concrete float," Palacios says. Throughout, the exposed concrete is warmed with wood and plaster. Window openings are lined with tzalam, a Yucatán hardwood that resists temperature changes and moisture. Light oak floors reflect light funneled through the stairwell, where a slim metal guardrail wafts upward.

Although the firm uses concrete only when necessary, the material "shows hand labor; it's a tribute to the people who build it," Palacios says. "It works well in Mexico, where there is no snow or need for insulation, and lasts forever. We think good architecture not only is good for its time but should age with dignity and be a timeless piece."

250 Casa Sierra Fria

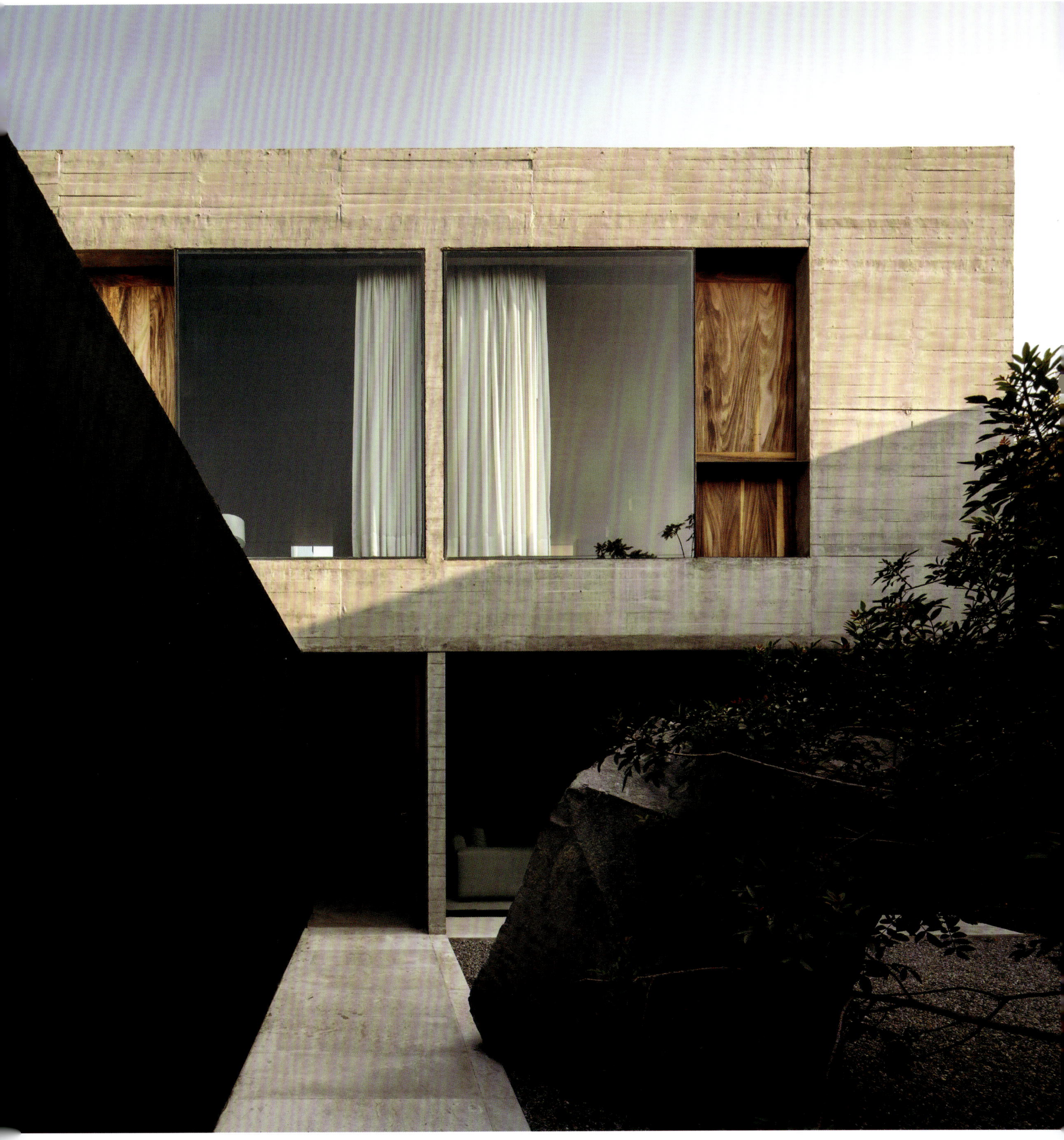

Casa Sierra Fria

The open ground floor literally carries a rock on top. It's the idea of lifting a huge rock from the ground. The circulation became the way we brought light into the house from the sky; there is literally a hole in the rock you're carrying.
—Pablo Pérez Palacios

The building looks straightforward from the outside, but inside there is a richness and a play of light. You discover space as you move through, and nature is framed in each space.
—Pablo Pérez Palacios

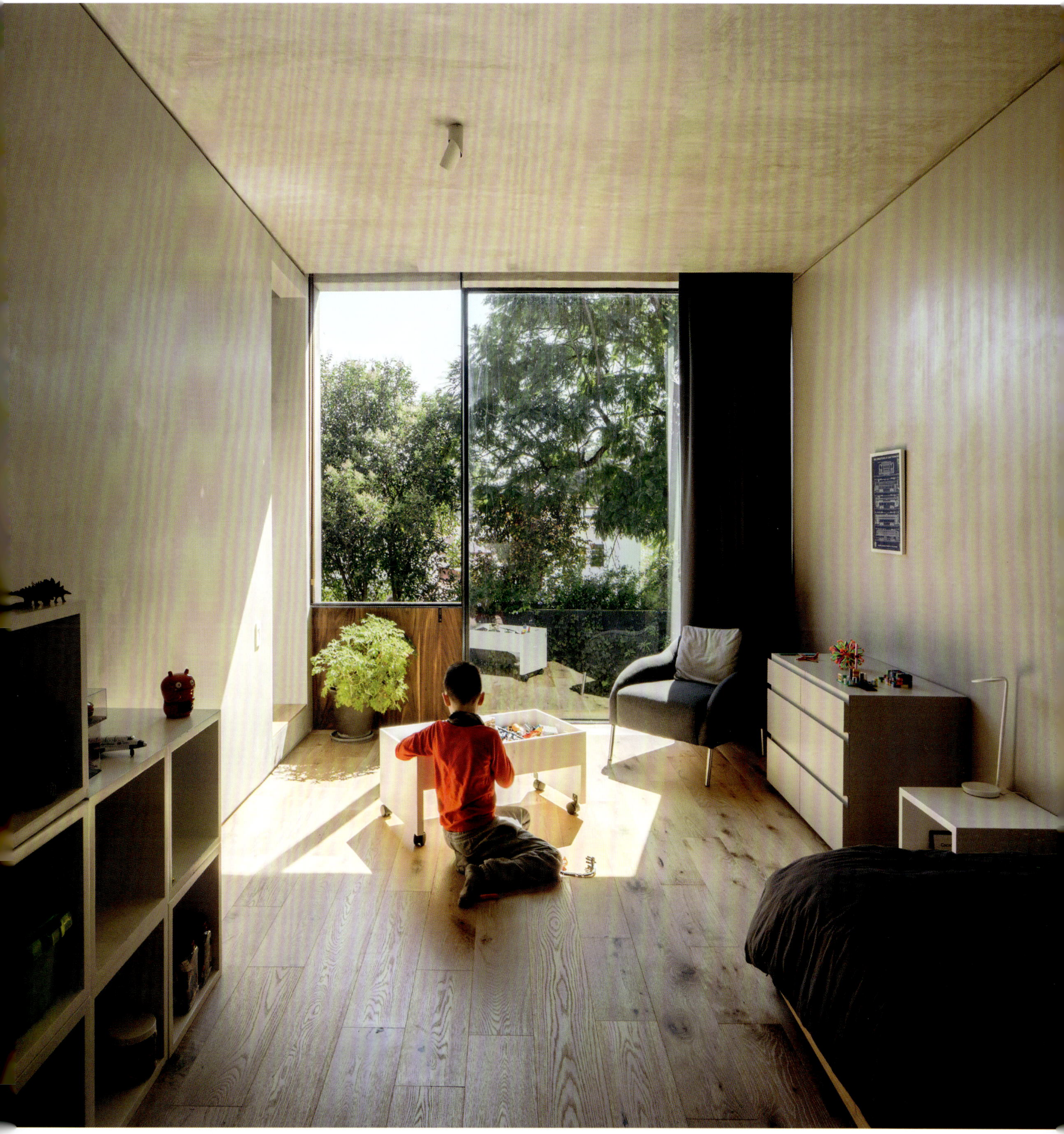

Casa Sierra Fria

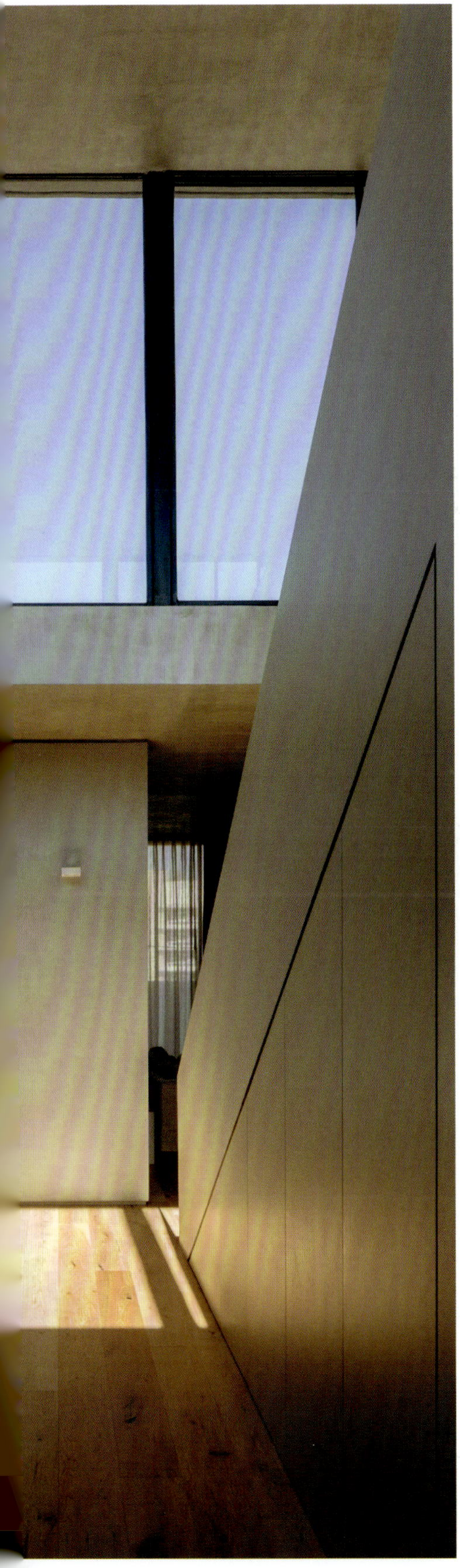

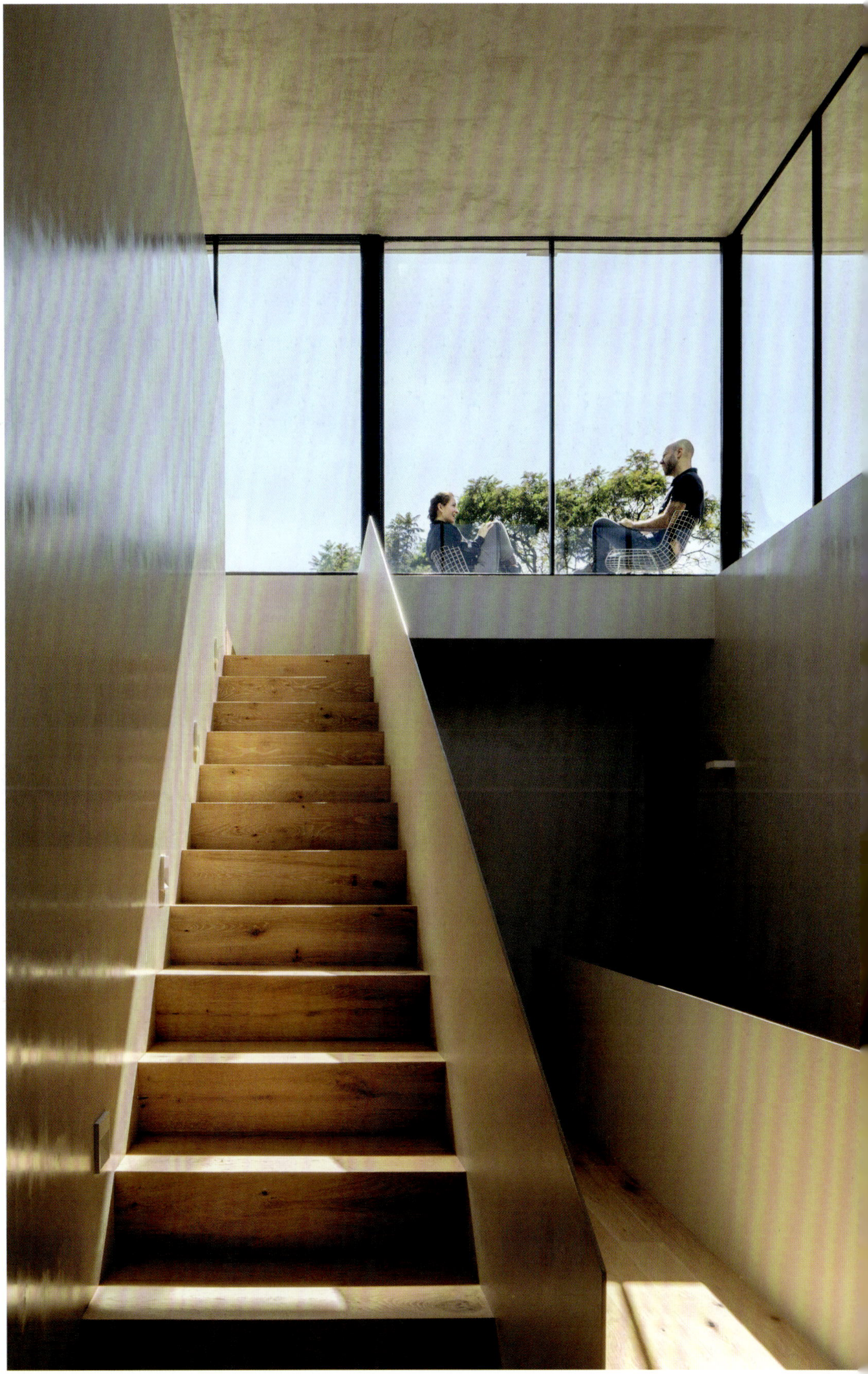

258 Casa Sierra Fria

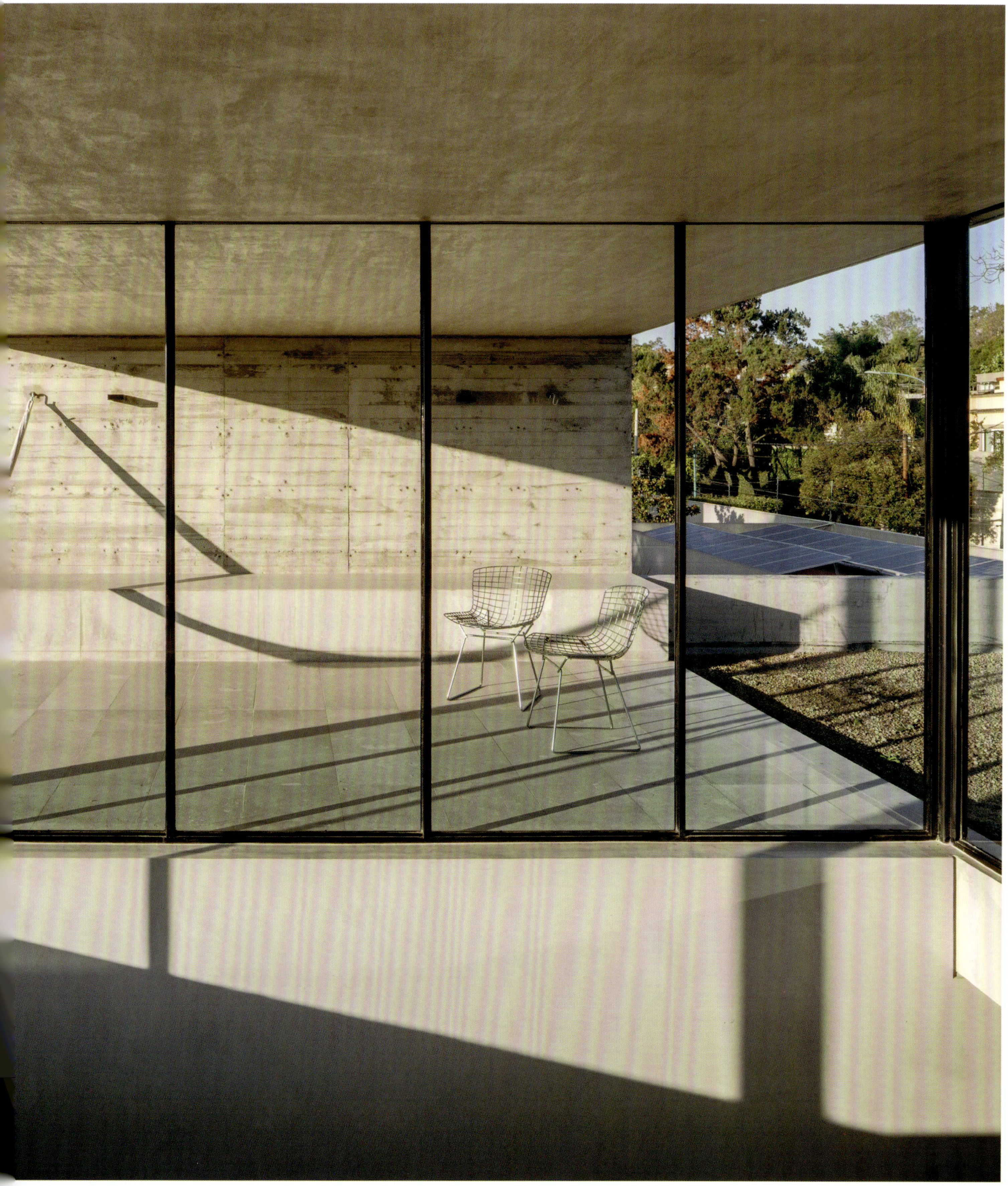

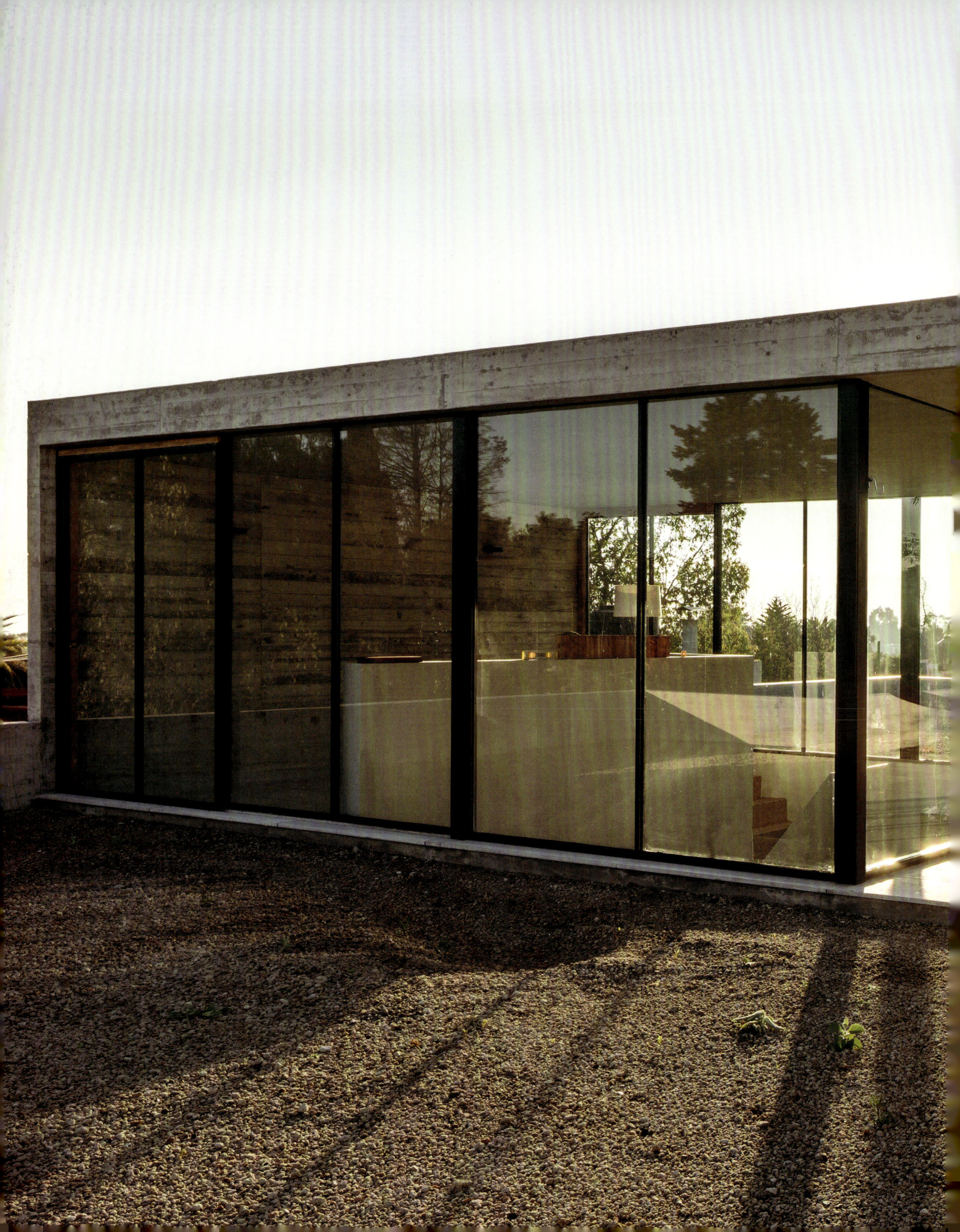

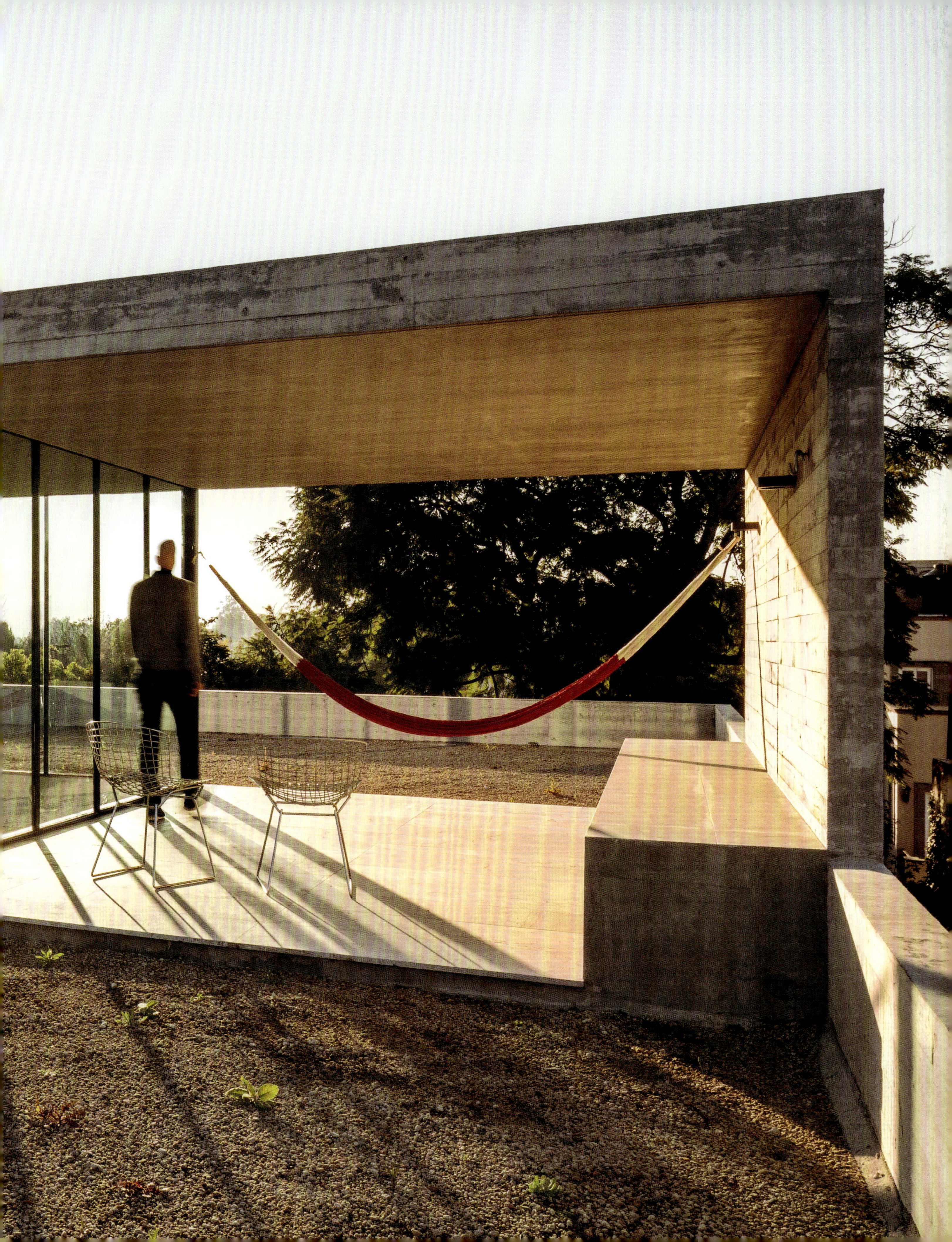

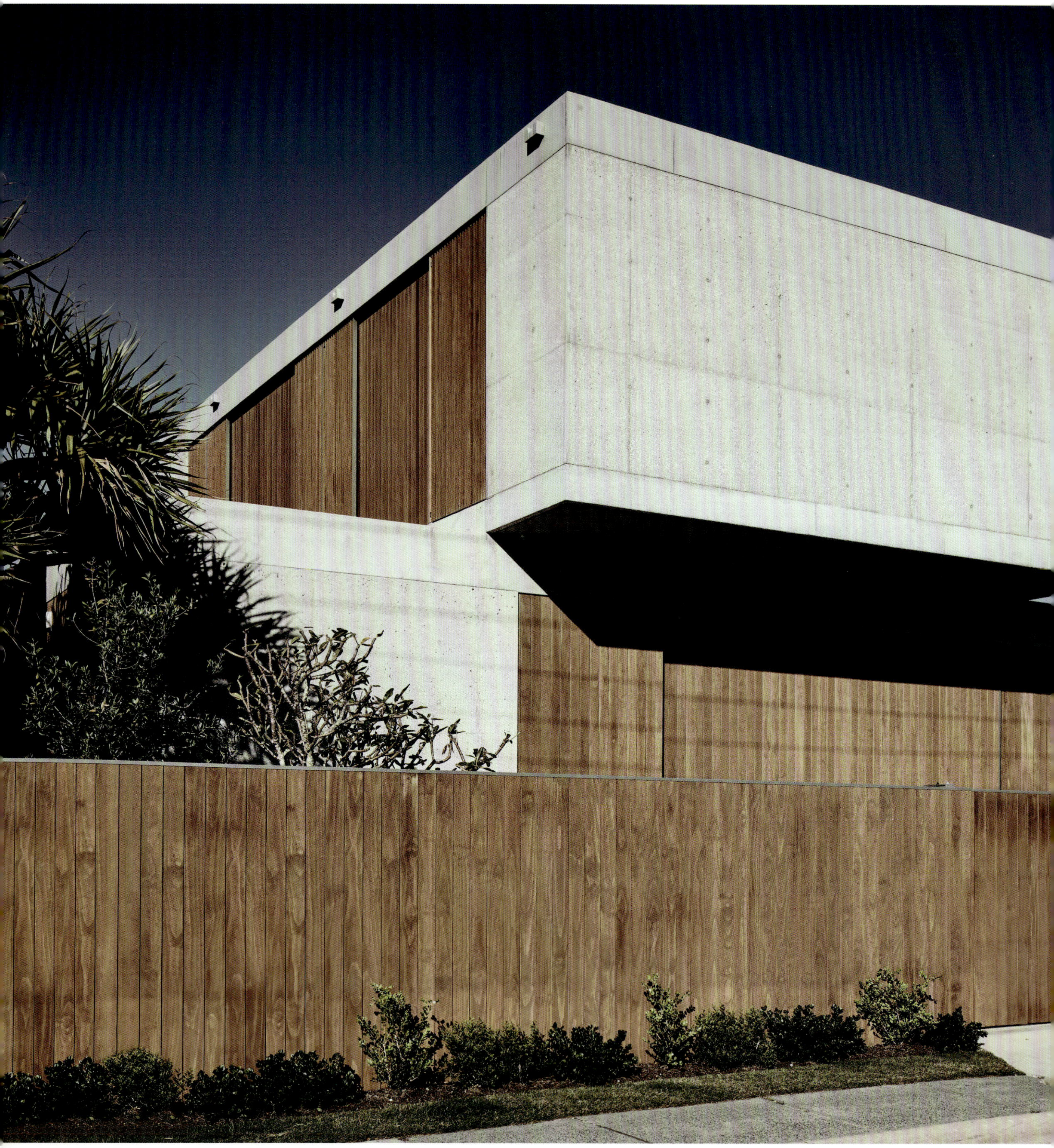

Gold Coast, Australia | 2019

MERMAID BEACH RESIDENCE

BE Architects

Photographs: Derek Swalwell and Andy McPherson

Fresh from a quaint, Cape Cod–style house just down the beach, these clients got their wish for something far more impervious to the mercurial coastal weather. "A lot of houses here on Australia's Gold Coast have led to preconceived ideas that beach shacks are made of whitened timber," says Andrew Piva, a principal at BE Architects. "We wanted to challenge that a bit, because it has to last a long time. Why can't you do something strong and quiet?"

On a site that's all about movement—shifting sands, harsh sunlight, and cyclonic winds and storms—the architects turned to concrete because of its permanence. Composed of two simple materials—timber and stacked concrete volumes that were poured in place—the top floor overhangs the lower one at each end, creating shaded terraces and walkways that provide relief from the heat. Along the busy road, the house's reductionist facade is a pause amid a cacophony of architectural styles, "like turning the volume down," Piva says.

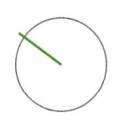

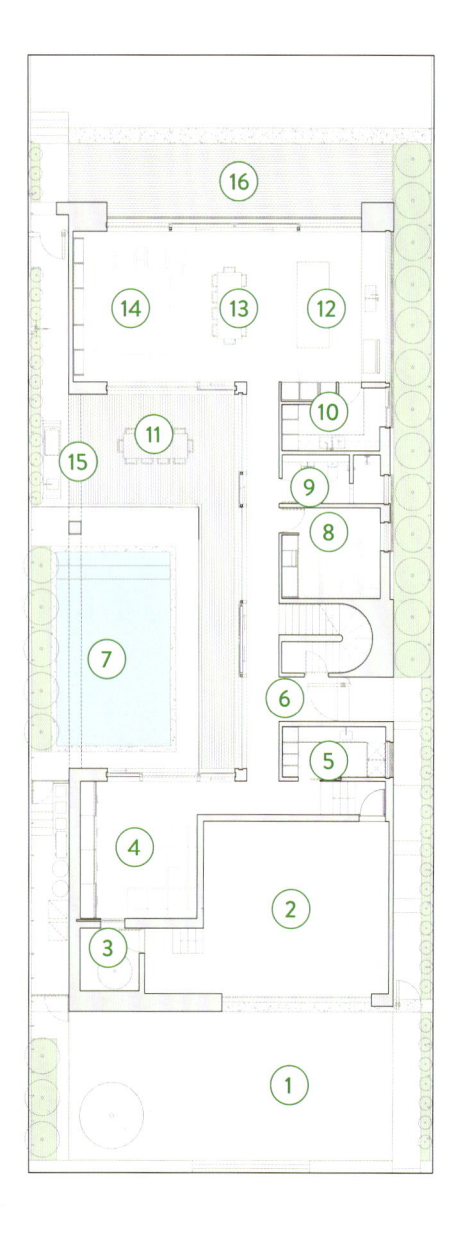

FIRST FLOOR

1. Entry court
2. Garage
3. Drying area
4. Rumpus room
5. Laundry
6. Entry
7. Pool
8. Guest room
9. Bath and laundry
10. Pantry
11. Courtyard
12. Kitchen
13. Dining
14. Living
15. Barbecue
16. Beach terrace

SECOND FLOOR

1. Courtyard
2. Yoga studio
3. Bedroom
4. Study
5. Stair
6. Main bedroom 1
7. Closet
8. Main bedroom 2
9. Bath
10. Deck

264　Mermaid Beach Residence • Floor Plan

In a beach community especially, not everyone will appreciate the facade's solidity. It challenges familiar notions of domesticity and turns its back unapologetically to the frenetic street. There is direct access to the beach at the back of the house, and that was the focus. "The big challenge is that concrete has a bit of a stigma, the feeling that it's too oppressive, heavy, and masculine," Piva says. "People associate concrete with car parks. We thought, How do we express it in a way that's more tactile and personal, softer?"

To achieve that effect, the architects experimented with pattern and texture. A series of horizontal bands add life and scale to the elevation, like timber or stone does. The base and top planes are smooth, while the midsection was exfoliated by hand, using a technique called scrabbling. "A pneumatic tool nibbles away at the face of the concrete and exposes some of the aggregate underneath," Piva says. "We played with different types of aggregate, mixing in white stones that reflect light." That treatment stops an inch short of the corners to preserve the building's crisp, creased form.

Mermaid Beach Residence

Further softening the monolithic concrete, accoya wood panels on the garage, privacy fence, and long upper sides of the house balance a heavy material with one that will weather softly. At the rear the panels become operable louvers; they combat glaring sunlight and strong winds coming from the sea but fold and stack to open the interior to the outdoors.

Visitors enter along the side of the house, stepping into the center of the U-shaped ground floor. Straight ahead is a pool courtyard facing the premium northern light. To the right, living spaces on the east spill out to the beach. Rooms along the courtyard have floor-to-ceiling glass, allowing light to penetrate deep into the house, while the solid west wall screens the street.

Another dramatic point of entry for the light is the large, round skylight that acts as a prism atop the central curved concrete stairwell. "We like reinforcing internally what our buildings are made of," Piva says. Sections of smooth, board-formed concrete appear on columns and select walls, while white oak floors and walnut joinery lend cozy warmth. Upstairs, the circular stair landing faces a courtyard planted with a tree and other greenery. On the east side of the stair, the main bedroom suite and balcony overlook the coastline. Toward the front are two kids' bedrooms and a bath, study, and yoga studio with a private courtyard.

The building's sturdy shell ensures that the house will be there for a very long time, while creating a relaxed, light-filled cocoon. "You're closing yourself off from the day you've had when you enter the door," Piva says. "It's a busy house with young kids. It's practical, not precious. These are people running out to the beach."

267

Mermaid Beach Residence

The big challenge is that concrete has a bit of a stigma, the feeling that it's too oppressive, heavy, and masculine. We thought, How do we express it in a way that's more tactile and personal, softer?
—Andrew Piva

Mermaid Beach Residence

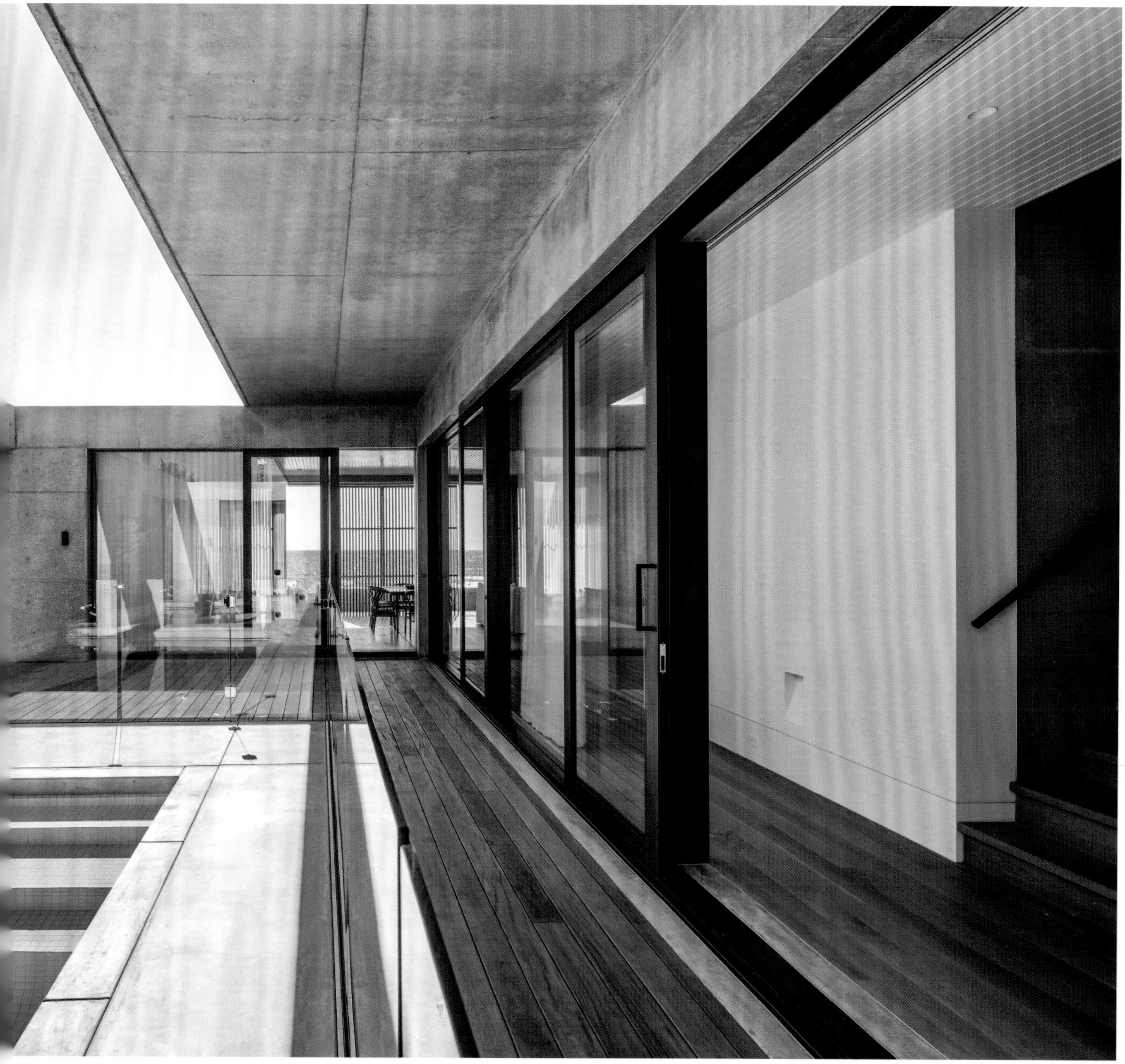

272 Mermaid Beach Residence

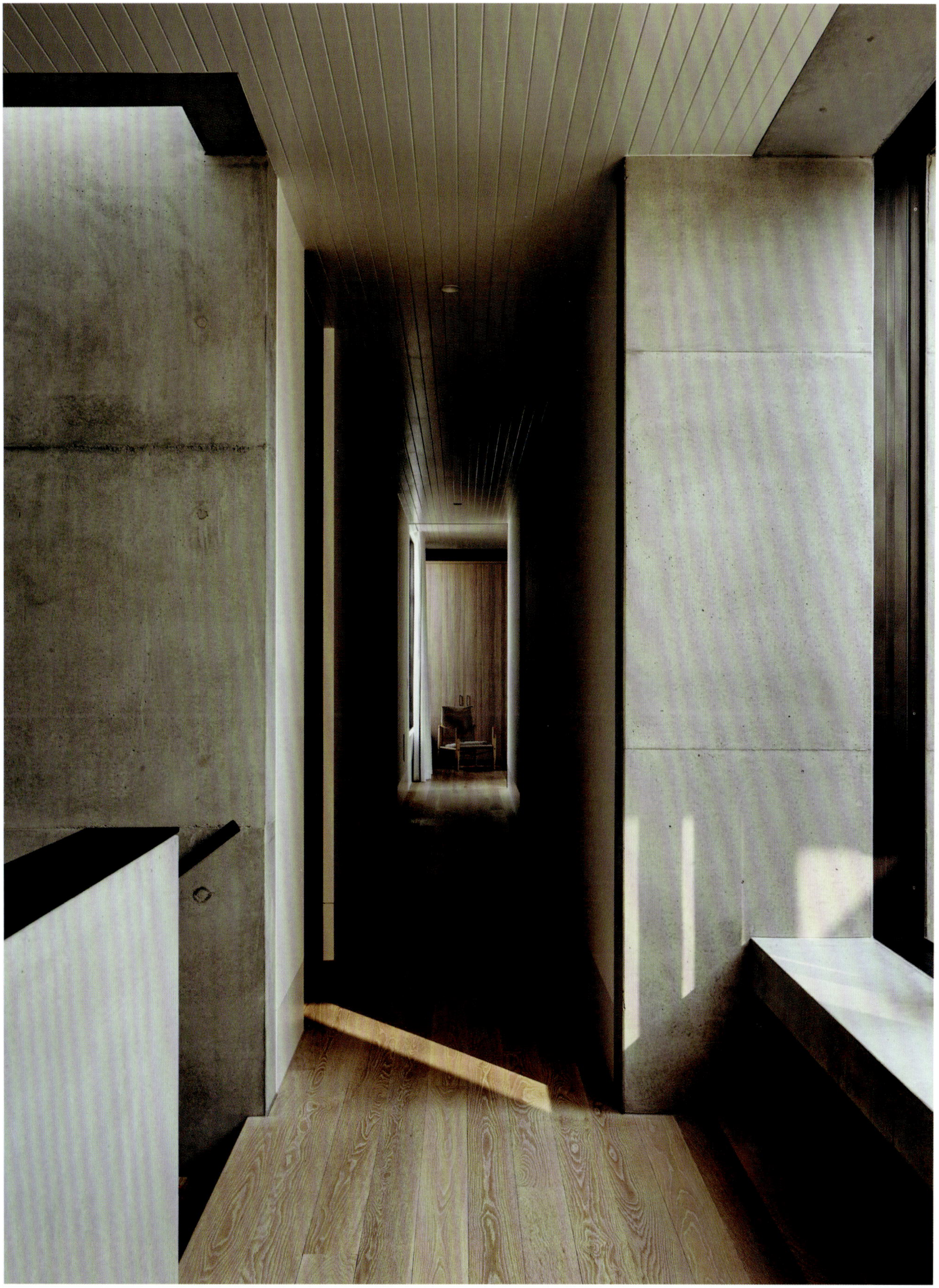

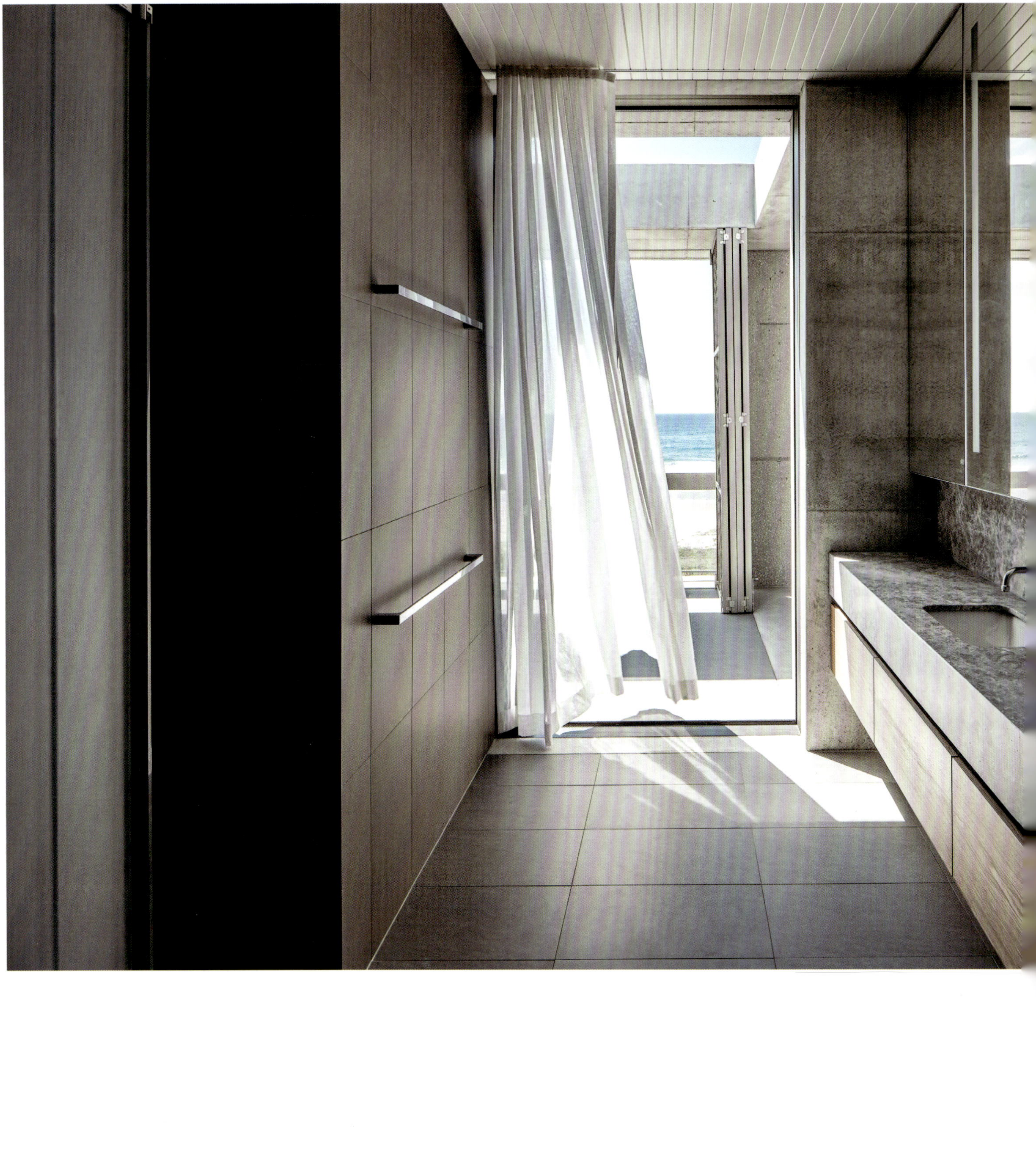

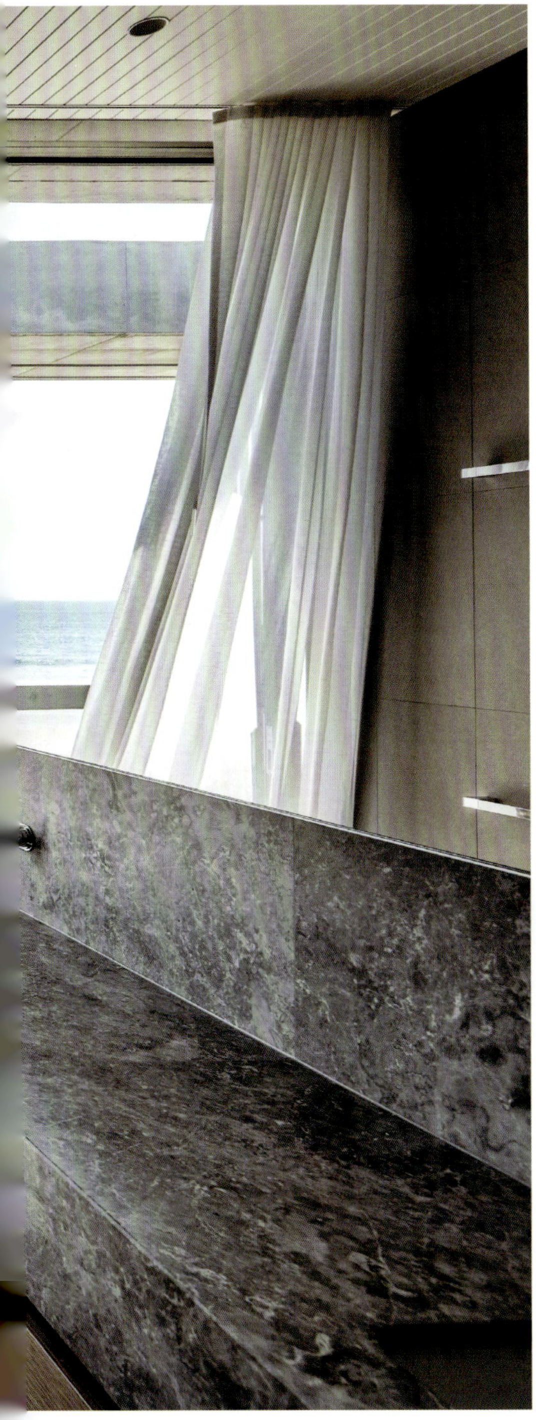

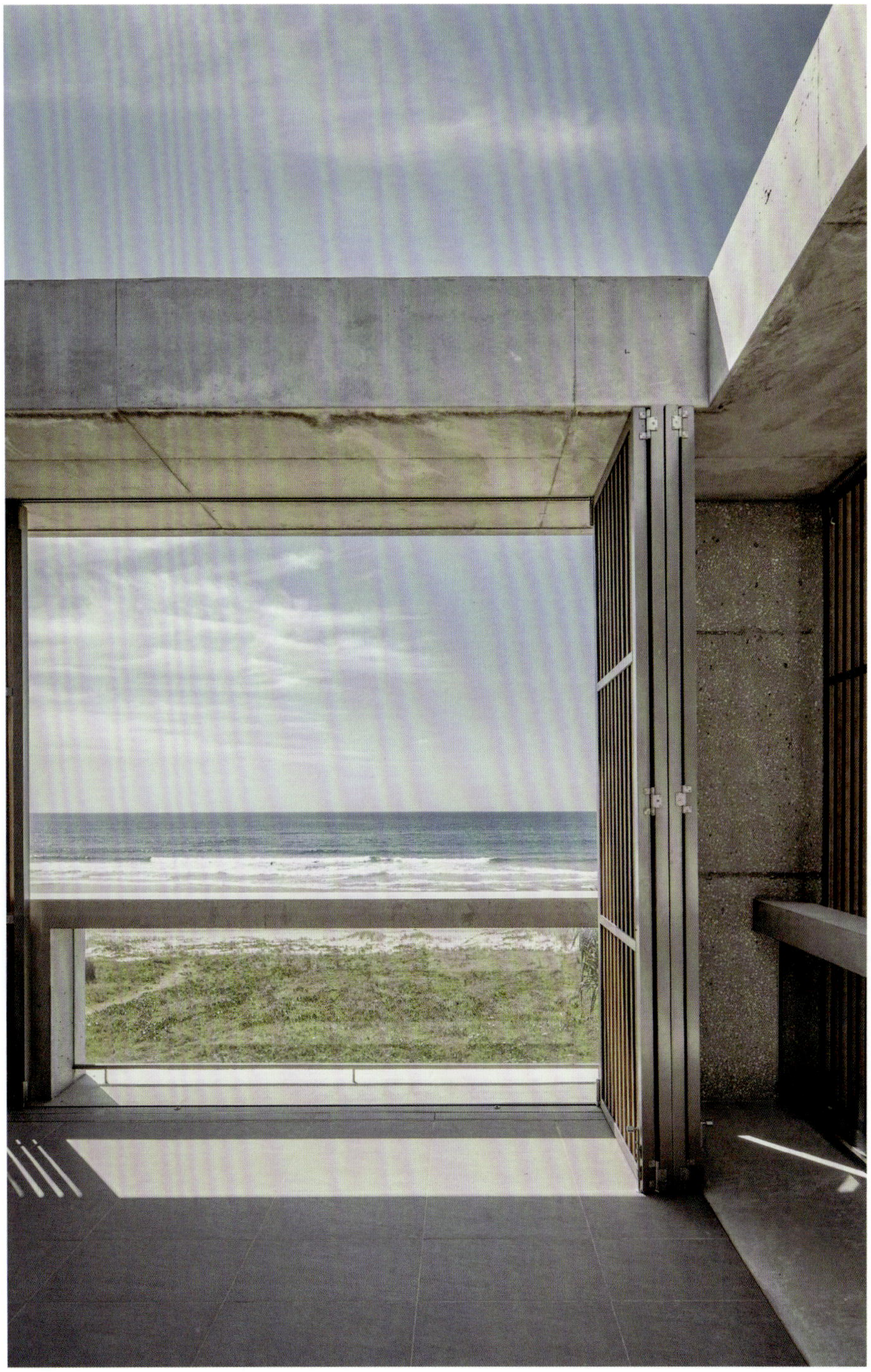

276   Mermaid Beach Residence

Accoya wood panels balance a heavy material with one that will weather softly. At the rear the panels become operable louvers; they combat glaring sunlight and strong winds coming from the sea but fold and stack to open the interior to the outdoors.

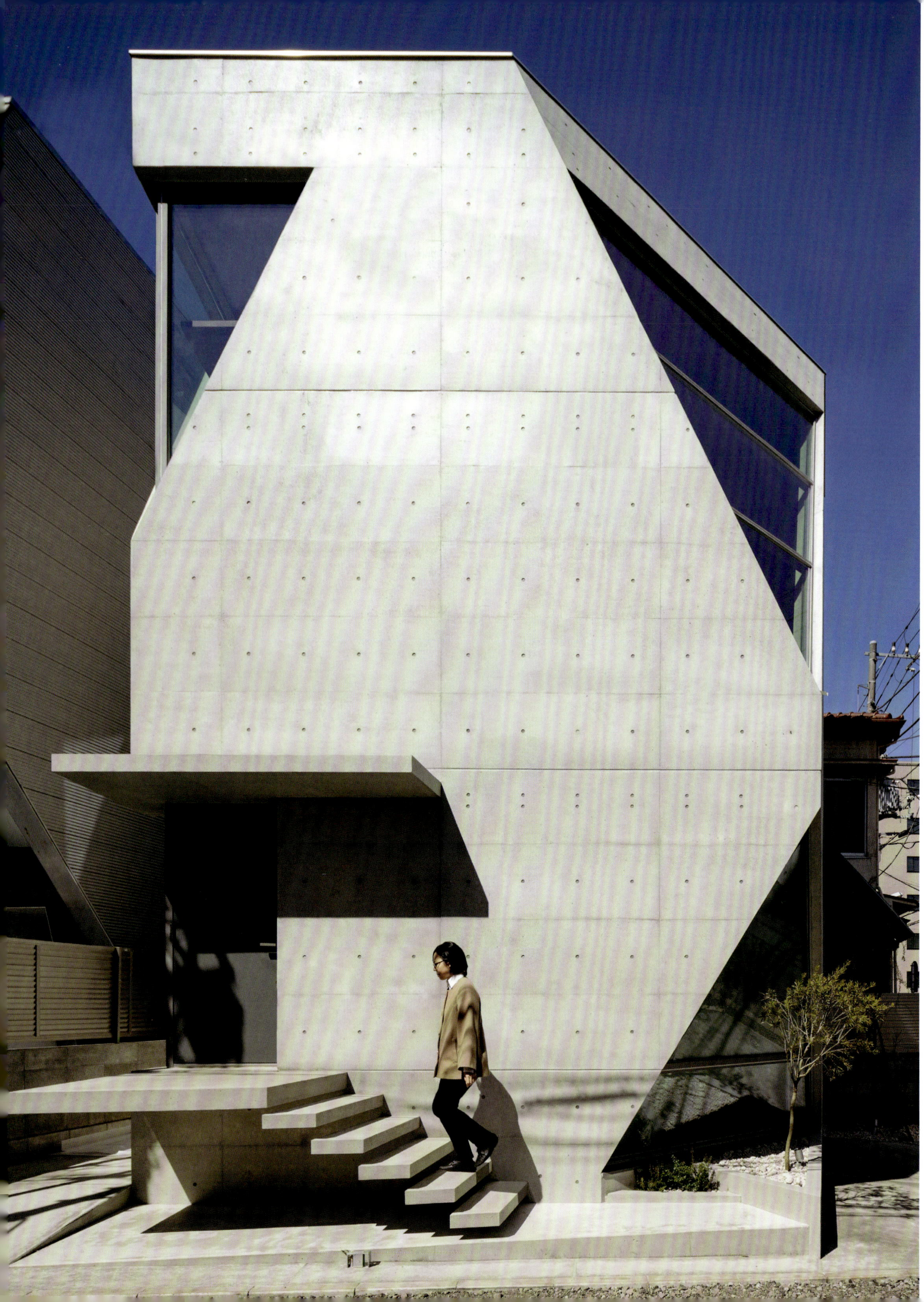

Tokyo, Japan | 2015

R TORSO C

Atelier Tekuto
Photographs: Jérémie Souteyrat and Toshihiro Sobajima

Squeezed into a micro lot in the center of Tokyo, this four-story house is a study in the power of sectional design. R Torso C has a blank concrete facade whose sliced, glazed angles create a sculptural form from the street. Inside, they make the house feel far larger than its 1,100 square feet by flooding it top to bottom with abstracted light and views.

The owners, who are chemists, asked Atelier Tekuto to use concrete with the lowest possible carbon footprint. The architects came up with a 100% recyclable concrete shell made with locally abundant volcanic ash deposit, which increases its strength over a long period and helps control humidity.

Often, architects execute their biggest ideas in the smallest spaces, and this house is a case in point. A short flight of cantilevered concrete stairs leads from the street to the front door, hinting at the dramatic interior stair layers that carry one up through the house. Inside, floating staircases blend the four levels into one fluid, vertically stacked space. The sequence starts with a lower-level gallery and media room, followed by a tearoom, gallery, and bath on the entry level, then the kitchen/dining/living room and bath, and a bedroom stacked on top.

Large, geometric windows and cutaways on each level create a shifting play of light and shadow across the suspended living spaces. Architect Yasuhiro Yamashita used the term *nuke*, which means to enlarge space through the use of visual and psychological connections between interior

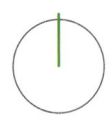

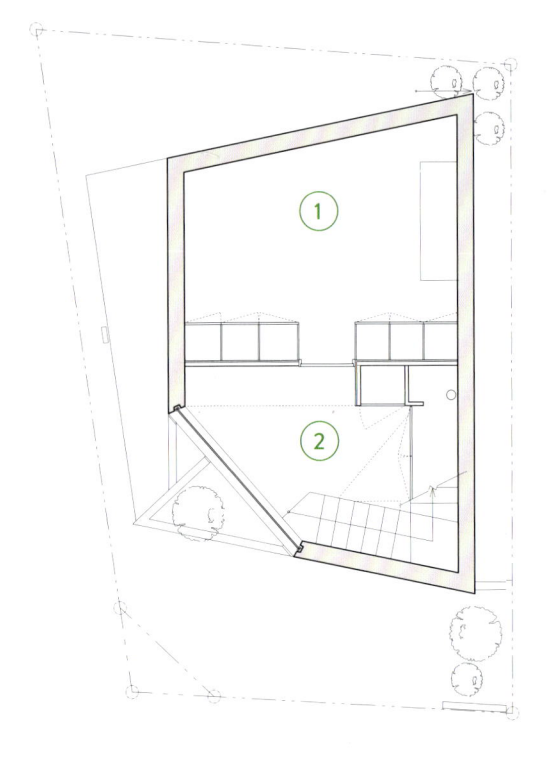

BASEMENT

1 Audio room
2 Gallery

FIRST FLOOR

1 Entrance
2 Tea room
3 Gallery
4 Powder room
5 Void
6 Stairs

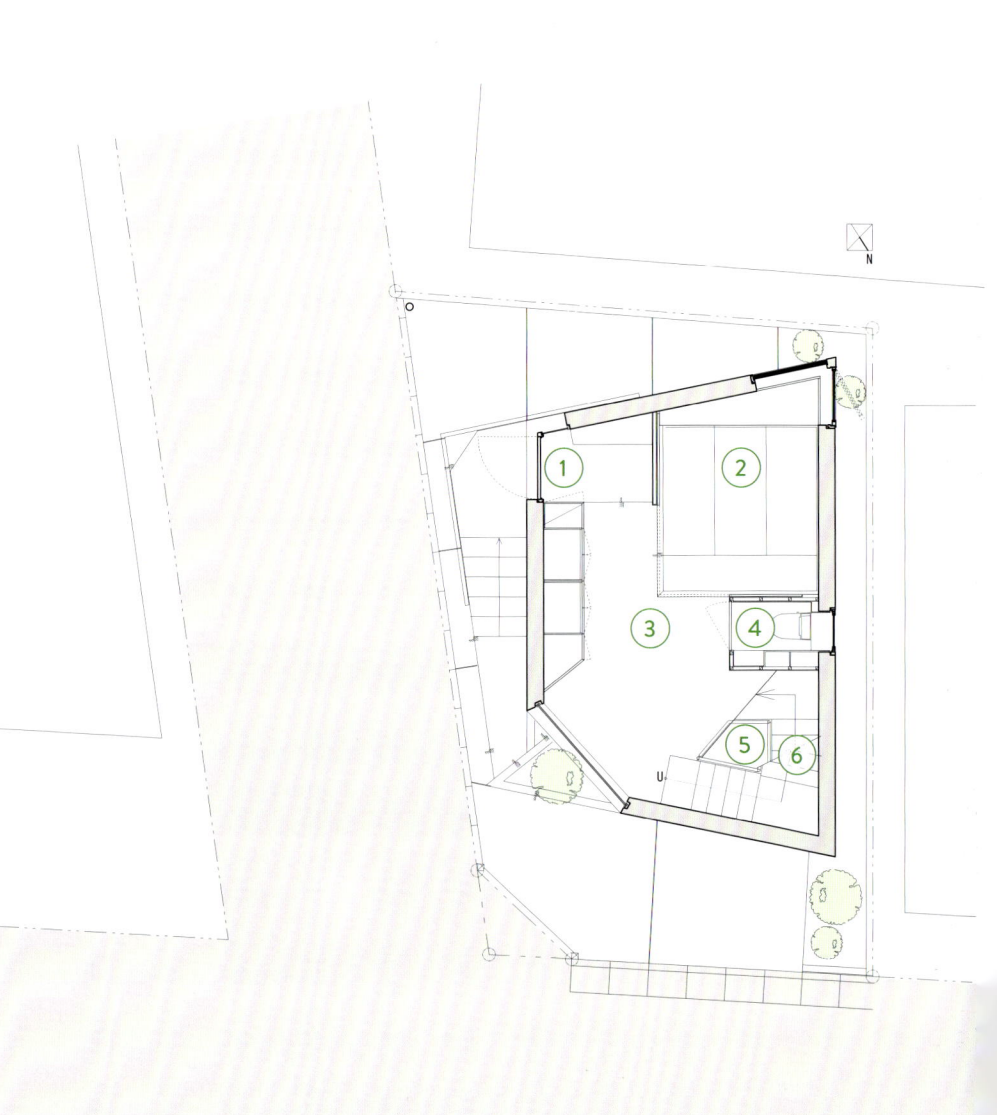

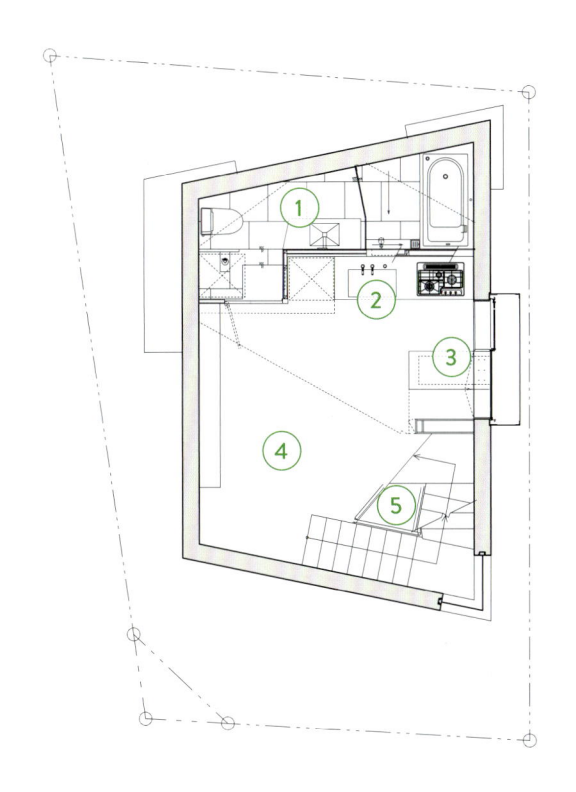

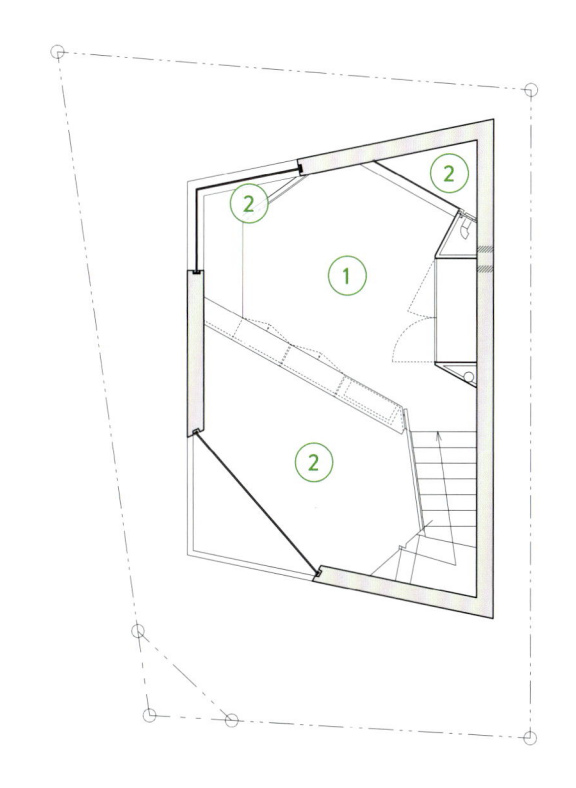

SECOND FLOOR

1 Bathroom
2 Kitchen
3 Dining room
4 Living room
5 Void

THIRD FLOOR

1 Bedroom
2 Void

SECTION

1 Storage
2 Audio room
3 Bathroom
4 Tea room
5 Dining
6 Kitchen
7 Bath
8 Storage

R Torso C • Floor Plan

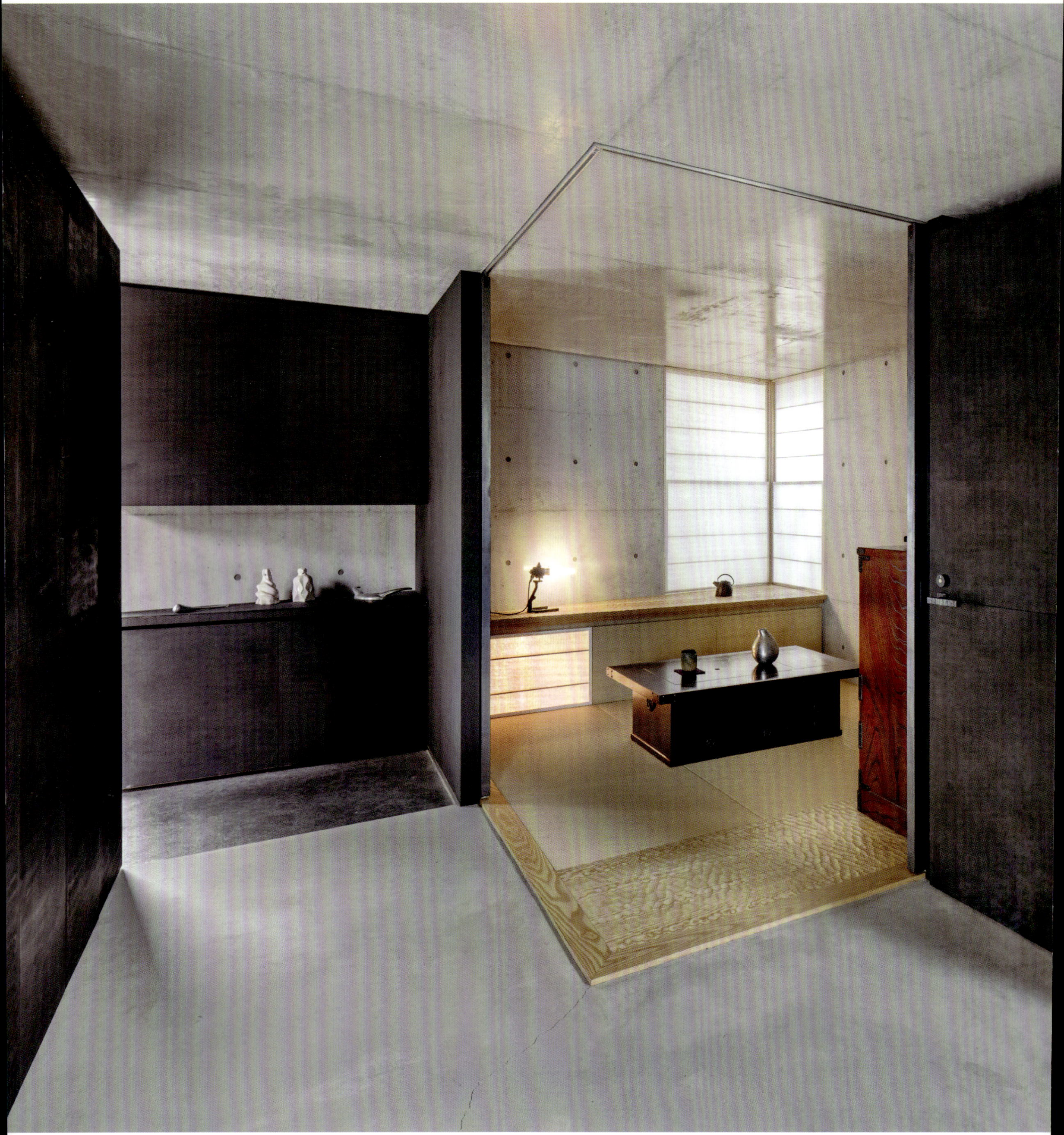

and exterior, and by layering walls and spatial volumes. "I pruned away some corners from the rectangular building to create *nuke* towards the sky, the last remaining vast piece of nature in Tokyo," he says. The living room is quite small, but its 16-foot ceiling and a large, oblique, triangular window make it seem exponentially more gracious.

Yamashita's team made many models to work out the spatial complexities. "I always draw plans and sections simultaneously and make numerous study models to create a multilayered space with an enhanced spaciousness," such as "the layering of concrete steps from the basement, the living space extending to the bedroom above, the toilet and high window leading to the sky and the bedroom, and the bathroom to the exterior via a skylight," Yamashita says. "These interconnections produce spatial richness that cannot be measured by area alone."

Tactile interior materials add to the physical and psychological richness: exposed concrete, charcoal-stained and persimmon-tanned wooden boards, hammered steel, black stainless steel, and oxidized black silver plate. These materials are unified by a matte texture and understated surfaces ranging from gray to black.

Tokyo's housing may be more tightly packed than almost any other metropolis, yet as this house remarkably shows, nature is never far away.

R Torso C

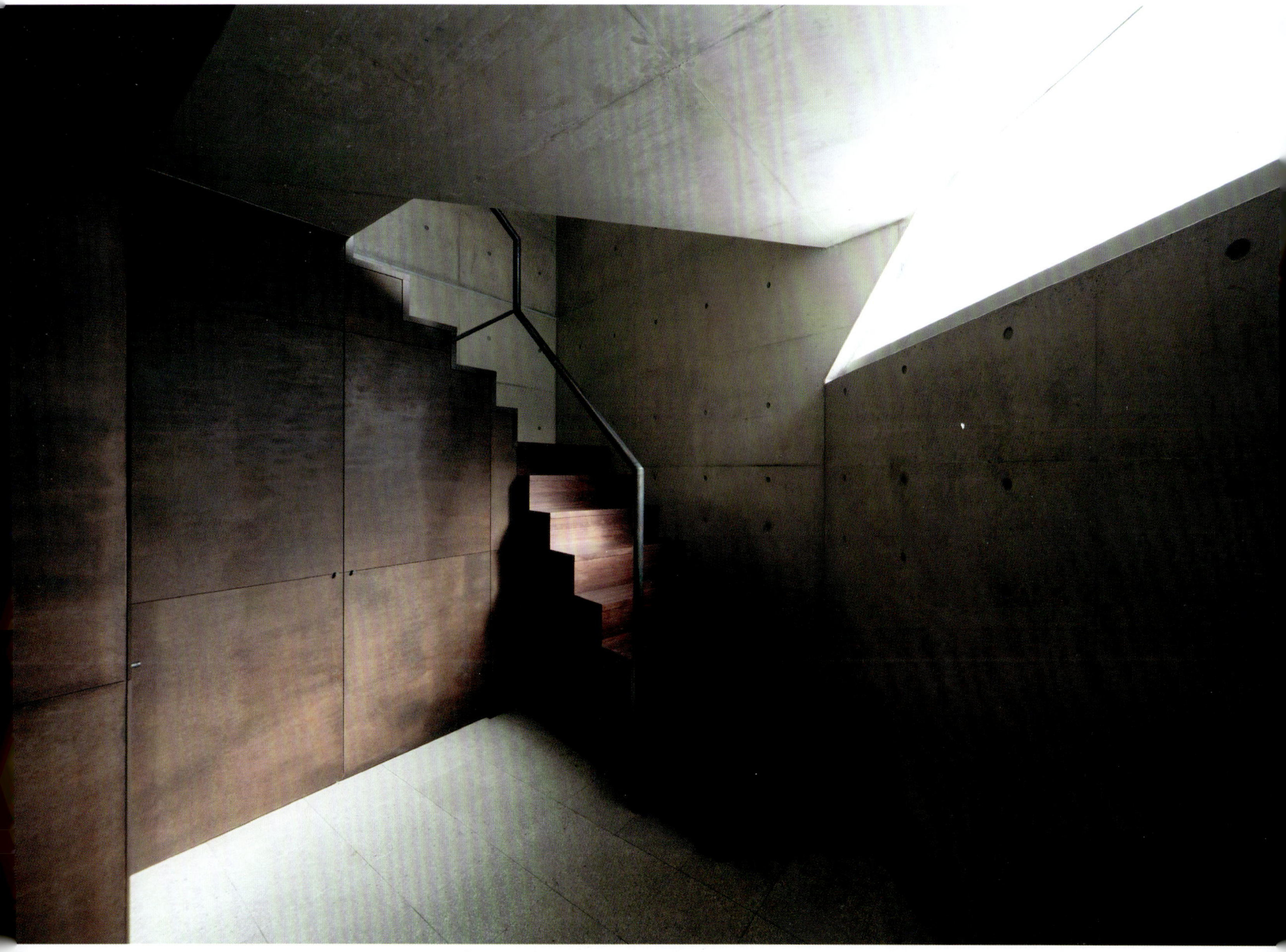

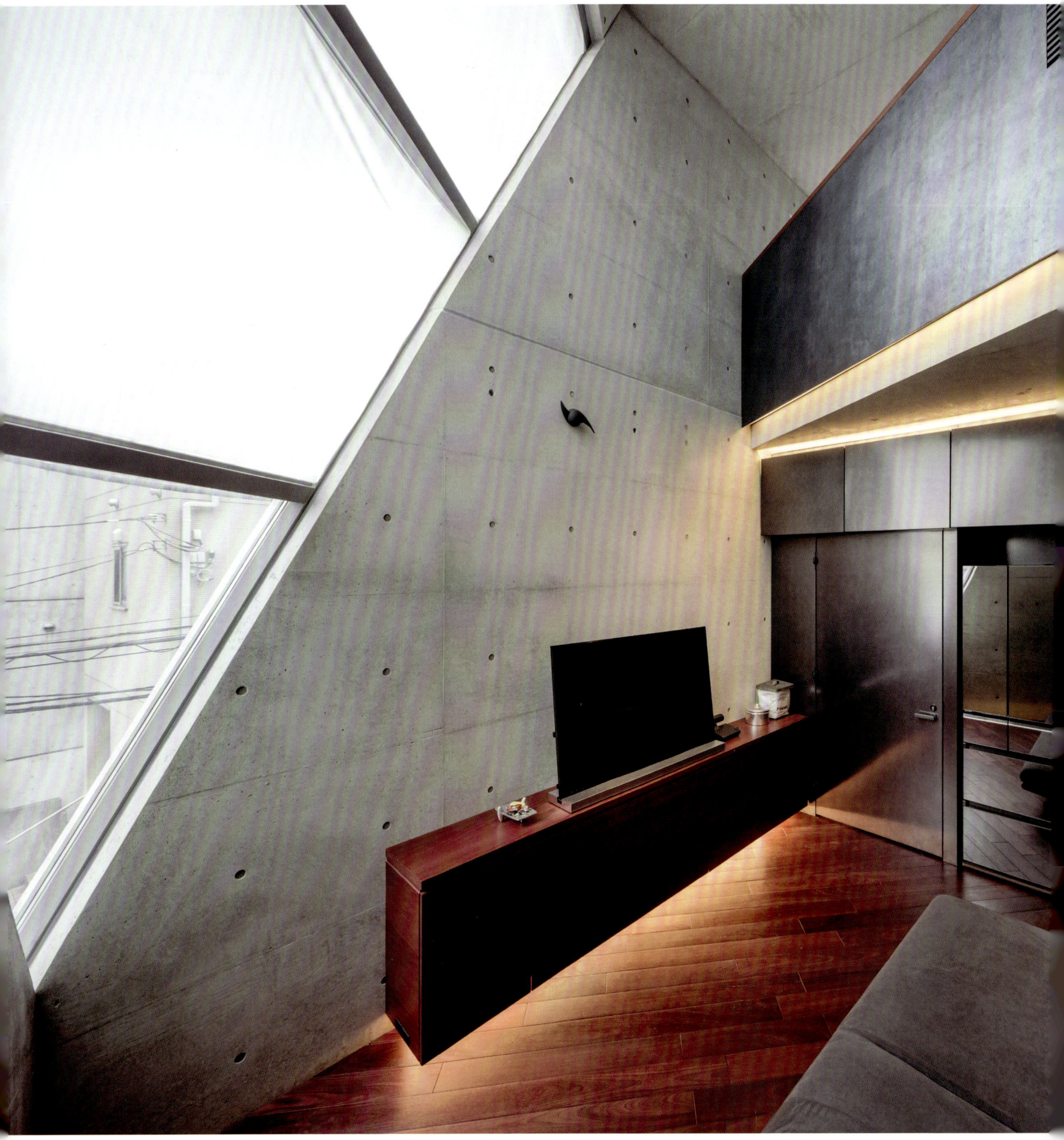

I pruned away some corners from the rectangular building to create *nuke* [visual and psychological connections between inside and outside] towards the sky, the last remaining vast piece of nature in Tokyo.
—Yasuhiro Yamashita

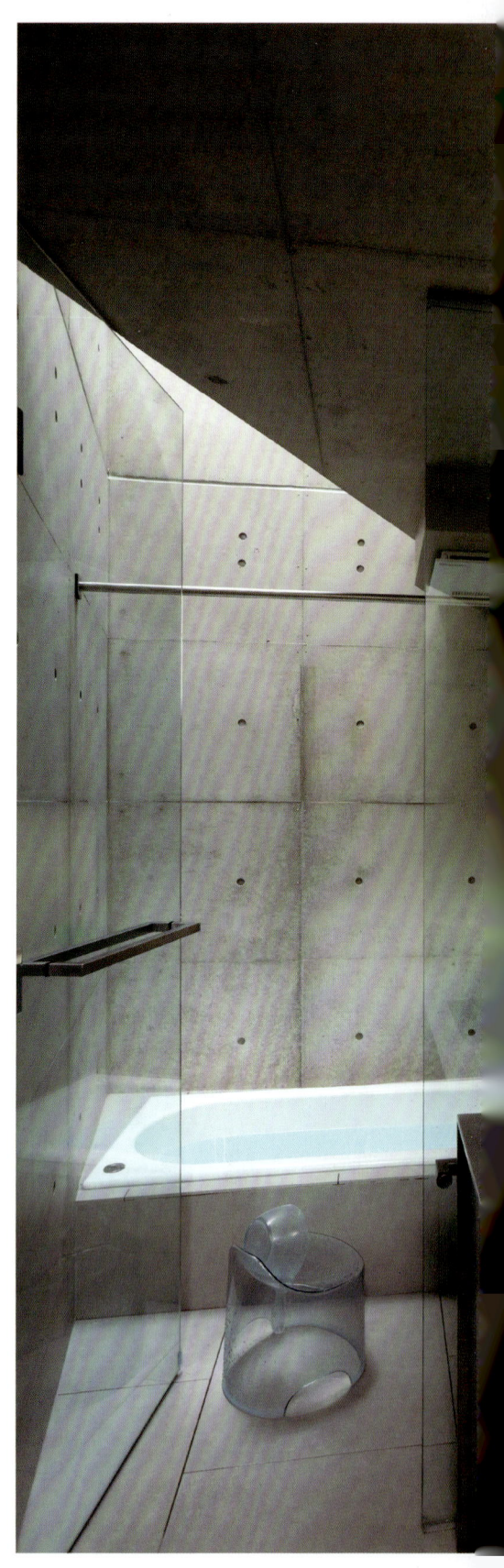

R Torso C

289

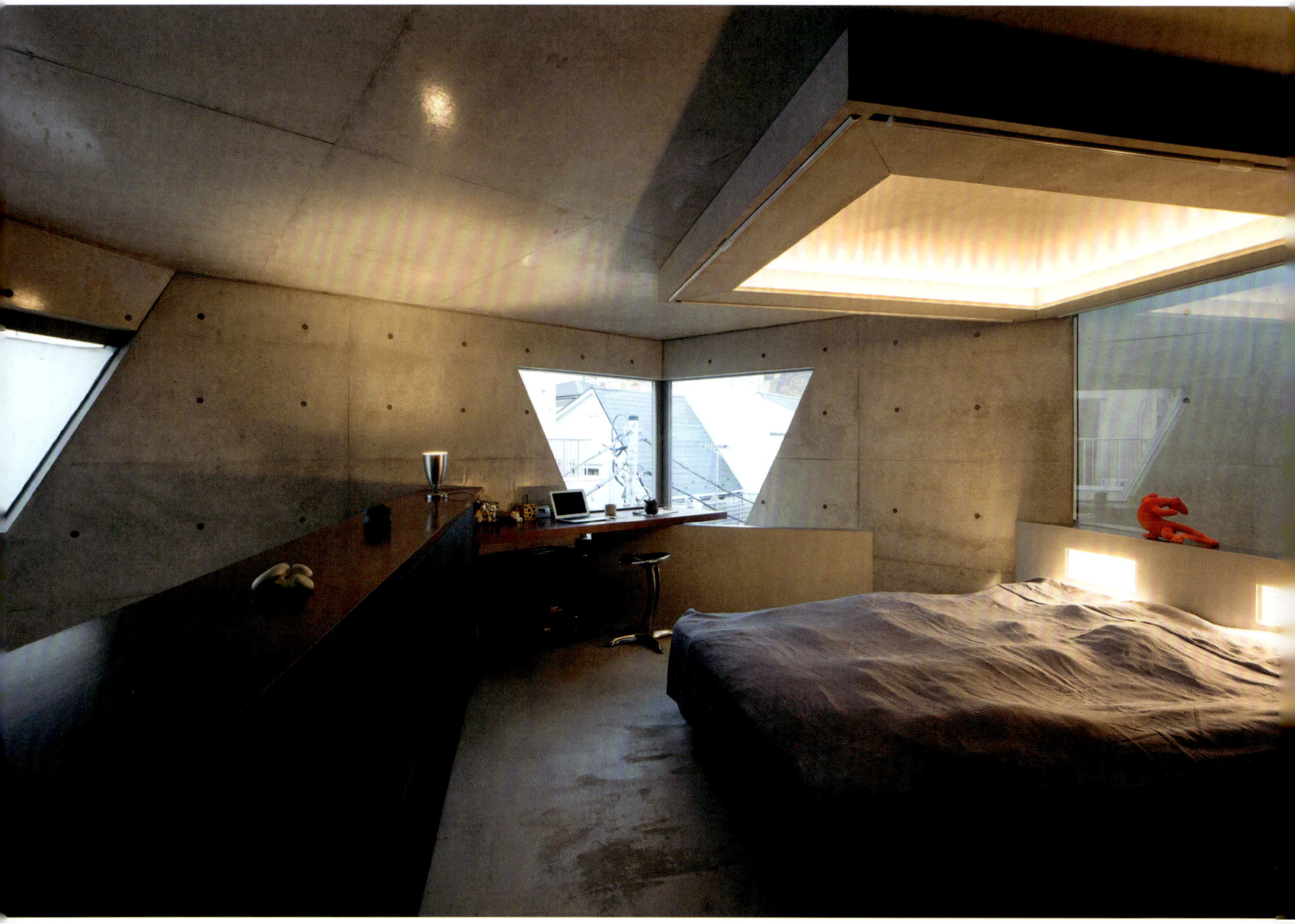

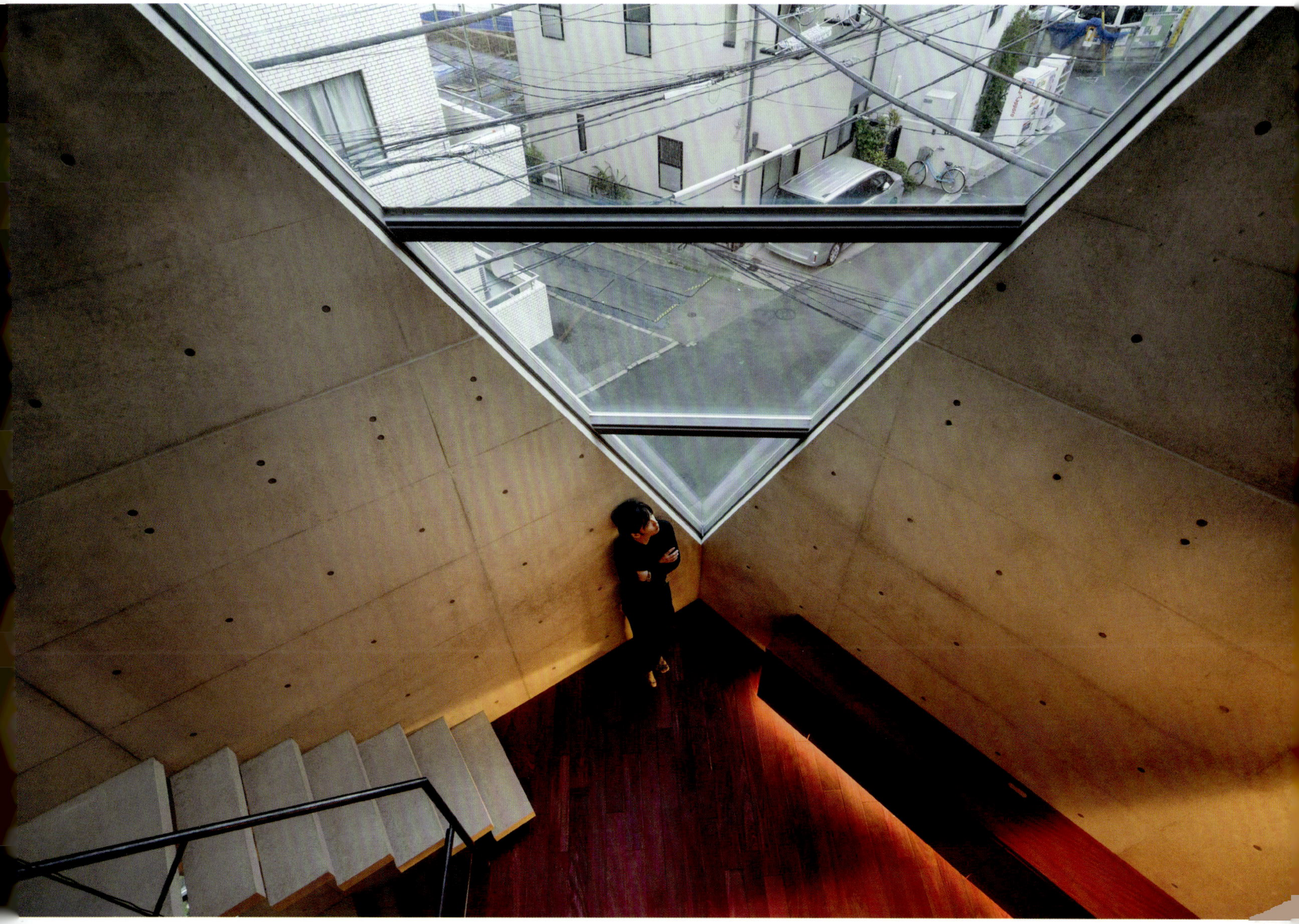

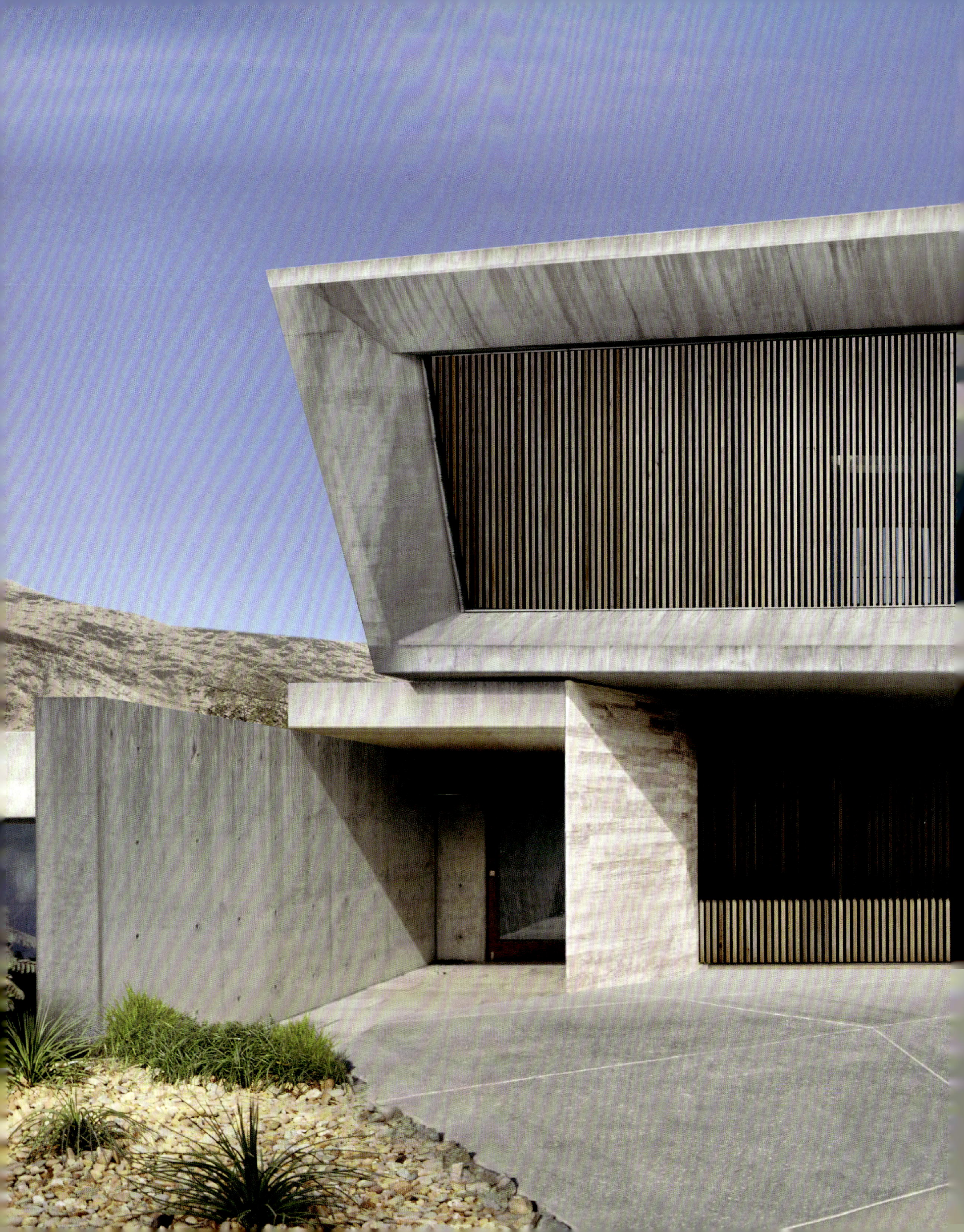

Australia

SHELL HOUSE

Wolf Architects
Photographs: Courtesy of Wolf Architects

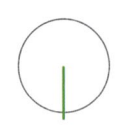

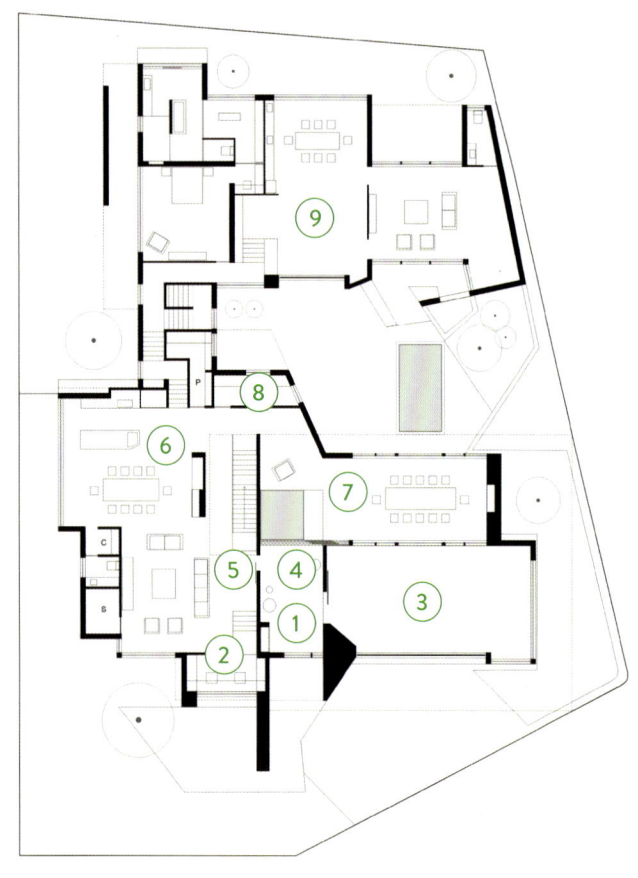

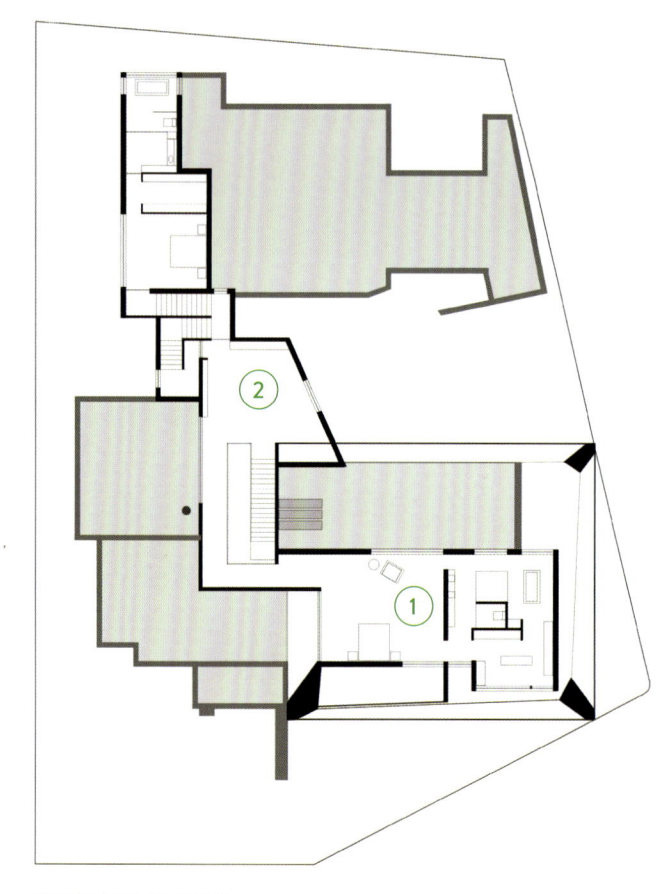

FIRST FLOOR

1 Entry
2 Study
3 Garage
4 Gallery
5 Living room
6 Kitchen
7 Dining room
8 Laundry
9 Game room

SECOND FLOOR

1 Main bedroom suite
2 Retreat

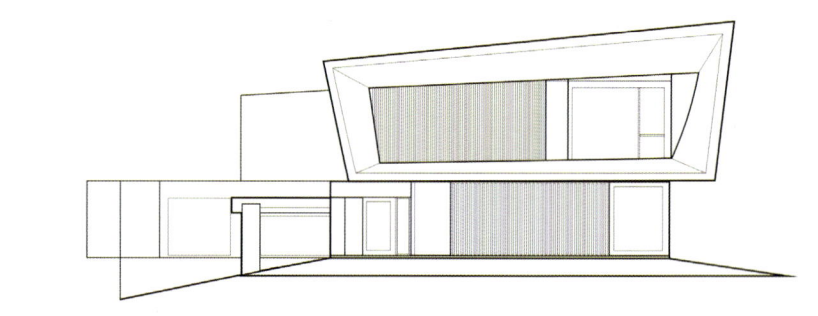

NORTH ELEVATION

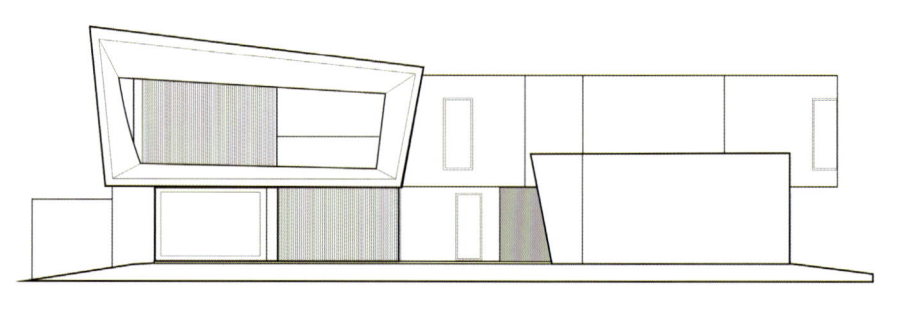

WEST ELEVATION

Once considered the norm, houses that remain in the family for generations have become the exception rather than the rule. But architect Taras Wolf and his clients aimed to uphold tradition in this third-generation family retreat. When Wolf was called in, the client's father was living in the modernist, 1960s family home—its provenance more Californian than Australian. It had been built near the back of a sloping, irregularly shaped lot, and they wanted to retain its historical character while inserting a new house into the established gardens. With three living and dining spaces, three en suite bedrooms, and a three-car garage, the new compound accommodates three generations.

By removing a part of the existing house and trimming the lap pool to spa size, Wolf was able to slot a sculptural dwelling into the front part of the lot, connecting the two with an internal bridge. "The site is irregular, and it was a matter of responding to the shape of the site," he says. "The old house, by the time of its 1990s renovation, had these angular shapes. It was a matter of trying to maximize the last time they would build on this property."

296 Shell House

While some might argue that a man-made object should try to disappear into a dramatic backdrop, this one's bold strokes sketch the lines of the mountain behind it. Perched atop the rambling first floor, a concrete frame enfolds the upper story like a sun visor, tapering to control the harsh desert light. Along the two-story street facade, thin, vertical cedar slats screen the light and views into the house and foreshadow the interior materials and textures.

Wolf thought of the house as a snail, with a hard shell and softer interior. The framing is steel and concrete, with an outer skin of poured concrete. "Concrete poured in situ is painstaking work, but any other kind of more cost-effective finish would probably break down over a period of time here," Wolf says. By contrast, interiors are moody, serene, and refined. Smooth or slatted American oak adds cocoon-like warmth on casework and some of the floors, ceilings, and walls. The wood ceilings echo the older house's exposed timber beams and complement the family's vintage furniture.

Points of drama counterpoint the tranquil domestic scenes. From the entry hall/gallery, a sliding glass wall opens to a skylit square pool at one end of the formal dining room, where sunlight is filtered through exposed rafters. A fireplace anchors the other end of this room, whose view looks across the courtyard to the old house's striking triangular fins. Adjacent to the formal dining room is an open kitchen and dining and living area. There, a cantilevered concrete kitchen island, recalling the exterior's angles, reads as a piece of sculpture against the marble and wood-clad walls.

Despite its feeling of permanence, the house was designed to live lightly in this extreme environment. The concrete allowed for long spans with deep eaves for shading. Interior and exterior water features also help keep the house cool. A cistern collects rainwater, and a rooftop solar array supplies the house's electricity. All of these gestures result in a house that is deeply attuned to its place. "When you put sculpture anywhere, it can complement rather than distract from its surroundings," Wolf says. "They collect art and came to the realization that the building could be a piece of art."

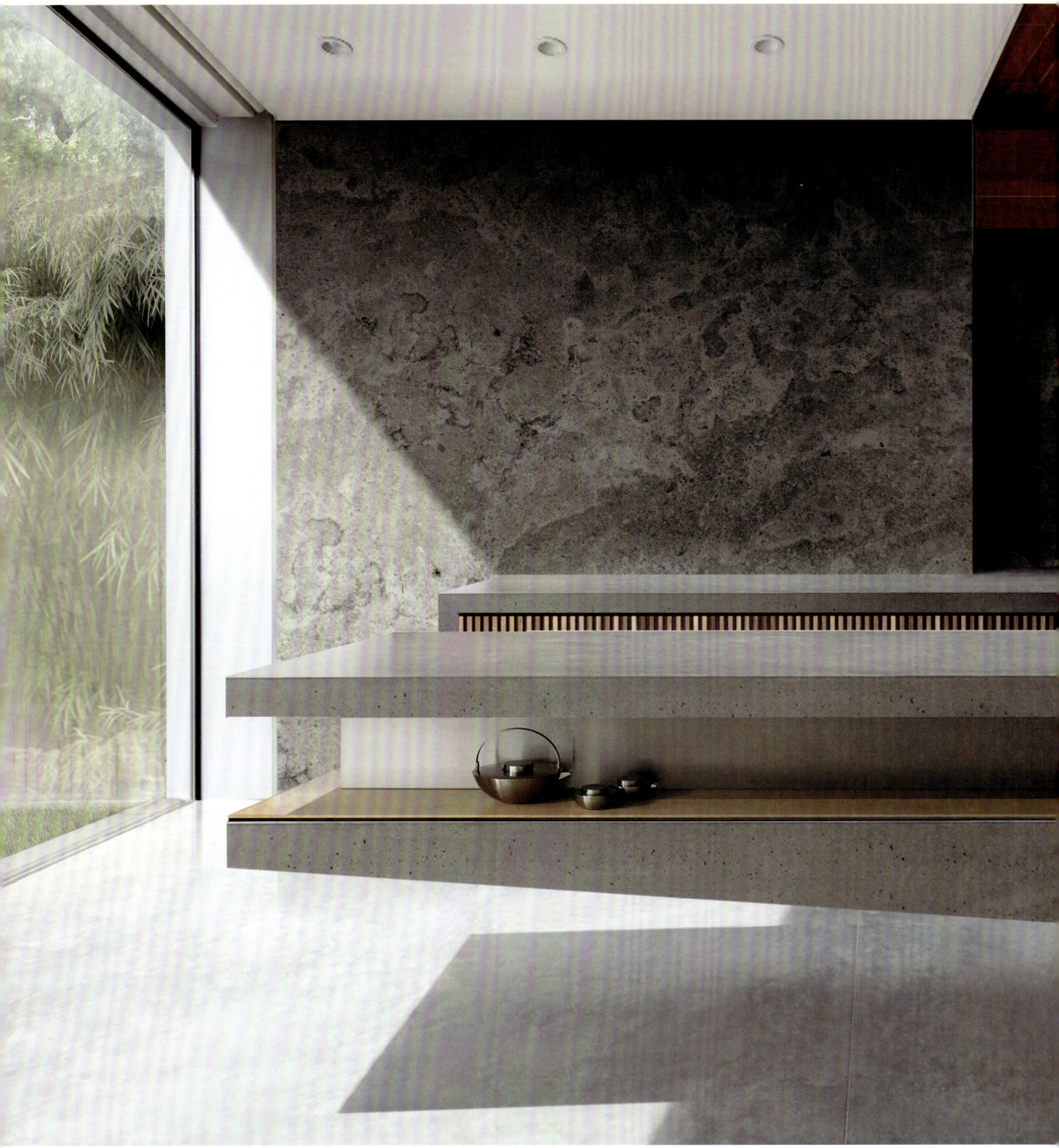

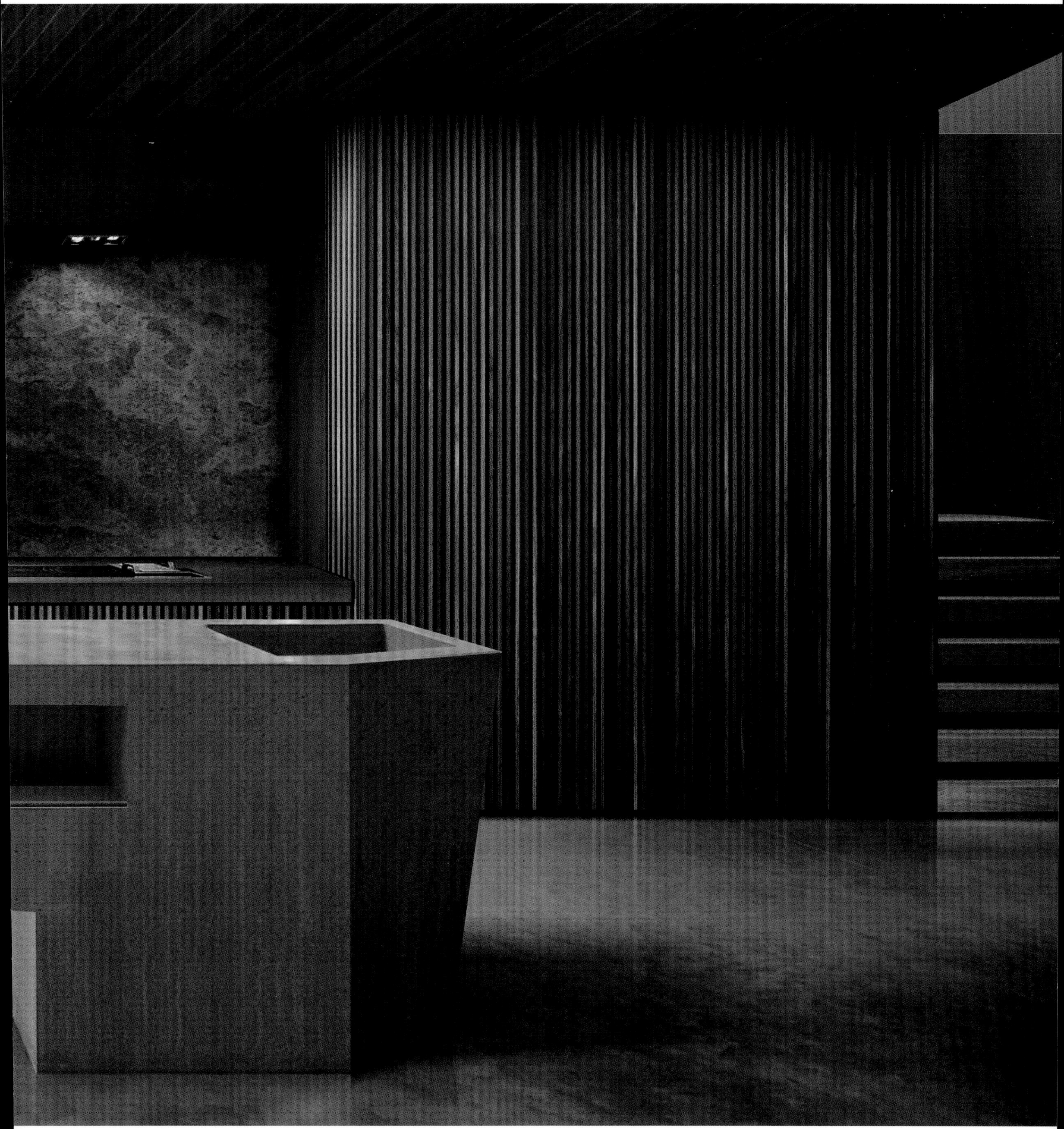

Shell House

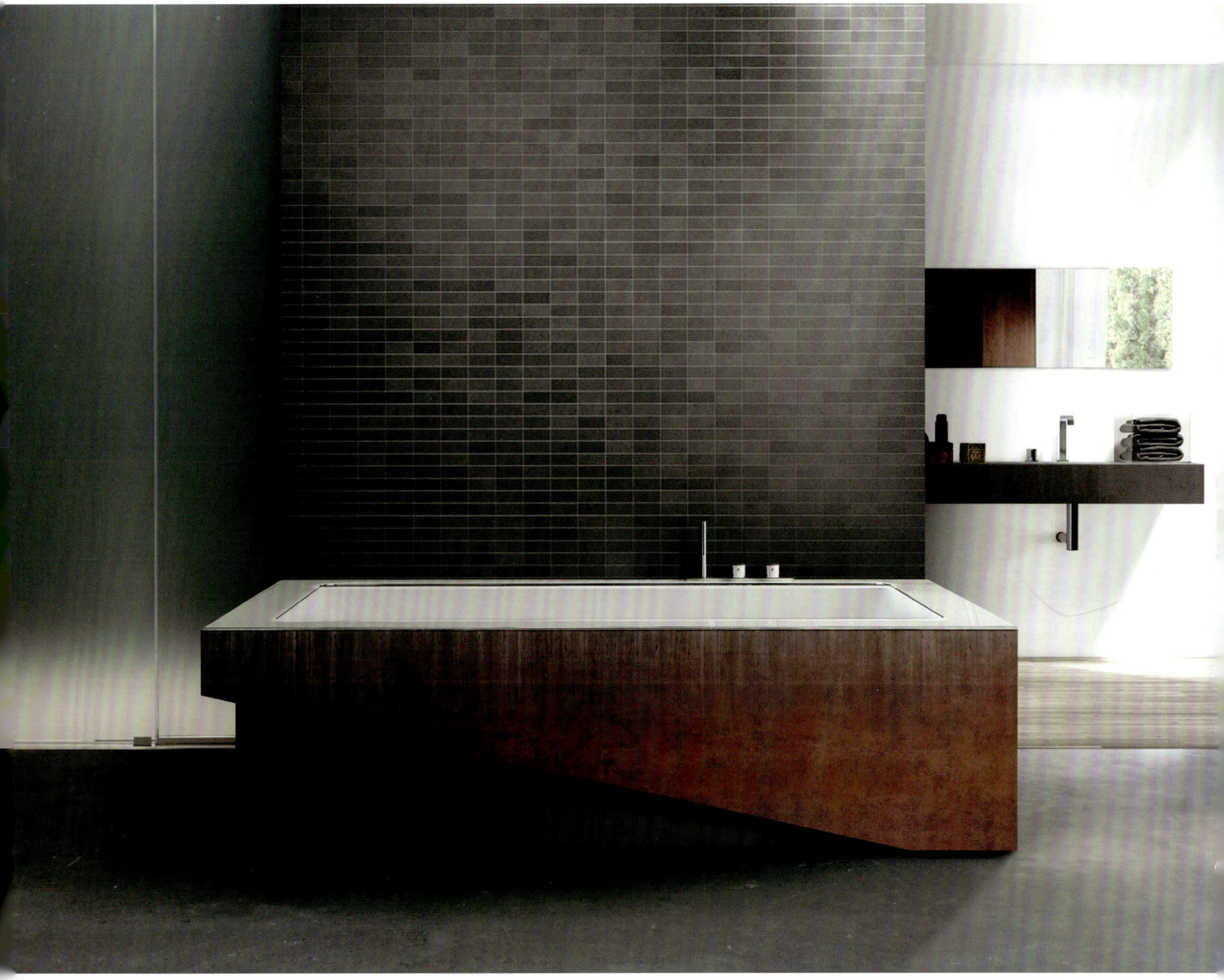

The dining room looks across a courtyard to the old house's striking fins.

Concrete was the only way to make it last forever, and it allowed for long spans with big eaves for shading. The material is beautiful, feels natural, and weathers well.
—Taras Wolf